Beginning SQL Queries

From Novice to Professional

Clare Churcher

Apress®

Beginning SQL Queries: From Novice to Professional

Copyright © 2008 by Clare Churcher

ISBN-13 (pbk): 978-1-59059-943-3

ISBN-13 (electronic): 978-1-4302-0550-0

Printed and bound in the United States of America (POD)

Lead Editor: Jonathan Gennick
Technical Reviewer: Darl Kuhn
Editorial Board: Clay Andres, Steve Anglin, Ewan Buckingham, Tony Campbell, Gary Cornell,
    Jonathan Gennick, Matthew Moodie, Joseph Ottinger, Jeffrey Pepper, Frank Pohlmann,
    Ben Renow-Clarke, Dominic Shakeshaft, Matt Wade, Tom Welsh
Project Manager: Beth Christmas
Copy Editors: Marilyn Smith, Kim Wimpsett
Associate Production Director: Kari Brooks-Copony
Production Editor: Ellie Fountain
Compositor: Susan Glinert
Proofreaders: Linda Seifert, Liz Welch
Indexer: Broccoli Information Management
Artist: April Milne
Cover Designer: Kurt Krames
Manufacturing Director: Tom Debolski

Distributed to the book trade worldwide by Springer-Verlag New York, Inc., 233 Spring Street, 6th Floor, New York, NY 10013. Phone 1-800-SPRINGER, fax 201-348-4505, e-mail orders-ny@springer-sbm.com, or visit http://www.springeronline.com.

For information on translations, please e-mail info@apress.com, or visit http://www.apress.com.

Apress and friends of ED books may be purchased in bulk for academic, corporate, or promotional use. eBook versions and licenses are also available for most titles. For more information, reference our Special Bulk Sales–eBook Licensing web page at http://www.apress.com/info/bulksales.

To Mark and Ali

Contents at a Glance

Contents

About the Author

CLARE CHURCHER holds a Ph.D. in physics and has designed several databases for a variety of large and small projects. She is a senior academic in the Applied Computing Group at Lincoln University, where she recently won an Excellence in Teaching Award for her contribution to developing and presenting courses in analysis and design, databases, and programming. She has supervised more than 70 undergraduate projects designing databases for small projects.

About the Technical Reviewer

 **DARL KUHN** is a senior database administrator with Sun Microsystems. Before joining Sun, his work as a consultant ranged from database administration to custom application development. Darl is a coauthor of *RMAN Recipes for Oracle Database 11g* and *Oracle RMAN Pocket Reference*. He is an affiliate professor at Regis University, where he teaches database courses for the department of computer information technology. Darl currently lives near Aguilar, Colorado, with his wife, Heidi, and two daughters, Lisa and Brandi.

Acknowledgments

Expecting your friends and family to put up with you writing a book is a tough call. Writing a second book the following year is really pushing their patience. So I am very indebted to my family and colleagues for putting up with me again. Special thanks to my two "first draft readers." My husband, Neville Churcher, and my friend and colleague Theresa McLennan both gave me many valuable suggestions on the first attempts at every chapter, and always did it in Clare time (i.e., now!) and with very good grace. Thanks also to all my good friends in the Applied Computing Group at Lincoln University, especially Alan McKinnon for his advice on Chapter 9.

Many thanks to my editor Jonathan Gennick for his insight, expertise, and encouragement, and to both Jonathan and Donna for showing us around their lovely hometown of Munising. Beth Christmas, my Apress project manager, has been a pleasure to work with, and Dahl Kuhn has been a most careful and expert technical reviewer. Thanks to you both.

Introduction

As a query language, SQL is really quite small and should be easy to learn. A few basic ideas and a handful of keywords allow you to tackle a huge range of queries. However, many users often find themselves completely stumped when faced with a particular problem. You may find yourself in that group. It isn't really a great deal of help for someone to say, "This is how I would do it." What you need is a variety of ways to get started on a tricky problem. Once you have made a start on a query, you need to be able to check, amend, and refine your solution until you have what you need.

Two-Pronged Approach

Throughout this book, I approach different types of queries from two directions. The two approaches have their roots in relational algebra and calculus. Don't be alarmed though— I won't be delving into any complex mathematics. However, understanding a question and developing an appropriate SQL query do require logical thinking and precise definitions. The relational algebra and calculus approaches are both useful ways to grasp the logic and precision that are required to get accurate results.

The first approach, which has its roots in relational algebra, looks at *how* tables need to be manipulated in order to retrieve the subset of data you require. I describe the different types of operations that you can perform on tables, including joins, intersections, selections, and so on, and explain how to decide which might help in particular situations. Once you understand what operations are needed, translating them into SQL is relatively straightforward.

The second approach is what I use when I just can't figure out which operations will give me the required results. This approach, based on relational calculus, lets you describe *what* an expected row in your result might be like; that is, what conditions it must obey. By looking at the data, it is surprisingly easy to develop a semiformal description of what a "correct" retrieved row would be like (and, by implication, how you would recognize an "incorrect" row). Because SQL was originally based on relational calculus, translating this semiformal description into a working query is particularly straightforward.

I am always surprised at which approach my students take when confronting a new problem. Some will instantly see the algebra operations that are needed; others will find the calculus approach more obvious. The choice of approach changes from query to query, from person to person, and (I suspect) from day to day. Having more than one way to get started means you are less likely to be completely baffled by a new problem.

Who This Book Is For

This book is for anyone who has a well-designed relational database and needs to extract some information from it. You might have noticed in the previous sentence that the database must be "well designed." I can't overemphasize this point. If your database is badly designed, it will not be able to store accurate and consistent data, so the information your queries retrieve will always be prone to inaccuracies. If you are looking to design a database from scratch, you should read my first book, *Beginning Database Design* (Apress, 2007). The final chapter of this book outlines a few common design problems you are likely to come across and gives some advice about how to mitigate the impact or correct the problem.

For this book, you do not need any theoretical knowledge of relational theory, as I will explain the relevant issues as they come up. The first chapter gives a brief overview of relational database theory, but it will help if you have had some experience working with databases with a few or more tables.

Objective of This Book

In this book, you will be introduced to all the main techniques and keywords needed to create SQL queries. You will learn about joins, intersections, unions, differences, selection of rows, and projection of columns. You will see how to implement these ideas in different ways using simple and nested queries, and you will be introduced to a variety of aggregate functions and summary techniques. You can try out what you learn using the sample data provided through the Apress web page for this book (http://www.apress.com/book/view/1590599438). There you will find the Access database used for the examples in the book and some scripts to create the database on a number of other platforms.

Most important of all, you will learn different ways to get started on a troublesome problem. In almost all cases, there are several different ways to express a query. My objective is, for any particular situation, to provide you with a method of attack that matches your psyche and mood (just kidding).

CHAPTER 1

∎∎∎

Relational Database Overview

A *query* is a way of retrieving some subset of information from a database. That information might be a single number such as a product price, a list of members with overdue subscriptions, or some sort of calculation such as the total amount of products sold in the past 12 months. Once we retrieve this subset of data, we might want to update the database records or include the information in some sort of report.

Before getting into the nuts and bolts of how to build queries, it is necessary to understand some of the ideas and terminology associated with relational databases. In particular, it is useful to have a way of depicting how a particular database is put together, that is, what data is being kept in what tables and how everything is interrelated.

It is imperative that any database has been designed to accurately represent the situation it is dealing with. With all the fanciest SQL in the world, you are unlikely to be able to get accurate responses to queries if the underlying database design is faulty. If you are setting up a new database, you should refer to a design book[1] before embarking on the project.

In this chapter, we will look at some of the basic ideas of data models and relational theory so we can get started on formulating queries in SQL. Later chapters will expand on these ideas, as required. You will also learn about two important ways to think about queries: relational algebra and relational calculus.

What Is a Relational Database?

In simple terms, a relational database is a set of tables.[2] Each table keeps information about aspects of one thing, such as a customer, an order, a product, a team, or a tournament. It is possible to set up constraints on the data in individual tables and also between tables. For example, when designing the database, we might specify that an order entered in the Order table must exist for a customer who exists in the Customer table. How the tables are interrelated can be usefully depicted with a data model.

---

1. For instance, you can refer to my other Apress book, *Beginning Database Design: From Novice to Professional* (Apress, 2007).
2. Really it's a set of relations, but I'll explain that in the "Introducing Tables" section.

Introducing Data Models

A *data model* provides us with information about how the data items in the database are interrelated. In this book, I will use an example of a golf club that has members who belong to teams and enter tournaments. One convenient way to give an overview of the different tables in a database is by using the class diagram notation from the Unified Modeling Language (UML).[3] In this section, we will look at how to interpret a class diagram.

A *class* is like a template for a set of things (or events, people, and so on) about which we want to keep similar data. For example, we might want to keep names and other details about the members of our golf club. Figure 1-1 shows the UML notation for a Member class. The name of the class is in the top panel, and the middle panel shows the *attributes*, or pieces of data, we want to keep about each member. Each member can have a value for LastName, FirstName, and so on.

Member
MemberID
LastName
FirstName
Phone
Handicap
JoinDate
Gender

Figure 1-1. *UML representation of a Member class*

Each class in a data model will be represented in a relational database as a *table*. The attributes are the *columns* (often referred to as *fields*) in the table, and the details of each member form the *rows* in the table. Figure 1-2 shows some example data.

The data model can also depict the way the different classes in our database depend on each other. Figure 1-3 shows two classes, Member and Team, and how they are related.

The pair of numbers at each end of the *plays for* line in Figure 1-3 indicates how many members play for one particular team, and vice versa. The first number of each pair is the minimum number. This is often 0 or 1 and is therefore sometimes known as the *optionality* (that is, it indicates whether a member *must* have an associated team, or vice versa). The second number (known as the *cardinality*) is the greatest number of related objects. It is usually 1 or many (denoted by *n* or ***), although other numbers are possible.

---

3. If you want more information about UML, then refer to *The Unified Modeling Language User Guide* by Grady Booch, James Rumbaugh, and Ivar Jacobsen (Addison Wesley, 1999).

MemberID	LastName	FirstName	Phone	Handicap	JoinDate	Gender
118	McKenzie	Melissa	963270	30	10-May-99	F
138	Stone	Michael	983223	30	13-May-03	M
153	Nolan	Brenda	442649	11	25-Jul-00	F
176	Branch	Helen	589419		18-Nov-05	F
178	Beck	Sarah	226596		06-Jan-04	F
228	Burton	Sandra	244493	26	21-Jun-07	F
235	Cooper	William	722954	14	15-Feb-02	M
239	Spence	Thomas	697720	10	04-Jun-00	M
258	Olson	Barbara	370186	16	11-Jul-07	F

Figure 1-2. *A table representing the instances of our Member class*

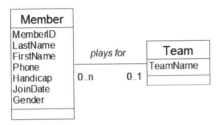

Figure 1-3. *A relationship between two classes*

Relationships are read in both directions. Reading Figure 1-3 from left to right, we have that one particular member doesn't have to *play for* a team and can *play for* at most one team (the numbers 0 and 1 at the end of the line nearest the Team class). Reading from right to left, we can say that one particular team doesn't need to have any members and can have many (the numbers 0 and n nearest the Member class). A relationship like the one in Figure 1-3 is called a 1-Many relationship (a member can belong to just one team, and a team can have many members). Most relationships in a relational database will be 1-Many relationships.

For members of a team, you might think there should be exactly four members (say for an interclub team). Although this might be true when the team plays a round of golf, our database might record different numbers of members associated with the team as we add and remove players through the year. A data model usually uses 0, 1, and many to model the relationships between tables. Other constraints (such as the maximum number in a team) are more usually expressed with business rules or with UML use cases.[4]

---

4. For more information, see *Writing Effective Use Cases* by Alistair Cockburn (Addison Wesley, 2001).

Introducing Tables

The earlier description of a relational database as a set of tables was a little oversimplified. A more accurate definition is that a relational database is a set of *relations*. When people refer to tables in a relational database, they generally assume (whether they know it or not) that they are dealing with relations. The reason for the distinction between tables and relations is that there is a well-defined set of operations on relations that allow them to be combined and manipulated in various ways.[5] This is exactly what we need in order to be able to extract accurate information from a database. We won't be covering the actual mathematics in this book, but we will be using the operations. So, in nonmathematical speak, what is so special about relations?

One of the most important features of a relation is that it is a set of *unique* rows.[6] No two rows in a relation can have identical values for every attribute. A table does not generally have this restriction. If we consider our member data, it is clear why this uniqueness constraint is so important. If, in the table in Figure 1-2, we had two identical rows (say for Brenda Nolan), we would have no way to differentiate them. We might associate a team with one row and a subscription payment with the other, thereby generating all sorts of confusion.

The way that a relational database maintains the uniqueness of rows is by specifying a primary key. A *primary key* is an attribute, or set of attributes, that is guaranteed to be different in every row of a given relation. For data such as the member data in this example, we cannot guarantee that all our members will have different names or addresses (a dad and son may share a name and an address and both belong to the club). To help distinguish different members, we have included an ID number as one of the member attributes, or fields. You will find that adding an identifying number (colloquially referred to as a *surrogate key*) is very common in database tables. If MemberID is defined as the primary key for the Member table, then the database system will ensure that in every row the value of MemberID is different. The system will also ensure that the primary key field always has a value. That is, we can never enter a row that has an empty MemberID field. These two requirements for a primary key field (uniqueness and not being empty) ensure that given the value of MemberID, we can always find a single row that represents that member. We will see that this is very important when we start establishing relationships between tables later in this chapter. Once a table has a primary key nominated, then it satisfies the uniqueness requirement of a relation.

Another feature of a relation is that each attribute (or column) has a domain. A *domain* is a set of allowed values and might be something very general. For example, the domain for the FirstName attribute in the Member table is just any string of characters, for example, "Michael" or "Helen." The domain for columns storing dates might be any valid date (so that February 29 is allowed only in leap years), whereas for columns keeping quantities,

---

5. The relational theory was first introduced by the mathematician E. F. Codd in June 1970 in his article "A Relational Model of Data for Large Shared Data Banks" in *Communications of the ACM: 13*.
6. More accurately, a relation is a set of *tuples*.

the domain might be integer values greater than 0. All database systems have built-in domains or types such as text, integer, or date that can be chosen for each of the fields in a table. Systems vary as to whether users can define their own more highly specified domains that they can use across different tables; however, all good database systems allow the designer to specify constraints on a particular attribute in a table. For example, in a particular table we might specify that a birth date is a date in the past, that the value for a gender field must be "M" or "F", or that a student's exam mark is between 0 and 100. The idea of domains becomes important for queries when we need to compare values of columns in different tables.

When I refer to a database *table* in this book, I mean a set of rows with a nominated primary key to ensure every row is different and where every column has a domain of allowed values. Listing 1-1 shows the SQL code for creating the Member table with the attribute names and domains specified. In SQL, the keyword INT means an integer or nonfractional number, and CHAR(n) means a string of characters n long. The code also specifies that MemberID will be the primary key. (Listing 1-1 doesn't create the relationship with the Team table yet.) The code is fairly self-explanatory.

Listing 1-1. *SQL to Create the Member Table*

```
CREATE TABLE Member (
MemberID INT PRIMARY KEY,
LastName CHAR(20),
FirstName CHAR(20),
Phone CHAR(20),
Handicap INT,
JoinDate DATETIME,
Gender CHAR(1))
```

Inserting and Updating Rows in a Table

The emphasis in this book is on getting accurate information out of a database, but the data has to get in somehow. Most database application developers will provide user-friendly interfaces for inserting data into the various tables. Often a form is presented to the user for entering data that may end up in several tables. Figure 1-4 shows a simple Microsoft Access form that allows a user to enter and amend data in the Member table.

It is also possible to construct web forms or mechanical readers—(such as the bar-code readers at supermarkets)—that collect data and insert it into a database. Behind all the different interfaces for updating data, SQL update queries are generated. I will show you three types of queries for inserting or changing data just so you get an idea of what they look like. I think you will find them quite easy to understand.

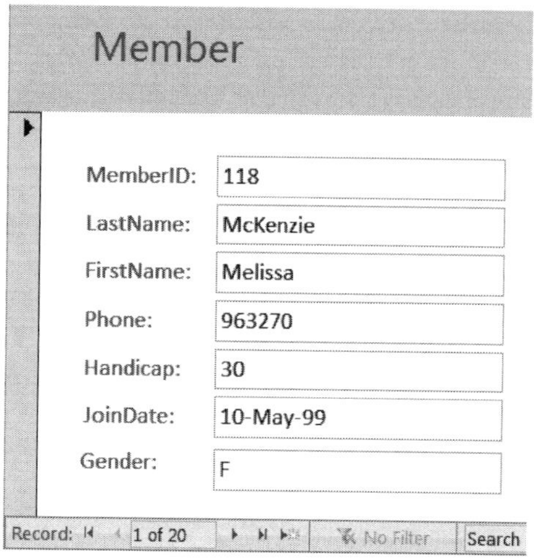

Figure 1-4. *A form allowing entry and updating of data in the Member table*

Listing 1-2 shows the SQL to enter one complete row in our Member table. The data items are in the same order as specified when the table was created (Listing 1-1). Note that the date and string values need to be enclosed in single quotes.

Listing 1-2. *Inserting a Complete Row into the Member Table*

```
INSERT INTO Member
VALUES (118, 'McKenzie', 'Melissa', '963270', 30, '05/10/1999', 'F')
```

If many of the data items are empty, we can specify which attributes or fields will have values. If we had only the ID and last name of a member, we could insert just those two values as in Listing 1-3. Remember that we always have to provide a value for the primary key field.

Listing 1-3. *Inserting a Row into the Member Table When Only Some Attributes Have Values*

```
INSERT INTO Member (MemberID, LastName)
VALUES (258, 'Olson')
```

We can also alter records that are already in the database with an update query. Listing 1-4 shows a simple example. The query needs to identify which records are to be changed (the WHERE clause in Listing 1-4) and then specify the field or fields to be updated (the SET clause).

Listing 1-4. *Updating a Row in the Member Table*

```
UPDATE Member
SET Phone = '875077'
WHERE MemberID = 118
```

Designing Appropriate Tables

Even a quite modest database system will have hundreds of attributes: names, dates, addresses, quantities, descriptions, ID numbers, and so on. These all have to find their way into tables, and getting them in the right tables is critical to the overall accuracy and usefulness of the database. Many problems can arise from having attributes in the wrong tables. As a simple illustration of what can go wrong, I'll briefly show the problems associated with having redundant information.

Say we want to add membership types and fees to the information we are keeping about members of our golf club. We could add these two fields to the Member table, as in Figure 1-5.

MemberID	LastName	FirstName	Phone	Handicap	JoinDate	Gender	MemberType	Fee
118	McKenzie	Melissa	963270	30	10/05/1999	F	Junior	150
138	Stone	Michael	983223	30	13/05/2003	M	Senior	300
153	Nolan	Brenda	442649	11	25/07/2000	F	Senior	300
176	Branch	Helen	589419		18/11/2005	F	Social	50
178	Beck	Sarah	226596		6/01/2004	F	Social	50
228	Burton	Sandra	244493	26	21/06/2007	F	Junior	150
235	Cooper	William	722954	14	15/02/2002	M	Senior	300
239	Spence	Thomas	697720	10	4/06/2000	M	Senior	280
258	Olson	Barbara	370186	16	11/07/2007	F	Senior	300

Figure 1-5. *Possible Member table*

If the fee for all senior members is the same (that is, there are no discounts or other complications), then immediately we can see there has been a problem with the data entry because Thomas Spence has a different fee from the other senior members. The piece of information about the fee for a senior member is being stored several times, so inevitably inconsistencies will arise. If we formulated a query to find the fee for seniors, what would we expect for an answer? Should it be $300, $280, or both?

The problem here is that (in database parlance) the table is not properly *normalized*. Normalization is a formal way of checking whether attributes are in the correct table. It is outside the scope of this book to delve into normalization, but I'll just briefly show you how to avoid the problem in this particular case.

The problem is that we are trying to keep information about two different things in our Member table: information about each member (IDs, names, and so on) and information about membership types (the different fees). This means the Fee attribute is in the wrong table. Figure 1-6 shows a better solution with two classes: one for information about members and one for information about membership types. The tables have a 1-Many relationship between them that can be read from left to right as "each member has one membership type" and in the other direction as "a particular membership type can have many associated members."

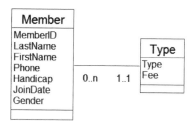

Figure 1-6. *Separating members and their types*

We can represent the model in Figure 1-6 with the two tables in Figure 1-7. (A few of the fields in the Member table have been hidden in Figure 1-7 just to keep the size manageable.) You can see that we have now avoided keeping the information about the fee for a senior member more than once, so inconsistencies do not arise. Also, if we need to change the value of the fee, we need to change it in only one place.

MemberID	LastName	FirstName	MemberType
118	McKenzie	Melissa	Junior
138	Stone	Michael	Senior
153	Nolan	Brenda	Senior
176	Branch	Helen	Social
178	Beck	Sarah	Social
228	Burton	Sandra	Junior
235	Cooper	William	Senior
239	Spence	Thomas	Senior
258	Olson	Barbara	Senior

Member

Type	Fee
Junior	150
Senior	300
Social	50

Type

Figure 1-7. *Member and Type tables*

If we need to find out what fee Thomas Spence pays, we now need to consult two tables: the Member table to find his type and then the Type table to find the fee for that type. The bulk of this book is about how to do just that sort of data retrieval. We can formulate queries to accurately retrieve all sorts of information from several tables in the database.

At the risk of repeating myself, I do want to caution you about the necessity of ensuring that the database is properly designed. The simple model in Figure 1-6 is almost certainly quite unsuitable even for the tiny amount of data it contains. A real club will probably want to keep track of fees and how they change over the years. They may need to keep records of when members graduated from junior to senior. They may offer discounts for prompt payments. Designing a useful database is a tricky job and outside the scope of this book.[7]

Maintaining Consistency Between Tables

Even the smallest database will have many, many tables. We saw in the previous section that keeping just a tiny amount of data for members required two tables if it was to be accurately maintained. Database systems provide domains or other constraints to ensure that values in particular columns of a given table are sensible, but we can also set up constraints between tables.

Look at the modified data in Figure 1-8. What fee does Melissa McKenzie pay now?

MemberID	LastName	FirstName	MemberType
118	McKenzie	Melissa	Junor
138	Stone	Michael	Senior
153	Nolan	Brenda	Senior
176	Branch	Helen	Social
178	Beck	Sarah	Social
228	Burton	Sandra	Junior
235	Cooper	William	Senior
239	Spence	Thomas	Senior
258	Olson	Barbara	Senior

Member

Type	Fee
Junior	150
Senior	300
Social	50

Type

Figure 1-8. *Inconsistent data between tables*

We can probably make an educated guess that Melissa is probably meant to be a "Junior" rather than a "Junor", but we don't want our database to be second-guessing what it thinks we mean. We can prevent typos like this by placing a constraint called a *foreign key* on the Member table. We tell the database that the MemberType column in the Member table can have only a value that already exists as a primary key value in the Type table (for this example, that means it must be either "Junior", "Senior", or "Social"). The terminology for this is to "create the MemberType field as a foreign key that references the Type table." With this constraint in place, "Junior" is OK because we have a row in the Type

---

7. For more information about database design, refer to my other Apress book, *Beginning Database Design: From Novice to Professional* (Apress, 2007).

table with "Junior" in the primary key, but "Junor" will not be accepted. In general, all 1-Many relationships between classes in a data model are set up this way.

Listing 1-5 shows the SQL for creating the Member table with a foreign key constraint.

Listing 1-5. *SQL to Create the Member Table with a Foreign Key*

```
CREATE TABLE Member(
MemberID INT PRIMARY KEY,
LastName CHAR(20),
FirstName CHAR(20),
Phone CHAR(20),
Handicap INT,
JoinDate DATETIME,
Gender CHAR(1),
MemberType CHAR(20) FOREIGN KEY REFERENCES Type)
```

Most database products also have graphical interfaces for setting up and displaying foreign key constraints. Figure 1-9 shows the interfaces for SQL Server and Access. These diagrams, which are essentially implementations of the data model, are invaluable for understanding the structure of the database so we know how to extract the information we require.

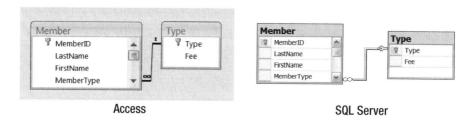

Access   SQL Server

Figure 1-9. *Diagrams for implementing 1-Many relationships using foreign keys*

Retrieving Information from a Database

Now that we have the starting point of a well-designed database consisting of a set of interrelated, normalized tables, we can start to look at how to extract information by way of queries. Many database systems will have a diagrammatic interface that can be very useful for many simple queries. Figure 1-10 shows the Access interface for retrieving the names of senior members from the Member table. The check marks denote which columns we want to see, and the Criteria row enables us to specify particular rows.

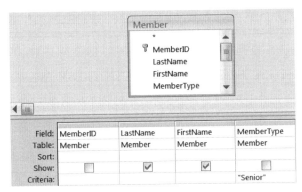

Figure 1-10. *Access interface for a simple query on the Member table*

We can express the same query in SQL as shown in Listing 1-6. It contains three clauses: SELECT specifies which columns to return, FROM specifies the table(s) where the information is kept, and WHERE specifies the conditions the returned rows must satisfy. We'll look at the structure of SQL statements in more detail later, but for now the intention of the query is pretty clear.

Listing 1-6. *SQL to Retrieve the Names of Senior Members from the Member Table*

```
SELECT FirstName, LastName
FROM Member
WHERE MemberType = 'Senior'
```

These two methods of expressing a simple query are quite straightforward, but as we need to include more and more tables connected in a variety of ways, the diagrammatic interface rapidly becomes unwieldy and the SQL commands more complex.

Often, it is easier to think about a query in a more abstract way. With a clear abstract understanding of what is required, it then becomes more straightforward to turn the idea into an appropriate SQL statement. There are two different abstract ways to consider queries on a relational database. Because relational theory was developed by a mathematician, it is couched in quite mathematical terms. The two equivalent ways of thinking about queries are called *relational algebra* and *relational calculus*. Do not be alarmed! We will not be getting into quadratic equations or integration—I promise. However, these two methods might take a bit of getting used to, so treat the examples in this chapter as just a taster; we will be going over the details in later chapters.

Relational Algebra: Specifying the Operations

With relational algebra, we describe queries by considering a sequence of operations or manipulations on the tables involved. Some operations act on one table, while others are different ways of combining data from two tables. (Remember that when I talk about tables, I really mean ones with unique rows.) Every time we use one of the operations on a table, the result is another table. This means we can build up quite complicated queries by taking the result of one operation and applying another operation to it.

We will look at all the different operations in detail throughout the book, but just as a simple example we will discuss how to use relational algebra to retrieve the names of the senior members of our golf club. We will need two operations. The *select* operation returns just those rows from a table that satisfy a particular condition. The *project* operation returns just the specified columns.

First we'll get just the rows we need. We can say it like this:

> *Apply the select operation to the Member table with the condition that the MemberType field must have the value "Senior".*

Clearly, this is all going to get a bit wordy as we apply more and more operations, so it is useful to introduce some shorthand, as shown in Listing 1-7. σ (the Greek letter sigma) stands for the select operation, and the condition is specified in the subscript. For convenience I have called the resulting table SenMemb.

Listing 1-7. *The Select Operation to Retrieve the Subset of Rows for Seniors*

$$\text{SenMemb} \leftarrow \sigma_{\text{MemberType='Senior'}} (\text{Member})$$

Figure 1-11 shows the result of this operation. Having retrieved a table with the appropriate rows, we now apply the project operation to get the right columns. Listing 1-8 shows the shorthand for this, where π (pi) denotes the project operation and the columns are specified in the subscript.

Listing 1-8. *The Project Operation to Retrieve a Subset of Columns*

$$\text{Final} \leftarrow \pi_{\text{LastName, FirstName}} (\text{SenMemb})$$

You can express the whole algebra expression in one go, as shown in Listing 1-9.

Listing 1-9. *The Complete Algebra Expression*

$$\text{Final} \leftarrow \pi_{\text{LastName, FirstName}} (\sigma_{\text{MemberType='Senior'}} (\text{Member}))$$

Figure 1-11 shows the original, intermediate, and final tables. Note that the intermediate and final tables are not permanent in the database.

The example in Figure 1-11 shows how we can apply two relational algebra operations in succession to retrieve a final relation with the required data. We do not really need the power of the relational algebra to visualize how to formulate a query this simple; however, most queries are not this simple.

$\sigma_{\text{MemberType="Senior"}}(\textbf{Member})$ $\qquad$ $\pi_{\text{LastName, FirstName}}(\sigma_{\text{MemberType="Senior"}}(\textbf{Member}))$

MemberID	LastName	FirstName	MemberType
118	McKenzie	Melissa	Junior
138	Stone	Michael	Senior
153	Nolan	Brenda	Senior
176	Branch	Helen	Social
178	Beck	Sarah	Social
228	Burton	Sandra	Junior
235	Cooper	William	Senior
239	Spence	Thomas	Senior
258	Olson	Barbara	Senior

MemberID	LastName	FirstName	MemberType
138	Stone	Michael	Senior
153	Nolan	Brenda	Senior
235	Cooper	William	Senior
239	Spence	Thomas	Senior
258	Olson	Barbara	Senior

LastName	FirstName
Stone	Michael
Nolan	Brenda
Cooper	William
Spence	Thomas
Olson	Barbara

Figure 1-11. *Result of two successive relational algebra operations*

Relational Calculus: Specifying the Result

Relational algebra lets us specify a sequence of operations that eventually result in a set of rows with the information we require. As we will see throughout this book, there may be several different ways of applying a sequence of relational operations that will retrieve the same data. The other method that relational theory provides for describing a query is relational calculus. Rather than specifying *how* to do the query, we describe *what* conditions the resulting data should satisfy. Once again, this may take a bit of getting used to, so we will go over all this more carefully in later chapters.

In nonformal language, a relational calculus description of a query has the following form:

I want the set of rows that obey the following conditions . . .

As with the algebra version, this can become very wordy, so shorthand is convenient, as shown in Listing 1-10.

Listing 1-10. *General Form of a Query Expressed in Relational Calculus*

```
{ m | condition(m) }
```

The part on the left of the bar will contain a description of the attributes or columns we want returned, while the part on the right describes the criteria they must satisfy. The letter m is a way of referring to a particular row (m) in a table, and we will need to introduce other labels when we have several tables to contend with. An example is the best way to clarify what a relational calculus expression means. Listing 1-11 shows the relational calculus for the query to retrieve senior club members.

Listing 1-11. *Relational Calculus to Retrieve Senior Members*

```
{m | Member(m) and m.MemberType = 'Senior'}
```

We can interpret Listing 1-11 like this:

> *Retrieve each row (m) from the* Member *table where the* MemberType *attribute of that row has the value "Senior".*

We can further refine the query as in Listing 1-12, which retrieves just the names of the senior members.

Listing 1-12. *Relational Calculus to Retrieve the Names of Senior Members*

```
{m.LastName, m.FirstName | Member(m) and m.MemberType = 'Senior'}
```

We can interpret Listing 1-12 like this:

> *Retrieve the values of the* FirstName *and* LastName *attributes from all the rows m where m comes from the* Member *table and the* MemberType *attribute of those rows has the value "Senior".*

Why are we doing this? Admittedly, it is over the top to introduce this notation for such a simple query, but as our queries become more complex and involve several tables, it is useful to have a way to express the criteria in an unambiguous way. Also, SQL is based on relational calculus. In Listing 1-12 if you replace the bar (|) with the SQL keyword FROM and the "and" with the keyword WHERE, then you essentially have the SQL query of Listing 1-6.

Why Do We Need Both Algebra and Calculus?

It would be reasonable to also ask, why do we need either? As mentioned earlier, we do not need these abstract ideas for simple queries. However, if all queries were simple, you would not be reading this book. In the first instance, queries are expressed in everyday language that is often ambiguous. Try this simple expression: "Find me all students who are younger than 20 or live at home and get an allowance." This can mean different things depending on where you insert commas. Even after we have sorted out what the natural-language expression means, we then have to think about the query in terms of the actual tables in the database. This means having to be quite specific in how we express the query. Both relational algebra and relational calculus give us a powerful way of being accurate and specific.

So, we need a way of expressing our queries. Why not skip all this abstract stuff and go right ahead and learn SQL? Well, the SQL language consists of elements of both calculus and algebra. Ancient versions of SQL were purely based on relational calculus in that you described *what* you wanted to retrieve rather than *how*. In the SELECT clause you specified the attributes, in the FROM clause you listed the tables, and in the WHERE clause you specified the criteria (much as in Listing 1-6). Modern implementations of SQL allow you to explicitly specify algebraic operations such as joins, products, and unions on the tables as well.

There are often several equivalent ways of expressing an SQL statement. Some ways are very much based on calculus, some are based on algebra, and some are a bit of both. I have been teaching queries to university students for several years. For some complicated queries, I often ask the class whether they find the calculus or algebra expressions more intuitive. The class is usually equally divided. Personally I find some queries just feel obvious in terms of relational algebra, whereas others feel much more simple expressed in relational calculus. Once I have the idea pinned down with one or the other, the translation into SQL (or some other query language) is usually straightforward.

The more tools you have at your disposal, the more likely you will be able to express complex queries accurately.

Summary

This chapter has presented an overview of relational databases. We have seen that a relational database consists of a set of tables that represent the different aspects of our data (for example, a table for members and a table for types). Each table has a primary key that is a field(s) that is guaranteed to have a different value for every row, and each field (or column) of the table has a set of allowed values (a domain).

We have also seen that it is possible to set up relationships between tables with foreign keys. A foreign key is a value in one table that has to already exist as the primary key in another table. For example, the value of MemberType in the Member table must be one of the values in the primary key field of the Type table.

It is often helpful to think about queries in an abstract way, and there are two ways to do this. Relational algebra is a set of operations that can be applied to tables in a database. It is a way of describing *how* we need to manipulate the tables to extract the information we require. Relational calculus is a way of describing *what* criteria our required information must satisfy.

SQL is a language for specifying queries on a database. There are usually many equivalent ways to specify a query in SQL. Some are like calculus, and some are like algebra. And some are a bit of both.

CHAPTER 2

■ ■ ■

Simple Queries on One Table

If a database has been designed correctly, the data will be in several different tables. For example, our golf database is likely to have separate tables for information about members, teams, and tournaments, as well as tables that connect these values, for example, which members play in which teams, enter which tournaments, and so on. To make the best use of our data, we will need to combine values from different tables. As we work through complicated combinations, we can imagine the set of rows resulting from each step being put into a "virtual" table. We can think of a virtual table as one that is made to order and is only temporary. At each step we may be interested in only some of the data in the virtual table. In this chapter, we will look at choosing values from just one table. The table may be one of the permanent tables in our database, or it may be a virtual table that has been temporarily put together as part of a more complicated query.

As an example in this chapter, we will look at the table containing information about members. We may want to see information about just some of the members (a subset of the rows), or we may want to see only some values for each member (a subset of the columns). Or, we may want a combination of both. We can think of a query to get a subset of information as "cutting" a subset of rows and columns from our table and then "pasting" them into a resulting virtual or temporary table, as shown Figure 2-1.

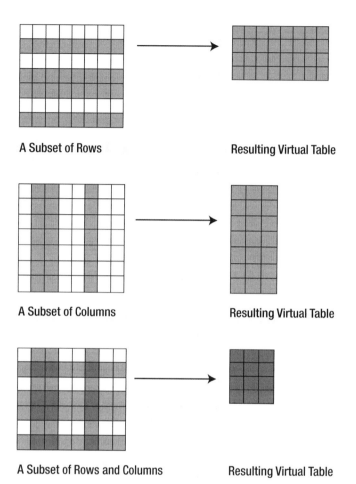

Figure 2-1. *Retrieving subsets of rows and columns from a single table*

Simple queries like this can provide information for reports, subsets of data for analysis, and answers to specific questions. Figure 2-2 shows some examples for the Member table from our golf club database.

MemberID	LastName	FirstName	Phone	Handicap	JoinDate	Gender	MemberType
323	Wilcox	Daniel	665393	3	30-Apr-03	M	Senior
461	Reed	Robert	994664	3	18-Jul-99	M	Senior
415	Taylor	William	137353	7	09-Nov-01	M	Senior
239	Spence	Thomas	697720	10	04-Jun-00	M	Senior
235	Cooper	William	722954	14	15-Feb-02	M	Senior
286	Pollard	Robert	617681	19	26-Jul-07	M	Junior
331	Schmidt	Thomas	867492	25	20-Mar-03	M	Senior
290	Sexton	Thomas	268936	26	10-Jul-02	M	Senior
138	Stone	Michael	983223	30	13-May-03	M	Senior

a) Subset of rows: All the information about men

LastName	FirstName	Phone
McKenzie	Melissa	963270
Stone	Michael	983223
Nolan	Brenda	442649
Branch	Helen	589419
Beck	Sarah	226596
Burton	Sandra	244493
Cooper	William	722954
Spence	Thomas	697720
Olson	Barbara	370186
Pollard	Robert	617681
Sexton	Thomas	268936
Wilcox	Daniel	665393
Schmidt	Thomas	867492
Bridges	Deborah	279087
Young	Betty	507813
Gilmore	Jane	459558
Taylor	William	137353
Reed	Robert	994664
Willis	Carolyn	688378
Kent	Susan	707217

b) Subset of columns:
Phone list for all members

LastName	FirstName	Handicap
Gilmore	Jane	5
Pollard	Robert	19
Burton	Sandra	26
Willis	Carolyn	29
McKenzie	Melissa	30

c) Subset of both rows and columns:
Handicaps for Junior members

Phone
244493

d) A tiny (1 cell) subset:
Member 228's phone number

Figure 2-2. *Examples of simple queries on the Member table*

Retrieving rows and columns uses the relational algebra operations *select* and *project*. Nearly all queries will at some stage include the select and project operations.

Retrieving a Subset of Rows

Retrieving a subset of rows is one of the most common operations we will carry out in a query. In the following sections, we will look at retrieving rows from one of the original tables in our database. The same ideas apply to selecting rows from virtual tables resulting from other manipulations of our data.

Relational Algebra for Retrieving Rows

The relational algebra select operation retrieves rows from a table. To decide which rows to retrieve, we need to specify a *condition* for the operation. Basically, a condition is a statement that is either true or false. We apply the condition to each row in the table independently, retaining those rows for which the condition is true and discarding the others. Say we want to find all the men our club, as in Figure 2-2a. Fortunately, when we designed our database in Chapter 1, we foresaw such a query and included an attribute Gender in the Member table. We want just that subset of rows where the value in the Gender field is "M", so this becomes the condition for the select operation.

Listing 2-1 shows the notation for this operation. The Greek letter sigma (σ) is short-hand for select, the table we are applying the operation to is in parentheses (Member), and the subscript Gender = 'M' is the condition.

Listing 2-1. *The Select Operation to Retrieve All the Men from the Member Table*

$\sigma_{\text{Gender='M'}}(\text{Member})$

What if we want to find everyone with a handicap under 12? This will again be a subset of rows from the Member table, so the select operation will do the trick. The condition this time depends on the value in the Handicap column. We want any rows where the value of Handicap is less than 12. Listing 2-2 shows the relational algebra for retrieving the required rows. We will look more closely at how to express more complex conditions in the next section.

Listing 2-2. *The Select Operation Used to Retrieve Members with Handicaps Under 12*

$\sigma_{\text{Handicap}<12}(\text{Member})$

Relational Calculus for Retrieving Rows

The relational algebra describes *how* we should retrieve the required information from our database; in the previous cases, it's by saying "Go and get the subset of rows that satisfy this condition." The relational calculus describes *what* the required information is like.

Listing 2-3 shows the shorthand for expressing the calculus for retrieving men from the Member table.

Listing 2-3. *The Calculus Expression to Retrieve All the Men from the Member Table*

```
{m | Member(m) and m.Gender = 'M'}
```

The part on the right of the vertical bar (|) is the description of the retrieved rows. The expression in Listing 2-3 can be interpreted as saying "I want a set of rows that come from the Member table, and each row must have 'M' as the value for the Gender attribute."

The letter m in Listing 2-3 is officially called a *tuple* variable, but I'll refer to it as a *row variable* (which is not strictly accurate but a bit easier to understand). I like to think of the variable acting like a finger, as in Figure 2-3. The finger (labeled m) points to each row in the Member table and checks to see whether it obeys the condition that its Gender attribute has the value "M". As our queries get more complex, we will have many different fingers pointing at different tables.

	LastName	FirstName	MemberType	Phone	Handicap	JoinDate	Gender
	McKenzie	Melissa	Junior	963270	30	10-May-99	F
	Stone	Michael	Senior	983223	30	13-May-03	M
m ☞	Nolan	Brenda	Senior	442649	11	25-Jul-00	F
	Branch	Helen	Social	589419		18-Nov-05	F
	Beck	Sarah	Social	226596		06-Jan-04	F
	Burton	Sandra	Junior	244493	26	21-Jun-07	F
	Cooper	William	Senior	722954	14	15-Feb-02	M
	Spence	Thomas	Senior	697720	10	04-Jun-00	M
	Olson	Barbara	Senior	370186	16	11-Jul-07	F

Figure 2-3. *Row variable m investigating each row of the Member table*

SQL for Retrieving Rows

Listing 2-4 shows the SQL statement for retrieving information about the men in our golf club.

Listing 2-4. *The SQL Statement to Retrieve All the Men from the Member Table*

```
SELECT *
FROM Member
WHERE Gender = 'M'
```

This query has three parts, or *clauses*: The SELECT[1] clause says what information to retrieve. In this case, * means retrieve all the columns. The FROM clause says which table(s)

---

1. Note that in SQL the keyword SELECT just means that a given statement is a query for retrieving information. It doesn't mean that the statement is necessarily going to involve an algebra select operation.

the query involves, and the WHERE clause describes the condition for deciding whether a particular row should be included in the result. Our condition says to check the value in the field Gender. In SQL when we specify an actual value for a character field, we need to enclose the value in single quotes, as in 'M'.

Retrieving a Subset of Columns

Now let's look at how we can specify that we want to see only some of the columns in our result, perhaps just names and phone numbers as in Figure 2-2b. Once again, this is an operation that we can apply to an original table in our database or to a virtual table resulting from some complex combination of several tables.

Relational Algebra for Retrieving Columns

The relational algebra operation for retrieving a subset of columns is project, and we represent it with the Greek letter pi (π). Listing 2-5 shows the algebra for selecting the names and phone numbers from our Member table.

Listing 2-5. *The Project Operation to Retrieve Names and Phone Numbers from the Member Table*

$$\pi_{\text{LastName, FirstName, Phone}}(\text{Member})$$

The columns we want to retrieve (LastName, FirstName, and Phone) are specified in the subscript.

Relational Calculus for Retrieving Columns

Our notation for expressing a calculus query is in two parts separated by a bar, as in Listing 2-6. The part on the left describes what information we want to retrieve (in this case the LastName, FirstName, and Phone columns), and the part on the right describes the condition. In this case, the condition is only that the row comes from the Member table because we want the information for all our members.

Listing 2-6. *The Calculus Expression to Retrieve Names and Phone Numbers from the Member Table*

```
{m.LastName, m.FirstName, m.Phone | Member(m) }
```

Once again, it is useful to think of the row variable m as being a finger pointing at each row, deciding whether it is to be included and then retrieving the specified attributes of that row.

SQL for Retrieving Columns

We specify what columns we want to retrieve in the SELECT clause of an SQL query. Whereas previously we used * to say "return all the columns," Listing 2-7 now specifies the subset of columns we want in our result.

Listing 2-7. *The SQL for Retrieving Names and Phone Numbers from the Member Table*

```
SELECT LastName, FirstName, Phone
FROM Member
```

Because we want to see all these column values for *every* row, this query doesn't need a WHERE clause.

Using Aliases

The query in Listing 2-7 works just fine, but as our queries get more complicated and involved, we will have a number of different tables. Some of the tables may have the same column names, and we might need to distinguish them. Therefore, we can preface each of the attributes in our query with the name of the table that they come from, as in Listing 2-8.

Listing 2-8. *Prefacing Attribute Names with the Table Name*

```
SELECT Member.LastName, Member.FirstName, Member.Phone
FROM Member
```

Because typing the whole table name can become tiresome and also because in some queries we might need to compare data in more than one row of a table, SQL has the notion of an *alias*. Have a look at Listing 2-9.

Listing 2-9. *Using an Alias*

```
SELECT m.LastName, m.FirstName, m.Phone
FROM Member m
```

In the FROM clause, we have declared an alias or alternative name for the Member table, in this case m. We can give our alias any name or letter we like; short is good. Then in the rest of the query we can use the alias whenever we want to specify an attribute from that table.

Now compare our relational calculus expression in Listing 2-6 and the SQL in Listing 2-9. We can think of the alias in the SQL as serving the same purpose as the row variable in the calculus expression. SQL syntax is based very much on relational calculus. This may all seem unnecessary for a simple query, but as our queries get more complicated, the idea of row variables will simplify things a great deal and make it much easier to get the SQL statements correct. I'll use aliases in all the SQL queries from now on.

Combining Subsets of Rows and Columns

In the previous sections, we saw the algebra operations select (a subset of rows) and project (a subset of columns) acting independently. One of the most powerful features of the algebra is that the result of an operation is another table (or, more formally, another set of unique rows). This means we can apply another operation to the result of the first operation and so build up complex queries.

We can use successive operations to create an algebra expression for the query in Figure 2-2c, retrieving the names and handicaps of junior members. First we find the rows for juniors using a select operation, and then we use a project operation to retrieve the required columns from the result. Listing 2-10 shows the full expression.

Listing 2-10. *Combining a Select and Project Operation*

$$\pi_{\text{LastName, FirstName, Handicap}} (\sigma_{\text{MemberType = 'Junior'}} (\text{Member}))$$

As you can see, the algebra tells us *how* to get the result we want. First get the appropriate rows, and then get the required columns. The calculus doesn't tell us *how* to carry out a series of steps; it just describes *what* the final set of rows will be like. Have a look at Listing 2-11.

Listing 2-11. *Calculus Expression to Retrieve Handicaps of Junior Members*

{m.Lastname, m.FirstName, m.Handicap | Member(m) and m.MemberType = 'Junior'}

The left side of the expression in Listing 2-11 says we are going to retrieve the LastName, FirstName, and Handicap values from some row m. The right side of the expression tells us which rows to include. Picture a finger labeled m, as in Figure 2-3. The expression in Listing 2-11 says that our finger m is going to scan rows in the Member table and include those rows where the value of MemberType is "Junior".

Now look at Listing 2-12, which shows the SQL for this query.

Listing 2-12. *SQL Statement to Retrieve Handicaps of Junior Members*

```
SELECT m.Lastname, m.FirstName, m.Handicap
FROM Member m
WHERE m.MemberType = 'Junior'
```

Compare the SQL in Listing 2-12 with the calculus expression in Listing 2-11, and you will see that they have all the same parts: an alias or row variable m declared for the Member table, a condition to say which rows to include, and a list of which attributes or columns to retrieve.

Saving Queries

I've been talking in a rather imprecise manner about "retrieving" rows and "returning" information. What happens to the rows that result from a query? In reality, we are not getting information and putting it anywhere; we are just looking at a subset of the information in the tables in our database. If the data in the underlying database changes, then the results of our query will change too. A query is like a window on our database through which we can see just the information we require. It doesn't hurt to think about the information that results from a query being in the form of a "virtual" table as long as you realize it is just temporary. The images in Figure 2-2 are results of queries, but they are not real tables—just different windows into the underlying Member table.

It is possible to keep the result of a query in a new permanent table (sometimes called a *snapshot*), but we usually don't want to do that because it will become out of date if the underlying data changes. What we usually want to do is save the instructions so that we can ask the same question another day. Consider our phone list query. Every so often after the membership of the club has been updated, we might want to see a new phone list. Rather than having to write the query in Listing 2-7 each time, we can save the instructions in what is known as a *view*. Listing 2-13 shows how we can create a view so we can see up-to-date phone lists. We have to give the view a name, which can be anything we want (PhoneList seems sensible), and then we supply the SQL statement (as in Listing 2-7) for retrieving the appropriate data.

Listing 2-13. *Creating a View So You Can Use the Same Query Many Times*

```
CREATE VIEW PhoneList AS
SELECT m.LastName, m.FirstName, m.Phone
FROM Member m
```

PhoneList now becomes a "virtual" table, and we can use it like one of our real tables in other queries. We just need to remember that the virtual table is created on the fly by running the query on the permanent Member table and is then gone. To get our phone list now, we can use the SQL statement in Listing 2-14.

Listing 2-14. *Using a View in a Query*

```
SELECT * FROM PhoneList
```

Specifying Conditions for Selecting Rows

In the queries we looked at in the previous sections, we used very simple conditions or criteria for determining whether to include a row in the result of a query. We looked at the value in just one field, such as MemberType = 'Junior'. In the following section, we will look more closely at the different ways you can specify quite complicated conditions.

Comparison Operators

A *condition* is a statement or expression that is either true or false, such as MemberType = 'Junior'. These types of expressions are called *Boolean expressions* after the 19th-century English mathematician George Boole who investigated their properties. The conditions we use to select rows from a table usually involve comparing the values of an attribute to some constant value. For example, we can ask whether the value of an attribute is the same, different, or greater than some value. Table 2-1 shows some comparison operators we can use in our queries.

Table 2-1. *Comparison Operators*

Operator	Meaning	Examples of True Statement
=	Equals	5=5, 'Junior' = 'Junior'
<	Less than	4<5, 'Ann' < 'Zebedee'
<=	Less than or equal	4<=5, 5<=5
>	Greater than	5>4, 'Zebedee' > 'Ann'
>=	Greater than or equal	5>=4, 5>=5
<>	Not equal	5<>4, 'Junior' <> 'Senior'

Just a quick note of caution. In Table 2-1, some of our examples compare numbers, and some compare text. When we compare text attributes, the comparison is alphabetical. "A" comes before "Z", so "A" < "Z". Similarly, "Ann" comes before "Azaria" alphabetically, so "Ann" < "Azaria," and so on. Recall from Chapter 1 that when we create a table, we specify the type of each field; for example, MemberID was an INT (integer or whole number), and LastName was CHAR(20) (a 20-character field). With numeric fields like INT, comparisons are numerical. With text or character fields, comparisons are alphabetical, and with date and time fields, comparisons are chronological. If we put numbers in a character field, they will sort alphabetically. This means you have things like "40" < "5" (because the first character, "4", in the left text is less than the first character, "5", on the right side[2]). So, make sure if a field in your table is going to contain numbers that you make it a numeric type, or you might get some rather surprising results from your queries.

---

2. The comparison for text is generally done by comparing the Unicode values of each character in turn. The character "4" has a value of 52, and "5" has a value of 53.

With these comparison operators, we can create many different queries. Often we will compare a value of an attribute (say MemberType) to a literal value (say "Junior"). Table 2-2 shows some examples of Boolean expressions that we can use as conditions in the WHERE clause of an SQL statement for selecting rows from the Member table.

Table 2-2. *Examples of Boolean Expressions on the Member Table*

Expression	Retrieved Rows
MemberType = 'Junior'	All junior members
Handicap <= 12	All members with a handicap of 12 or less
JoinDate < '01/01/2000'	Everyone who has been a member since before the beginning of 2000
Gender = 'F'	All the women

Some implementations of SQL are case sensitive when comparing text, and others are not. Being case sensitive means that, in comparisons, the different cases of the letters will make a difference; in other words, "Junior" is different from "junior", which is different from "JUNIOR". I usually check out any new database system I use to see what it does. If you do not care about the case of the attribute you are considering (that is, you are happy to retrieve rows where MemberType is "Junior" or "jUnIoR" or whatever), you can use the SQL function UPPER as in Listing 2-15. This will turn the value of each text attribute into uppercase before you do the comparison so that you know what is happening.

Listing 2-15. *Selecting Rows Where the Case of a Text Value Is Not Important*

```
SELECT *
FROM Member m
WHERE UPPER(m.MemberType) = 'JUNIOR'
```

Logical Operators

We can also combine Boolean expressions to create more interesting conditions. For example, we can specify that two expressions must both be true before we retrieve a particular row.

Let's assume we want to find all the junior girls. This requires two conditions to be true: they must be female, and they must be juniors. We can easily express each of these conditions independently. After that, we can use the logical operator AND, as in Listing 2-16, to say that *both* conditions must be true.

Listing 2-16. *Finding All the Junior Girls*

```
SELECT *
FROM Member m
WHERE m.MemberType = 'Junior' AND m.Gender = 'F'
```

Here we will look at three logical operators: AND, OR, and NOT. We have already seen how AND works. If we use OR between two expressions, then we require only one of the expressions to be true (but if they are both true, that is OK as well). NOT is used before an expression. For example, for our Member table, we might ask for rows obeying the condition NOT (MemberType = 'Social'). This means check each row, and if the value of MemberType is "Social", then we don't want that row. Table 2-3 gives some examples for the Member table. In the diagrams, each circle represents a set of rows (that is, those for social members or those for members with handicaps under 12). The shaded area represents the result of the operation.

Table 2-3. *Examples of Logical Operators*

Expression	Description of Retrieved Data	Diagram of Retrieved Data
MemberType = 'Senior' AND Handicap < 12	Seniors with a handicap under 12	
MemberType = 'Senior' OR Handicap < 12	All the senior members as well as anyone else with a good handicap (those less than 12)	
NOT MemberType = 'Social'	All the members except the social ones (for the current data, that would be just the seniors and juniors)	

The little truth tables in Figure 2-4 can be helpful in understanding and remembering how the Boolean operators work. You read them like this: In Figures 2-4a and 2-4b, we have two expressions, one along the top and one down the left. Each expression can have one of two values: True (T) or False (F). If we combine them with the Boolean expression AND, then Figure 2-4a shows that the overall statement is True only if both the contributing statements are True (the square in the top left). If we combine them with an OR statement, then the overall statement is False only if both contributing statements are False (bottom right of Figure 2-4b). The table in Figure 2-4c says that if our original statement is True and we put NOT in front, then the result is False (left column), and vice versa.

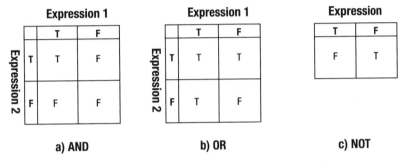

Figure 2-4. *Truth tables for logical operators (T = True, F = False)*

Sometimes it can be a bit tricky turning natural-language descriptions into Boolean expressions. If you were asked for a list that included *all the woman and all the juniors* (don't ask why!), you might translate this literally and write the condition MemberType = 'Junior' AND Gender = 'F'. However, the AND means *both* conditions must be true, so this would give us junior women. What our natural-language statement really means is "I want the row for any member if they are either a woman OR they are a junior (or both)." Be careful.

Dealing with Nulls

The example data in the Member table shown earlier in Figure 2-2 is all very accurate and complete. Every row has a value for each attribute except for Handicap, which doesn't apply to some members. Real data is usually not so clean. Let's consider some different data, as in Figure 2-5.

MemberID	LastName	FirstName	MemberType	Phone	Handicap	Gender
118	McKenzie	Melissa	Junior	963270	30	F
178	Beck	Sarah	Social	226596		F
235	Cooper	William	Senior	722954	14	M
239	Spence	Thomas	Senior	697720	10	M
258	Olson	Barbara		370186	16	F
283	Jones	Kim	Junior	617681	19	
290	Sexton	Thomas	Senior	268936	26	M
323	Wilcox	Daniel	Senior	665393	3	M
331	Schmidt	Thomas	Senior	867492	25	M

Figure 2-5. *Table with missing data*

When there is no value in a cell in a table, it is said to be *Null*. Nulls can cause a few headaches in a database. For example, if we ran two queries, one to produce a list of male members and the other a list of females, we might assume that all the members of the club would appear on one list or the other. However, for the data in Figure 2-5, we would miss Kim Jones. Now, you could argue that the data shouldn't be like that—but we are talking about real people and real clubs with less than accurate and complete data. Maybe Kim forgot (or refused) to fill in the gender part of the application form. It is possible to insist that Nulls are not allowed in a field when we create a table. Listing 2-17 shows how we could make Gender a field that always requires a value.

Listing 2-17. *SQL for Creating a Table with a Required Field*

```
CREATE TABLE Member (
MemberID INT PRIMARY KEY,
...
Gender CHAR(1) NOT NULL,

...)
```

It is worth bearing in mind, however, that making fields required can create more headaches than it cures. If Kim Jones did not fill all the boxes on his/her membership application but sent a bank draft for the subscription, then we want to make him/her a member and worry about the full details later. However, if we make Gender a required field, then we can't enter a record for him/her in the table—or we have to guess what his/her gender is. Neither of these options is very good, so it is best to be sparing about making fields required. Remember that our primary key fields (by definition) always need a value.

Not all values of Null mean there is a problem with the data. In our Member table, a field might be Null because it does not apply to a particular member. Sarah Beck's handicap may be genuinely Null because she does not have a handicap. However, it is fair to assume that every member should have a value for MemberType and Gender, so the Nulls in these columns are because we do not know the value. In the real world, therefore, expect that your tables will have missing data.

Comparing Null Values

Given that we are going to have unexpected Nulls in our tables, it is important to know how to deal with them. What rows will match the two conditions in Listing 2-18?

Listing 2-18. *What Rows Will Match Each of These Conditions*

```
Gender = 'F'
NOT (Gender = 'F')
```

If we run two queries with the conditions in Listing 2-18, will we get all the rows in the table? You might think that if we get all the rows that match a condition and all the ones that don't, then we will get the lot. But in fact we don't. Kim will not be included with the first condition because clearly the value of Gender does not equal "F", But when we ask whether the value is NOT ("F"), we can't say because we don't know what the value is. It might be "F" if it had a value. This probably makes more sense if we think about handicaps. If we ask for everyone with Handicap > 12, NOT (Handicap > 12), or Handicap <=12, then Sarah's row will never be retrieved because the question doesn't apply to her—she doesn't have a handicap.

So once we take Nulls into consideration, our expressions for conditions might actually have one of three values: True, False, or "don't know." That is pretty much how the world actually works if you think about it. Only rows that are True for a condition are retrieved in a query. If the condition is False or if we "don't know," then the row is not retrieved.

The truth tables, when we include "don't know," look like those in Figure 2-6. For an AND operation, if one expression is False, then it doesn't matter about the others—the result will be False. For an OR operation, if one expression is True, then it doesn't matter about the others, so the result will be True.

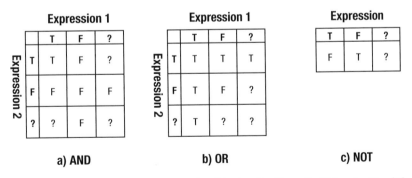

Figure 2-6. *Truth tables with three valued logic (T = True, F= False, ? = Don't know)*

Finding Nulls

Given that in our tables we may have Nulls that might cause us problems, it is useful to be able to find them. After we have entered a lot of new members into our database, we should check for problems. We might want to get a list of all the members who don't have a value for MemberType, say. The SQL phrase to do this is IS NULL, as in Listing 2-19.

Listing 2-19. *Finding the Members with No Value for MemberType*

```
SELECT *
FROM Member m
WHERE m.MemberType IS NULL
```

Alternatively, we might want to retrieve just those members who do have a value in a cell. If we wanted the names and handicaps of those members who have a value for Handicap, we could use the NOT operator to write a query like that in Listing 2-20.

Listing 2-20. *Retrieving Information About Members Who Have a Handicap*

```
SELECT *
FROM Member m
WHERE NOT (m.Handicap IS NULL)
```

Managing Duplicates

Let's get a little more formal for a moment. In Chapter 1, I explained that relational theory is based on mathematics and one of its main premises is that we are working with relations. A relation is a set of distinct rows. The fact that all the rows are different is important. Not only would it make no sense to have two identical rows about one of our members, but it would also get us into all sorts of trouble. I've been using the term *table* rather than *relation* but on the understanding that all our tables have a primary key, which ensures they meet the requirement that the rows are unique. When we use a project operation to retrieve a subset of columns, we may no longer have that primary key field in the result. Relational algebra depends on the result of each operation being another relation, and this is why it is possible to build up a series of operations to create quite complex queries. What do we do about possible duplicates? Let's look at an example.

Consider the relational project operation to retrieve just the FirstName column from the Member table. Figure 2-7 shows two possible results.

FirstName
Melissa
Michael
Brenda
Helen
Sarah
Sandra
William
Thomas
Barbara
Robert
Thomas
Daniel
Thomas
Deborah
Betty
Jane
William
Robert
Carolyn
Susan

FirstName
Barbara
Betty
Brenda
Carolyn
Daniel
Deborah
Helen
Jane
Melissa
Michael
Robert
Sandra
Sarah
Susan
Thomas
William

a) With duplicates   b) Without duplicates

Figure 2-7. *Projecting the FirstName column from the Member table*

From a mathematical perspective, there is no question that in terms of the relational algebra the project operation will give us Figure 2-7b, a set of unique rows with the duplicates for William and Thomas removed. What would you have expected? It is useful to think about why we might carry out a query retrieving just names. Perhaps the query is to help prepare a set of nametags for a club party. If that is the case, then two Thomases and a William are going to feel a bit left out if we use the unique output.

For the previous example you might think, what's all the fuss? Of course we want to keep all the rows. But let's look at a different project operation to retrieve a list of membership types. Figure 2-8 shows the outputs with duplicates included and removed.

It's pretty difficult to think of a situation where you want the duplicated rows in Figure 2-8a. The two project operations we have considered sound similar in natural language. "Give me a list of first names" and "Give me a list of membership types" sound like the same sort of question, but they mean something quite different. The first means "Give me a name for each member," and the other means "Give me a list of unique membership types."

MemberType
Junior
Senior
Senior
Social
Social
Junior
Senior
Senior
Senior
Junior
Senior
Senior
Senior
Senior
Senior
Junior
Senior
Senior
Junior
Social

MemberType
Junior
Senior
Social

a) With duplicates   **b) Without duplicates**

Figure 2-8. *Projecting the MemberType column from the Member table*

What does SQL do? If we say `SELECT MemberType FROM Member`, we will get the output in Figure 2-8a with all the duplicates included. If we do not want the duplicates, then we can use the keyword DISTINCT, as in Listing 2-21.

Listing 2-21. *Retrieving a List of Unique Membership Types*

```
SELECT DISTINCT m.MemberType
FROM Member m
```

Whether you keep the duplicates depends very much on the information you require, so you need to give it some careful thought. If you were expecting the set of rows in Figure 2-8b and got Figure 2-8a, you would most likely notice. With the two sets of rows in Figure 2-7, it is much more difficult to spot that you have perhaps made a mistake. Get into the habit of thinking about duplicates for all your queries.

Ordering Output

Every now and then I refer to a "set of rows" rather than a table or a virtual table. Our formal definition of a database is a "set of tables," and for a table the definition is a "set of rows."[3] The word *set* has two implications. One is that there are no duplicates (and we have discussed that a lot!). The other implication is that there is no particular order to the rows in our set. In theory, we don't have a first row or a last row or a next row. If we run a query to retrieve all the rows, or just some of the rows, from a table, then we have no guarantee in what order they will be returned. However, sometimes we might like to display the result in a particular order. We can do this with the key phrase ORDER BY. Listing 2-22 shows how to retrieve member information ordered alphabetically by LastName.

Listing 2-22. *Retrieving the Members in Order of LastName*

```
SELECT *
FROM Member m
ORDER BY m.LastName
```

We can also order by two or more values. For example, if we want to order members with the same LastName by the value of their FirstName, we can include those two attributes (in that order) in the ORDER BY clause. The ORDER BY clause is the final clause in an SQL query. Listing 2-23 shows how to list all the senior members ordered by LastName and where the last names are the same by FirstName.

Listing 2-23. *Retrieving the Senior Members Ordered by LastName and Then FirstName*

```
SELECT *
FROM Member m
WHERE m.MemberType = 'Senior'
ORDER BY m.LastName, m.FirstName
```

The type of a field determines how the values will be ordered. Text fields will be ordered alphabetically, number fields will be ordered numerically, and date and time fields will be ordered chronologically.

Performing Simple Counts

As well as retrieving a subset of rows and columns from a table, we can also use SQL queries to retrieve some statistics. There are SQL functions that allow us to count records, total or average values, find maximum and minimum values, and so on. In this section, we will look at some simple queries for counting records. (We will return to this topic in Chapter 8.)

---

3. To be really formal, a database is actually a "set of relations," and a relation is a "set of tuples."

Listing 2-24 shows a simple query to return the number of records in the Member table. COUNT is a function in SQL, and * means count each record.

Listing 2-24. *Retrieving the Number of Records in a Table*

```
SELECT COUNT(*) FROM Member
```

We can also count a subset of rows by adding a WHERE clause to specify those rows we want to include. Listing 2-25 shows how to count the number of senior members.

Listing 2-25. *Retrieving the Number of Senior Members*

```
SELECT COUNT(*) FROM Member m
WHERE m.MemberType = 'Senior'
```

Because we have just been talking about Nulls and duplicate values, it is worth briefly mentioning here how these will affect our counts. Rather than use * as a parameter to the COUNT function so that it counts all the rows, we can put an attribute such as Handicap in parentheses, as shown in Listing 2-26. This will count the number of records that have a value for the Handicap attribute.

Listing 2-26. *Retrieving the Number of Records with a Non-Null Value for Handicap*

```
SELECT COUNT(Handicap) FROM Member
```

We can also specify that we want to count the number of unique values for an attribute, that is, how many different handicaps there are. Listing 2-27 shows how to do this.

Listing 2-27. *Retrieving the Number of Different Values for Handicap*

```
SELECT COUNT(DISTINCT Handicap) FROM Member
```

It is worth reiterating that different database software will support different parts of the SQL standard syntax. For example, Microsoft Access does not support the statement in Listing 2-27. There is usually a way to work around this and find an equivalent query, and we will look at that and other issues related to aggregates and summaries in Chapter 8.

Avoiding Common Mistakes

The select and project operations for retrieving a subset of rows and columns from a single table are the simplest of the relational operations. However, you have seen that you still need to be careful. It is important to remember that there will be Null values in your tables and to think carefully about how your selection conditions will treat them. You also need to remember that if you do not retrieve the primary key fields from your tables, there is the potential to have duplicate rows, and you must deal with them appropriately.

There are a couple of other mistakes that are commonly made with a select operation. They don't become apparent with a table like Member, so I'll introduce some more of the tables in our golf club database. Figure 2-9 shows part of the Member table and two other tables: Entry and Tournament. The first row in the Entry table records that person 118 (Melissa McKenzie) entered tournament 24 (Leeston) in 2005.

MemberID	LastName	FirstName
118	McKenzie	Melissa
138	Stone	Michael
153	Nolan	Brenda
176	Branch	Helen
178	Beck	Sarah
228	Burton	Sandra
235	Cooper	William
239	Spence	Thomas
258	Olson	Barbara
286	Pollard	Robert
290	Sexton	Thomas
323	Wilcox	Daniel
331	Schmidt	Thomas
332	Bridges	Deborah
339	Young	Betty
414	Gilmore	Jane
415	Taylor	William
461	Reed	Robert
469	Willis	Carolyn
487	Kent	Susan

MemberID	TourID	Year
118	24	2005
228	24	2006
228	25	2006
228	36	2006
235	38	2004
235	38	2006
235	40	2005
235	40	2006
239	25	2006
239	40	2004
258	24	2005
258	38	2005
286	24	2004
286	24	2005
286	24	2006
415	24	2006
415	25	2004
415	36	2005
415	36	2006
415	38	2004
415	38	2006
415	40	2004
415	40	2005
415	40	2006

TourID	TourName	TourType
24	Leeston	Social
25	Kaiapoi	Social
36	WestCoast	Open
38	Canterbury	Open
40	Otago	Open

a) Member (some columns)   b) Entry   c) Tournament

Figure 2-9. *Introducing the Tournament and Entry tables*

We can try some of our select and project operations on the Entry table to answer questions such as which tournaments (just the ID number) has person 258 entered, who (just the ID number) has ever entered tournament 24, or who entered tournament 36 in 2006. Listing 2-28 shows the SQL for the last question. (Recall that e is just an alias referring to the Entry table.)

Listing 2-28. *Who Entered Tournament 36 in 2006*

```
SELECT e.MemberID
FROM Entry e
WHERE e.TourID = 36 AND e.Year = 2006
```

Misusing Select to Answer Questions with the Word "both"

The select operation to find subsets of rows can very simply give us the answer to many questions as in the previous section. However, there is a bit of a temptation to write similar queries such as that in Listing 2-29 to try to retrieve people who have entered *both* tournaments 36 and 38.

Listing 2-29. *Incorrect SQL to Retrieve People Who Have Entered Both Tournaments 36 and 38*

```
SELECT e.MemberID
FROM Entry e
WHERE e.TourID = 36 AND e.TourID= 38
```

Can you work out what this query will return? This is where thinking of our row variable (finger) e investigating each row in table Entry can help. We can see part of the Entry table in Figure 2-10.

MemberID	TourID	Year
286	24	2005
286	24	2006
415	24	2006
415	25	2004
415	36	2005
415	36	2006
415	38	2004
415	38	2006
415	40	2004
415	40	2005
415	40	2006

Figure 2-10. *The row variable e investigates each row independently.*

Imagine our finger is pointing at the row shown in the diagram. Does this row (415, 38, 2004) satisfy the condition e.TourID = 36 AND e.TourID= 38? It satisfies the second part, but the AND operator requires the row to satisfy both conditions. No single row in our table will have *both* 36 and 38 in the tournament column because each row is for just one entry. The SQL in Listing 2-29 will never find any rows; it will always return an empty table. If we change the Boolean operator to OR, we will get the row indicated in Figure 2-10 returned; however, we will also then get anyone who has entered 36 or 38 but not necessarily both.

This particular query cannot be solved with a simple select operation. By definition, the condition in a select applies to *each row independently*. To answer the question about who has entered *both* competitions, we need to look at more than one row of the Entry table at the same time (that is, two fingers). If we have two fingers, one pointing at the row shown in Figure 2-10 and another pointing at the previous row, then we can deduce that 415 has been in both tournaments. We'll look at how to do this in Chapter 5.

Misusing Select Operations to Answer Questions with the Word "not"

Now let's consider another common error. It is easy to find the people who have entered tournament 36 with the condition e.TourID = 36. It is tempting to try to retrieve the people who have *not* entered tournament 36 by changing the condition slightly, as in Listing 2-30.

Listing 2-30. *Incorrect SQL to Retrieve People Who Have Not Entered Tournament 36*

```
SELECT e.MemberID
FROM Entry e
WHERE e.TourID <> 36
```

Can you figure out what rows the SQL query in Listing 2-28 will retrieve? What about the row that the finger is pointing to in Figure 2-10? Does this satisfy e.TourID <> 36? It certainly does. But this doesn't mean 415 hasn't entered tournament 36 (the previous row says he did). The query in Listing 2-28 returns all the people who have entered some tournament that isn't 36 (which is unlikely to be a question you'll ever want to ask!).

This is another type of question that can't be answered with a simple select operation that looks at independent rows in a table. In fact, we can't even do this with a query that involves just the Entry table. Member 138 Michael Stone has not entered tournament 36, but he doesn't even get a mention in the Entry table because he has never entered any tournaments at all. We'll see how to deal with questions like this in Chapter 7.

Summary

In this chapter, we looked at the relational algebra operations select and project on a single table, the equivalent relational calculus expressions, and the equivalent SQL statements.

The select operation returns a subset of rows that satisfy a given condition. The condition is a Boolean expression, which is a statement that is either true or not true. The expression usually compares the values in fields and—with the use of the Boolean operators AND, OR, and NOT—can be very descriptive. The condition is applied to each row of the table independently.

The project operation returns a subset of columns. Table 2-4 summarizes the SQL for the select and project operations.

Table 2-4. *SQL for Select and Project Operations*

SQL for Select	SQL for Project

`SELECT *`
`FROM <table>`
`WHERE <condition>`
	`SELECT <column 1>, <column 2> , ...`
	`FROM <table>`

Because relational operations always result in another table (really a relation), we can do several operations in succession. We can follow a select by a project to get a subset of both rows and columns.

Because the result of a query is a *set* of rows, we cannot guarantee the order in which the rows will be returned. If we want to display the result in a particular order, we can use the ORDER BY key phrase.

It is possible to create a view, which essentially stores an SQL command so that you can run it over and over again as the data in the base tables changes.

The following are some other key points to remember from this chapter:

- Tables are likely to have Null values (both on purpose and by mistake). Always check how your conditions will apply to Null values.

- When you project a subset of columns using an SQL command, the default is to retain duplicate rows in the result. Always think about whether you want the duplicates, and use the keyword DISTINCT if you want unique rows.

- The select operation considers only one row at a time. Don't use it for queries that require you to look at several rows at once, as in who entered *both* tournaments or who did *not* enter this tournament.

■ ■ ■

A First Look at Joins

In the previous chapter, we looked at how to retrieve subsets of rows and/or columns from a single table. We saw in Chapter 1 that to keep data accurately in a database, different aspects of our information need to be separated into normalized tables. Most of our queries will require information from two or more tables. You can combine data from two tables in several different ways depending on the nature of the information you are trying to extract. The most often encountered two-table operation is the join.

Joins in Relational Algebra

The join is one of the relational algebra operations, so we will first look at the definition in terms of the algebra. The algebra tells us *how* to get the result we are looking for, and a join has two steps. The first step involves an operation called a *Cartesian product*.

Cartesian Product

A Cartesian product is the most versatile operation between two tables because it can be applied to any two tables of any shape. Having said that, it rarely produces particularly useful information on its own, so its main claim to fame is as the first step of a join.

A Cartesian product is a bit like putting two tables side by side. Let's have a look at two tables in Figure 3-1: an abbreviated Member table and the Type table.

The virtual table resulting from the Cartesian product will have a column for each column in the two contributing tables. The rows in the resulting table consist of every combination of rows from the original tables. Figure 3-2 shows the first few rows of the Cartesian product.

MemberID	LastName	FirstName	MemberType
118	McKenzie	Melissa	Junior
138	Stone	Michael	Senior
153	Nolan	Brenda	Senior
176	Branch	Helen	Social
178	Beck	Sarah	Social
228	Burton	Sandra	Junior
235	Cooper	William	Senior
239	Spence	Thomas	Senior
258	Olson	Barbara	Senior

Type	Fee
Junior	150
Senior	300
Social	50

a) (Abbreviated) Member table   b) Type table

Figure 3-1. *Two permanent tables in our database*

From Member table   From Type table

MemberID	LastName	FirstName	MemberType	Type	Fee
118	McKenzie	Melissa	Junior	Junior	150
118	McKenzie	Melissa	Junior	Senior	300
118	McKenzie	Melissa	Junior	Social	50
138	Stone	Michael	Senior	Junior	150
138	Stone	Michael	Senior	Senior	300
138	Stone	Michael	Senior	Social	50
153	Nolan	Brenda	Senior	Junior	150
153	Nolan	Brenda	Senior	Senior	300
153	Nolan	Brenda	Senior	Social	50
176 Branch	Hel...				...50

Figure 3-2. *First few rows of the Cartesian product between Member and Type*

We have the four columns from the Member table and the two columns from the Type table, which gives us six columns total. Each row from the Member table appears in the resulting table alongside each row from the Type table. We have Melissa McKenzie appearing on three rows—once with each of the three rows in the Type table (junior, senior, social). The total number of rows will be the number of rows in each table multiplied together; in other words, for this cut-down Member table, we have 9 rows times 3 rows (from Type), giving a total of 27 rows. Cartesian products can produce very, very large result tables, which is why they don't give us much useful information on their own. Listing 3-1 shows the relational algebra expression for the Cartesian product resulting in the table in Figure 3-2. The symbol X represents the Cartesian product operation.

Listing 3-1. *Cartesian Product Between Two Tables*

```
Member X Type
```

Inner Join

If you look at the table in Figure 3-2, you can see that most of the rows are quite meaningless. For example, the second and third rows that have our junior member Melissa McKenzie alongside information about the senior and social membership types are pointless. However, the first row where the member types from each table match is useful because it allows us to see what fee Melissa pays. If we take just the subset of rows where the value in the MemberType column matches the value in the Type column, then we have useful information about the fees for each of our members. This combination of a Cartesian product followed by a select operation is known as an *inner join* (often just called a *join*). The condition for the rows we want to retrieve is known as the *join condition*. Listing 3-2 shows the algebra expression to retrieve members with their appropriate fees. On the left side of the equation, the bow tie symbol represents the join between the two tables Member and Type, and the join condition is expressed in the subscript. On the right side of the equation, we perform a select operation on the result of the Cartesian product.

Listing 3-2. *A Join (Left Side) Is Defined As a Cartesian Product Followed by a Select*

$$\text{Member} \bowtie_{\text{MemberType}=\text{Type}} \text{Type} = \sigma_{\text{MemberType}=\text{Type}}(\text{Member X Type})$$

Figure 3-3 depicts the process.

a) Cartesian product → select → **b) Join**

MemberID	LastName	FirstName	MemberType	Type	Fee
118	McKenzie	Melissa	Junior	Junior	150
118	McKenzie	Melissa	Junior	Senior	300
118	McKenzie	Melissa	Junior	Social	50
138	Stone	Michael	Senior	Junior	150
138	Stone	Michael	Senior	Senior	300
138	Stone	Michael	Senior	Social	50
153	Nolan	Brenda	Senior	Junior	150
153	Nolan	Brenda	Senior	Senior	300
153	Nolan	Brenda	Senior	Social	50
176	Branch	Helen			

MemberID	LastName	FirstName	MemberType	Type	Fee
118	McKenzie	Melissa	Junior	Junior	150
138	Stone	Michael	Senior	Senior	300
153	Nolan	Brenda	Senior	Senior	300
176	Branch	Helen	Social	Social	50
178	Beck	Sarah	Social	Social	50
228	Burton	Sandra	Junior	Junior	150
235	Cooper	William	Senior	Senior	300
239	Spence	Thomas	Senior	Senior	300
258	Olson	Barbara	Senior	Senior	300

Select just those rows where these two columns have the same value

Figure 3-3. *A join is a Cartesian product followed by a select.*

The two columns that we are comparing for equality (MemberType and Type) must be what is sometimes referred to as *join compatible*. In the pure relational theory, this means they must both come from the same set of possible values (formally known as a *domain*). In practical terms, join compatibility usually means that the columns in each of the tables have the same data type. For example, they are both integers or both dates. Different database products may interpret join compatibility differently. Some might let you join on a float (number with a decimal point) in one table and an integer in another. Some may be fussy about whether text fields are the same length (such as CHAR(10) or CHAR(15)), and others may not. I recommend you don't try to join on fields with different types unless you are very clear what your particular product does. As always, the best thing is to make sure that when you design your tables, those fields that are likely to be joined have the same types.

SQL for Cartesian Product and Join

As I pointed out in the previous section, not all versions of SQL are the same. In 1992 keywords representing some algebra operations were added to the SQL standard,[1] and there have been a number of updates since then. However, not all vendors incorporate all parts of the standard, and some add extras. You might find that some SQL versions may not implement all the algebra-related keywords that we use in this book, but there are usually a number of ways to retrieve the information required. You can express all the relational algebra operations using relational calculus expressions, and they will always work for you. In the meantime, let's look at the SQL statements that reflect the algebra operations. We'll look at other equivalent calculus statements later in this chapter.

The SQL key phrase for a Cartesian product is CROSS JOIN. It is not often that you have a question that requires a CROSS JOIN, but for completeness Listing 3-3 shows it being used to retrieve the table shown in Figure 3-3a. As in all our other SQL queries, SELECT * just means retrieve all the columns.

Listing 3-3. *SQL for a Cartesian Product to Produce Table in Figure 3-3a*

```
SELECT *
FROM Member m CROSS JOIN Type t
```

The SQL phrase for a join is INNER JOIN. The join condition (which in this case allows us to select those rows where the member type is the same in both tables) follows the keyword ON, as shown in Listing 3-4.

Listing 3-4. *SQL for a Join to Produce Table in Figure 3-3b*

```
SELECT *
FROM Member m INNER JOIN Type t ON m.MemberType = t.Type
```

---

1. International Organization for Standardization. *Information technology — Database languages — SQL.* ISO, Geneva, Switzerland, 1992. ISO/IEC 9075:1992.

Joins in Relational Calculus

Now let's take a look at joins from a calculus perspective. Remember, calculus expressions tell us *what* we would like the resultant table to look like as opposed to *how* we get it.

Let's start with the Cartesian product: we want a set of rows made up of combinations of rows from each of the contributing tables. Figure 3-4 shows how we can envisage this. We are looking at two tables, so we need two fingers to keep track of the rows. Finger m looks at each row of the Member table in turn. Currently it is pointing at row 3. For each row in the Member table, finger t will point to each row in the Type table.

	MemberID	LastName	FirstName	MemberType
	118	McKenzie	Melissa	Junior
	138	Stone	Michael	Senior
m ☞	153	Nolan	Brenda	Senior
	176	Branch	Helen	Social
	178	Beck	Sarah	Social
	228	Burton	Sandra	Junior
	235	Cooper	William	Senior
	239	Spence	Thomas	Senior
	258	Olson	Barbara	Senior

	Type	Fee
	Junior	150
t ☞	Senior	300
	Social	50

Member table   Type table

Figure 3-4. *Row variables m and t point to each row of their respective tables.*

Listing 3-5 shows the relational calculus expression.

Listing 3-5. *Relational Calculus for Cartesian Product*

```
{m, t | Member(m), Type(t)}
```

Listing 3-6 shows the SQL that is very similar to this relational calculus expression.

Listing 3-6. *Alternative SQL for a Cartesian Product to Produce Table in Figure 3-3a*

```
SELECT *
FROM Member m , Type t
```

The SQL statement in Listing 3-6 is equivalent to the one in Listing 3-3 that used the CROSS JOIN keyword. They will both return the same set of rows. Which you use doesn't matter—in fact, in some products when you type Listing 3-6, it will automatically replace it with Listing 3-3. Other products do not implement the key phrase CROSS JOIN, so you have to use the alternative statement.

Now let's consider the join. As the two fingers traverse the two tables, they cover every combination of rows. For the join we have the extra condition that we want to retrieve rows only where the membership type from each table is the same. The pair of rows depicted in Figure 3-4 satisfies that condition and so will be retrieved. If m stays where it is and t moves, then the condition will no longer be satisfied. We can express this in calculus notation as in Listing 3-7 where we have just added the extra condition to the right side.

Listing 3-7. *Relational Calculus for Join*

```
{m, t | Member(m), Type(t) and m.MemberType = t.Type}
```

We can translate the calculus expression directly into an SQL statement as in Listing 3-8. The extra condition is represented by a WHERE clause.

Listing 3-8. *Alternative SQL for a Join to Produce the Table in Figure 3-3b*

```
SELECT *
FROM Member m , Type t
WHERE m.MemberType = t.Type
```

The SQL statement in Listing 3-8 is based on relational calculus in that it says *what* the rows to be retrieved are like. We want combinations of rows from Member and Type where the membership types are the same. The statement is equivalent to the statement in Listing 3-4, which uses the INNER JOIN key phrase. Once again, which one you use does not matter—it just depends how you find yourself thinking about the query. Sometimes there is a possibility that the way you express the query may affect the performance, and we will talk about this more in Chapter 9. Actually, most database products are pretty smart at optimizing or finding the quickest way to perform a query regardless of how you express it. For example, in SQL Server, the queries in Listings 3-4 and 3-8 are carried out in the same way. In fact, in SQL Server, if you type the code in Listing 3-8 into the default interface, that code will be replaced by Listing 3-6.

Even though the expression in Listing 3-8 is not based directly on the algebra, we can see how the algebra is reflected. The second line is the Cartesian product, and the last line is a select—and there we have our algebra definition of a join.

Extending Join Queries

Now that we have added joins to our arsenal of relational operations, we can perform numerous types of queries. Because the result of a join (as with any operation) is another table, we can then join that result to a third table (and then another) and then apply select and project operations to the result as required. Let's look at an example using the tables in Figure 3-5. The Member and Tournament tables provide details of members and tournaments (not surprisingly!), and the Entry table has information about which members have entered the different tournaments. In the Entry table, we have the ID numbers of members and tournaments as foreign keys, and if we want any additional information (say the name of a member or type of tournament), we need to find this from the Member and Tournament table, respectively. Say we want to find the names of everyone who entered an Open tournament in 2006.

MemberID	LastName	FirstName
118	McKenzie	Melissa
138	Stone	Michael
153	Nolan	Brenda
176	Branch	Helen
178	Beck	Sarah
228	Burton	Sandra
235	Cooper	William
239	Spence	Thomas
258	Olson	Barbara
286	Pollard	Robert
290	Sexton	Thomas
323	Wilcox	Daniel
331	Schmidt	Thomas
332	Bridges	Deborah
339	Young	Betty
414	Gilmore	Jane
415	Taylor	William
461	Reed	Robert
469	Willis	Carolyn
487	Kent	Susan

MemberID	TourID	Year
118	24	2005
228	24	2006
228	25	2006
228	36	2006
235	38	2004
235	38	2006
235	40	2005
235	40	2006
239	25	2006
239	40	2004
258	24	2005
258	38	2005
286	24	2004
286	24	2005
286	24	2006
415	24	2006
415	25	2004
415	36	2005
415	36	2006
415	38	2004
415	38	2006
415	40	2004
415	40	2005
415	40	2006

TourID	TourName	TourType
24	Leeston	Social
25	Kaiapoi	Social
36	WestCoast	Open
38	Canterbury	Open
40	Otago	Open

a) Member (some columns)   b) Entry   c) Tournament

Figure 3-5. *Permanent tables in the club database*

We can approach the question "What are the names of people who entered an Open tournament in 2006?" in many different ways. I'll describe an algebra and a calculus approach, and you will probably find that one appeals to you more than the other.

An Algebra Approach

We are starting with three tables, so we need some relational operation that combines data from more than one table. Let's start with Member and Entry.

The first row in the Entry table is for the member with ID 118, and to find his or her name, we need the corresponding row in the Member table, that is, one where the member IDs match. A join between these two tables as in Listing 3-9 will give us that information for all entries.

Listing 3-9. *Join the Member and Entry Tables*

Member ⋈ $_{MemberID=MemberID}$Entry

This join will result in the table in Figure 3-6.

From Member table (m)			From Entry table (e)		
m.MemberID	LastName	FirstName	e.MemberID	TourID	Year
118	McKenzie	Melissa	118	24	2005
228	Burton	Sandra	228	24	2006
228	Burton	Sandra	228	25	2006
228	Burton	Sandra	228	36	2006
235	Cooper	William	235	38	2004
235	Cooper	William	235	38	2006
235	Cooper	William	235	40	2005
235	Cooper	William	235	40	2006
239	Spence	Thomas	239	40	2004
239	Spence	Thomas	239	25	2006
258	Olson	Barbara	258	24	2005
258	Olson	Barbara	258	38	2005
286	Pollard	Robert	286	24	2004
286	Pollard	Robert	286	24	2005
286	Pollard	Robert	286	24	2006
415	Taylor	William	415	25	2004
415	Taylor	William	415	36	2005
415	Taylor	William	415	36	2006
415	Taylor	William	415	38	2004
415	Taylor	William	415	38	2006
415	Taylor	William	415	40	2004
415	Taylor	William	415	40	2005
415	Taylor	William	415	40	2006
415	Taylor	William	415	24	2006

Join condition requires values in these two columns to be the same

Figure 3-6. *Joining the Member and Entry tables*

Now we can see the names of the members along with their entry. To find the additional information about each tournament, we need to take the result of the join between Member and Entry and join that to the Tournament table. The algebra is in Listing 3-10, and the resulting table in Figure 3-7. It doesn't matter which of the joins we specify as being done first because the result will be the same.

Listing 3-10. *Join the Tournament Table to the Result of Joining the Member and Entry Tables*

(Member ⋈ $_{MemberID=MemberID}$Entry) ⋈ $_{TourID=TourID}$Tournament

	Member joined with Entry					Tournament	
m.MemberID	LastName	FirstName	e.MemberID	e.TourID	Year	t.TourID	TourType
118	McKenzie	Melissa	118	24	2005	24	Social
228	Burton	Sandra	228	24	2006	24	Social
228	Burton	Sandra	228	25	2006	25	Social
228	Burton	Sandra	228	36	2006	36	Open
235	Cooper	William	235	38	2004	38	Open
235	Cooper	William	235	38	2006	38	Open
235	Cooper	William	235	40	2005	40	Open
235	Cooper	William	235	40	2006	40	Open
239	Spence	Thomas	239	40	2004	40	Open
258	Olson	Barbara	258	24	2005	24	Social
258	Olson	Barbara	258	38	2005	38	Open
286	Pollard	Robert	286	24	2004	24	Social
286	Pollard	Robert	286	24	2005	24	Social
286	Pollard	Robert	286	24	2006	24	Social
415	Taylor	William	415	25	2004	25	Social
415	Taylor	William	415	36	2005	36	Open
415	Taylor	William	415	36	2006	36	Open
415	Taylor	William	415	38	2004	38	Open
415	Taylor	William	415	38	2006	38	Open
415	Taylor	William	415	40	2004	40	Open
415	Taylor	William	415	40	2005	40	Open
415	Taylor	William	415	40	2006	40	Open
239	Spence	Thomas	239	25	2006	25	Social
415	Taylor	William	415	24	2006	24	Social

Join condition requires values in these two columns to be the same

Figure 3-7. *Join the Tournament table to the result of joining the Member and Entry table.*

The table in Figure 3-7 now has all the information we need to answer our question about who entered Open tournaments in 2006. It is going to be a useful table for us to be able to re-create from time to time, so we might want to create a view as described in the previous chapter. Listing 3-11 shows the SQL to make a view that we can reuse. Although the SQL statement looks quite long, it is easy to understand if you start with the individual bits. I've split the query into different lines to make it easier to read. On the third line you can see the join between Member and Entry in brackets and then on the fourth line the result joined to the Tournament table. (I haven't repeated the duplicated MemberID and TourID columns in the view in Listing 3-11.)

Listing 3-11. *SQL to Create a View to Join Three Tables*

```
CREATE VIEW AllTourInfo AS
SELECT m.MemberID, m.LastName, m.FirstName, e.TourID, e.Year, t.TourName, t.TourType
FROM ( Member m INNER JOIN Entry e ON m.MemberID = e.MemberID )
        INNER JOIN Tournament t ON e.TourID = t.TourID
```

Although the table in Figure 3-7 and the corresponding view in Listing 3-11 are both useful, they contain more information than our original question required. We can take the result of our view and use select and project operations to retrieve a subset of rows and columns as we did in Chapter 2. We are interested in only some of the rows—so we need a select operation with the condition TourType = 'Open' AND Year = 2006. Then we want to see only the names, that is, a subset of the columns, so we can use a project operation to retrieve those. Altogether, the algebra looks like the expression in Listing 3-12 and can be implemented by the SQL expression in Listing 3-13.

Listing 3-12. *Algebra to Retrieve Subset of Information from the View AllTourInfo*

$$\pi_{\text{LastName, FirstName}} \left(\sigma_{\text{Year=2006 AND Type='Open'}}(\textbf{AllTourInfo}) \right)$$

Listing 3-13. *SQL to Retrieve Subset of Information from the View AllTourInfo*

```
SELECT LastName, FirstName
FROM  AllTourInfo
WHERE TourType = 'Open' AND Year = 2006
```

If we didn't want to have the intermediate step of creating a view, we could combine all the operations into one SQL query as in Listing 3-14 where the name of the view has been replaced with the SQL SELECT statement, Listing 3-11, that we used to define it.

Listing 3-14. *SQL to Retrieve Information from Original Tables*

```
SELECT LastName, FirstName
FROM ( Member m INNER JOIN Entry e ON m.MemberID = e.MemberID)
        INNER JOIN Tournament t ON e.TourID = t.TourID
WHERE TourType = 'Open' AND Year = 2006
```

Order of Algebra Operations

In our relational algebra description, we joined all the tables first and then selected the appropriate rows and columns. The result of the join is an intermediate table (as in Figure 3-7) that is potentially extremely large if there are lots of members and tournaments. We could have done the algebra in a different order. We could have first selected just the Open tournaments from the Tournament table and the 2006 tournaments from the

Entry tables, as shown in Figure 3-8. Joining these two smaller tables with each other and then joining that result with Member would result in a much smaller intermediate table.

Selecting 2006 entries

MemberID	TourID	Year
228	25	2006
228	24	2006
228	36	2006
235	40	2006
235	38	2006
286	24	2006
415	40	2006
415	38	2006
415	36	2006

Select Open tournaments

TourID	TourName	TourType
36	WestCoast	Open
38	Canterbury	Open
40	Otago	Open

Figure 3-8. *Selecting rows from the Entry and Tournament tables before joining them*

So, should we worry about the order of the operations? The answer is "yes"—order of operation makes a huge difference—but if you are using SQL, then it is not your problem to worry about it. The SQL statement is always going to look like the one in Listing 3-14 (but with the tables possibly in a different order). The SQL statement is sent to the engine of whatever database program you are using, and the query will be *optimized*. This means the database program figures out the best order to do things. Some products do this extremely well, and others not so well. Many products have analyzer tools that will let you see in what order things are being done. For many queries, writing your SQL differently doesn't make much difference, but you can make things more efficient by providing indexes for your tables. We will look at these issues more carefully in Chapter 9.

A Calculus Approach

The reason that the way we write our SQL statements often doesn't affect the efficiency of a query is that SQL is fundamentally based on relational calculus. The original SQL standards did not even have algebra keywords like INNER JOIN. SQL statements without these algebra keywords describe *what* the retrieved rows should be like, so they do not have anything to say about *how*. Let's look at a calculus approach to our question "Who entered Open tournaments in 2006?"

We want to just retrieve some names from the Member table. Forget joins, and think how you would know whether a particular name should be retrieved if you were shown just the three tables and knew nothing about databases or foreign keys or anything. Imagine a finger m tracing down the table as in Figure 3-9.

MemberID	LastName	FirstName
118	McKenzie	Melissa
138	Stone	Michael
153	Nolan	Brenda
176	Branch	Helen
178	Beck	Sarah
228	Burton	Sandra
235	Cooper	William
239	Spence	Thomas
258	Olson	Barbara
286	Pollard	Robert
290	Sexton	Thomas
323	Wilcox	Daniel
331	Schmidt	Thomas
332	Bridges	Deborah
339	Young	Betty
414	Gilmore	Jane
415	Taylor	William
461	Reed	Robert
469	Willis	Carolyn
487	Kent	Susan

MemberID	TourID	Year
118	24	2005
228	24	2006
228	25	2006
228	36	2006
235	38	2004
235	38	2006
235	40	2005
235	40	2006
239	25	2006
239	40	2004
258	24	2005
258	38	2005
286	24	2004
286	24	2005
286	24	2006
415	24	2006
415	25	2004
415	36	2005
415	36	2006
415	38	2004
415	38	2006
415	40	2004
415	40	2005
415	40	2006

TourID	TourName	TourType
24	Leeston	Social
25	Kaiapoi	Social
36	WestCoast	Open
38	Canterbury	Open
40	Otago	Open

a) Member (some columns)   b) Entry   c) Tournament

Figure 3-9. *Using row variables to describe the rows that satisfy the query conditions*

Do we want to write out William Cooper, the name to which m is currently pointing? How would we know? Well, first we have to find a row with his ID (235) in the Entry table for the year 2006 such as the one where finger e is pointing (where TourID is 40). Then we have to find a row with that tournament ID (40) in the Tournament table and check whether it is an Open tournament. Looking at Figure 3-9, we see that the rows where the three fingers are pointing give us enough information to know that William Cooper did indeed enter an Open tournament in 2006. This set of conditions describes *what* a row in the result table should be like.

Now let's write that last paragraph a bit more succinctly. Read the following sentence with reference to the rows denoted in Figure 3-9:

> *I'll write out the names from row m, where m comes from the* Member *table, if there exists a row (e) in the* Entry *table where* m.MemberID *is the same as* e.MemberID *and* e.Year *is 2006 and there also exists a row (t) in the* Tournament *table where* e.TourID *is the same as* t.TourId *and* t.TourType *has the value "Open".*

And now (if you prefer), Listing 3-15 shows the same sentence represented in calculus notation. The construction ∃(e) means "There exists a row e," and Entry(e) means "where e comes from the Entry table."

Listing 3-15. *Relational Calculus Expression to Find Members Entered in 2006 Open Tournaments*

```
{m.LastName, m.FirstName | Member(m) and ∃ (e) Entry(e) and ∃ (t) Tournament(t) and
m.MemberID = e.MemberID and e.TourID = t.TourID and t.TourType = 'Open' and e.Year = 2006}
```

The expression in Listing 3-16 describes *what* a particular row in our resulting table must look like. The SQL statement is very similar. Compare Listing 3-16 with the calculus expression and with Figure 3-9. The last three lines are all part of one big WHERE clause. I've indented them to make that easier to interpret.

Listing 3-16. *SQL to Find Members Entered in 2006 Open Tournaments*

```
SELECT m.LastName, m.FirstName
FROM Member m, Entry e, Tournament t
WHERE m.MemberID = e.MemberID
        AND e.TourID = t.TourID
        AND t.TourType = 'Open' AND e.Year = 2006
```

You can see how the SQL statement in Listing 3-16 is like the calculus in that it describes *what* a retrieved row should be like. If you look carefully at the statement, you can pick out all the algebra operations. The second line (FROM) is a big Cartesian product, the next two lines are the join conditions (which would give us a table like the one in Figure 3-7), the final line is our select operation, and the first line tells us what columns to project.

The two SQL statements in Listings 3-14 and 3-16 are equivalent. They will return the same set of rows: Listing 3-14 reflects the underlying algebra of *how*, and Listing 3-16 reflects the underlying calculus of *what*.

You may be wondering why I've been bothering with the calculus expressions and their somewhat obscure symbols like ∃, and so on. For the particular example in this section, the calculus and SQL statements are so similar that we don't really need the intermediate step of writing the calculus statement. However, for more complicated queries, I find having a shorthand notation for describing a typical row very helpful. As you get more proficient, you will find that for many queries you can just write the SQL statement directly, but when you get stumped, the more approaches at your disposal, the more likely you will be able to find a solution.

Expressing Joins Through Diagrammatic Interfaces

This book is about queries in SQL, but most database products also provide a diagrammatic interface to express queries. Just for completeness, I'll show you what a typical diagrammatic interface looks like for retrieving the names of members who entered an Open tournament in 2006.

Figure 3-10 shows the Microsoft Access interface, but most products have something very similar. The tables are represented by the rectangles in the top section with the lines showing the joins between them. The columns to be retrieved have a check mark (√) in the row marked Show, and the select conditions are shown for the relevant fields in the row marked Criteria.

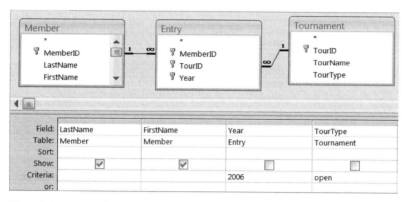

Figure 3-10. *Access diagrammatic interface for the query to find names of members entering an Open tournament in 2006*

Other Types of Joins

The joins we have been looking at in this chapter are *equi-joins*. An equi-join is one where the join condition has an equals as in m.MemberID = e.MemberID. This is the most common type of condition, but you can have different operators. A join is just a Cartesian product followed by a select, and the select condition can consist of different comparison operators (for example, <> or >) and also logical operators (for example, AND or NOT). These sorts of joins don't turn up all that often. On the tables we have been looking at, I can't for the life of me think of a sensible query that would need one.

The joins up to now have also been what are more accurately called *inner joins*. You will recall that the SQL key phrase (for example, in Listing 3-11) was INNER JOIN. There are also joins called *outer joins*. The best way to understand an outer join is to see where they are useful. Have a look at the (modified) Member and Type tables in Figure 3-11.

You might want to produce different lists from the Member table, such as numbers and names, names and membership types, and so on. In these lists you expect to see all the members (for the table in Figure 3-11, that would be nine rows). Then you might think that as well as seeing the numbers and names in your member list, you will also include the membership fee. You join the two tables (with the condition MemberType = Type) and find that you "lose" one of your members—Barbara Olson (Figure 3-12).

MemberID	LastName	FirstName	MemberType
118	McKenzie	Melissa	Junior
178	Beck	Sarah	Social
235	Cooper	William	Senior
239	Spence	Thomas	Senior
258	Olson	Barbara	
283	Jones	Kim	Junior
290	Sexton	Thomas	Senior
323	Wilcox	Daniel	Senior
331	Schmidt	Thomas	Senior

(modified) Member table

Type	Fee
Junior	150
Senior	300
Social	50

Type table

Figure 3-11. *Member and Type tables*

MemberID	LastName	FirstName	MemberType	Type	Fee
323	Wilcox	Daniel	Senior	Senior	300
239	Spence	Thomas	Senior	Senior	300
178	Beck	Sarah	Social	Social	50
235	Cooper	William	Senior	Senior	300
283	Jones	Kim	Junior	Junior	150
331	Schmidt	Thomas	Senior	Senior	300
290	Sexton	Thomas	Senior	Senior	300
118	McKenzie	Melissa	Junior	Junior	150

Figure 3-12. *Inner join between Member and Type, and we "lose" Barbara Olson*

The reason is that Barbara Olson has no value of MemberType in the Member table. Let's look at the Cartesian product that is the first step for doing a join. Figure 3-13 shows those rows of the Cartesian product that include Barbara.

MemberID	LastName	FirstName	MemberType	Type	Fee
178	Beck	Sarah	Social	Social	50
235	Cooper	William	Senior	Junior	150
235	Cooper	William	Senior	Senior	300
235	Cooper	William	Senior	Social	50
258	Olson	Barbara		Junior	150
258	Olson	Barbara		Senior	300
258	Olson	Barbara		Social	50
283	Jones	Kim	Junior	Junior	150
283	Jones	Kim	Junior	Senior	300

Figure 3-13. *Part of the Cartesian product between the Member and Type tables*

Having done the Cartesian product, we now need to do the final part of our join operation, which is to apply the condition (MemberType = Type). As you can see in Figure 3-13, there is no row for Barbara Olson that satisfies this condition because she has a Null or empty value in MemberType.

Consider the following two natural-language questions: "Get me the fees for members" and "Get me all member information including fees." The first one has an implication of "Just get me the members that have fees," while the second has more of a feel of "Get me all the members and include the fees for those that have them." One of the biggest difficulties about writing queries is actually trying to decide exactly what it is you want. It is even more difficult if you are trying to understand what someone else is asking for!

Let's say that what we want is a list of all our members, and where we can find the fee information, we'd like to include that. In this case, we want to see Barbara Olson included in the result but with no fee displayed. That is what an outer join does. Outer joins can come in three types: left, right, and full outer joins. Look at Listing 3-17, which shows a left outer join (denoted by the equal sign to the left of the join symbol) between the Member and Type tables. Figure 3-14 shows the rows retrieved.

Listing 3-17. *Algebra Expression for Left Outer Join Between Member and Type Tables*

Member= ⋈ $_{\text{MemberType=Type}}$ Type

MemberID	LastName	FirstName	MemberType	Type	Fee
323	Wilcox	Daniel	Senior	Senior	300
239	Spence	Thomas	Senior	Senior	300
178	Beck	Sarah	Social	Social	50
235	Cooper	William	Senior	Senior	300
258	Olson	Barbara			
283	Jones	Kim	Junior	Junior	150
331	Schmidt	Thomas	Senior	Senior	300
290	Sexton	Thomas	Senior	Senior	300
118	McKenzie	Melissa	Junior	Junior	150

Figure 3-14. *Result of left outer join between Member and Type tables*

What the left outer join does is retrieve all the rows from the left table, even those with a Null value in the join field. So, we see that as well as all the rows from the inner join (Figure 3-12), we also have a row from the Member table for Barbara who had a Null for the join field MemberType. The fields in that row that would have come from the table on the right (Type and Fee) have Null values.

Listing 3-18 shows the SQL for the outer join depicted in Figure 3-14. It is the same as for the ordinary join, but the key phrase INNER JOIN is replaced with LEFT OUTER JOIN.

Listing 3-18. *SQL Statement for an Outer Join*

```
SELECT *
FROM Member m LEFT OUTER JOIN Type t ON m.MemberType = t.Type
```

You might quite reasonably say that we wouldn't have needed an outer join if all the members had a value for the MemberType field (as they probably should). That may be true for this case—but remember my cautions in Chapter 2 about assuming that fields that *should* have data *will* have data. In many situations, the data in the join field may be quite legitimately empty. We will see in later chapters queries like "List all members and the names of their coaches—if they have one." "Losing" rows because you have used an inner join when you should have used an outer join is a very common problem and sometimes quite hard to spot.

What about right and full outer joins? Left and right outer joins are the same and just depend on which order you put the tables in the join statement. Listing 3-19 will return the same information as Listing 3-18, although the columns may be presented in a different order.

Listing 3-19. *SQL Statement for an Outer Join*

```
SELECT *
FROM Type t RIGHT OUTER JOIN Member m ON m.MemberType = t.Type
```

In Listing 3-19, any rows with a Null in the join field of the right table (Member) will be included. A full outer join will retain rows with a Null in the join field in either table. The SQL is the same as Listing 3-19 but with the key phrase FULL OUTER JOIN. Let's assume that our Type table in Figure 3-11 has another row for an associate member type. The full outer join would result in the table in Figure 3-15.

MemberID	LastName	FirstName	MemberType	Type	Fee
				Associate	70
118	McKenzie	Melissa	Junior	Junior	150
178	Beck	Sarah	Social	Social	50
235	Cooper	William	Senior	Senior	300
239	Spence	Thomas	Senior	Senior	300
258	Olson	Barbara			
283	Jones	Kim	Junior	Junior	150
290	Sexton	Thomas	Senior	Senior	300
323	Wilcox	Daniel	Senior	Senior	300
331	Schmidt	Thomas	Senior	Senior	300

Figure 3-15. *Result of a full outer join between Member and Type tables*

We have our row for Barbara Olson padded with Null values for the missing columns from the Type table. We also have the first row, which shows us the information about the associate membership type even though there are no rows in the Member table with "Associate" as a member type. Here each missing value from the Member table is replaced with a Null.

Not all implementations of SQL necessarily have a full outer join implemented explicitly. Access 2007 doesn't. However, there are always alternative ways in SQL to retrieve the information you want. In Chapter 7 I'll show you how to get the equivalent of a full outer join by using a union operator between a left and right outer join (which is what I had to do to get the screen shot in Figure 3-15!).

Summary

Joins are the most often used of the operations that involve combining two tables. The resulting table has a column for each column in the two contributing tables. A join condition tells us which combinations of rows from the two contributing tables we will retain. The most common condition is equality between a field in each table. In the example in this chapter, the value of MemberType in the Member table had to equal the value of Type in the Type table.

There are a number of equivalent ways of expressing joins in SQL. Table 3-1 shows a couple.

Table 3-1. *SQL for Simple Joins*

SQL Reflecting Algebra	SQL Reflecting Calculus
SELECT *	SELECT *…
FROM <table1> INNER JOIN <table2>	FROM <table1>, <table2>
ON <condition>	WHERE <condition>

If one (or both) of the tables has rows with a Null in the field involved in the join condi-tion, then that row will not appear in the result of an inner join. If that row is required, you can use an outer join. A left outer join will include all rows in the left table, including those with a Null in the join field—the corresponding fields from the right table will contain Nulls. A right outer join is the same but includes all rows from the right table, and a full outer join includes all rows from both tables.

CHAPTER 4

■ ■ ■

Nested Queries

In the previous chapters, we looked at the select and project operations, which retrieve a subset of rows and columns from a single table, and we also looked at Cartesian products and joins, which combine two tables on a common field. We saw that there are several different ways to write SQL statements to perform combinations of these operations.

As queries become more complicated, we might find that we can think of SQL expressions for different parts of the query but we need a way to tie them all together. In this chapter, we will look at nested queries and two new SQL keywords, EXISTS and IN. We will see how to use nesting to perform some of the queries we have already done and also how this will open up some other possibilities.

IN Keyword

The IN keyword allows us to select rows from a table, where an attribute can have one of several values. For example, if we wanted to retrieve the member IDs from the rows in our Entry table for tournaments with ID 36, 38, or 40, we could do this with a Boolean OR operator, as in the SQL statement in Listing 4-1.

Listing 4-1. *Using OR Operations*

```
SELECT e.MemberID
FROM Entry e
WHERE e.TourID= 36 OR e.TourID= 38 OR e.TourID=  40
```

Clearly, the sort of expression shown in Listing 4-1 will start to become unwieldy as the number of possible options grows. Using the IN keyword, we can construct a more compact statement, as in Listing 4-2, where the set of possible values are enclosed in parentheses and separated by commas. Each row of Entry is investigated, and if TourID is one of the values in the set, then the WHERE condition is true, and that row will be returned.

Listing 4-2. *Using the IN Keyword*

```
SELECT e.MemberID
FROM Entry e
WHERE e.TourID IN (36, 38, 40)
```

We can combine IN with the logical operator NOT, as shown in Listing 4-3. The query will return all the IDs of members who have entered any tournament that is not in the list. We will look more carefully at using NOT later in the chapter.

Listing 4-3. *Using NOT IN Keyword*

```
SELECT e.MemberID
FROM Entry e
WHERE e.TourID NOT IN (36, 38, 40)
```

Using IN with a Nested Query

The real usefulness of the IN keyword is that we can use another SQL statement to generate the values in the set. For example, the reason that someone may have been interested in the set of tournaments (36, 38, 40) might have been because they are the Open tournaments. Thus, we might want to generate a list of Open tournaments and feed that list into the IN clause.

Let's look at a specific example of a query feeding into IN. I've reproduced a few of the columns of the Member table along with the Entry and Tournament tables in Figure 4-1.

In Listings 4-1 and 4-2, the Open tournaments were explicitly stated in the query by listing each ID. If a new Open tournament is added to the Tournament table, then the query will need to be changed to include that tournament's ID in the set. However, we can construct another query to retrieve the IDs of all the Open tournaments, as shown in Listing 4-4.

Listing 4-4. *Finding the IDs of All Open Tournaments*

```
SELECT t.TourID
FROM Tournament t
    WHERE t.TourType = 'Open'
```

MemberID	LastName	FirstName
118	McKenzie	Melissa
138	Stone	Michael
153	Nolan	Brenda
176	Branch	Helen
178	Beck	Sarah
228	Burton	Sandra
235	Cooper	William
239	Spence	Thomas
258	Olson	Barbara
286	Pollard	Robert
290	Sexton	Thomas
323	Wilcox	Daniel
331	Schmidt	Thomas
332	Bridges	Deborah
339	Young	Betty
414	Gilmore	Jane
415	Taylor	William
461	Reed	Robert
469	Willis	Carolyn
487	Kent	Susan

MemberID	TourID	Year
118	24	2005
228	24	2006
228	25	2006
228	36	2006
235	38	2004
235	38	2006
235	40	2005
235	40	2006
239	25	2006
239	40	2004
258	24	2005
258	38	2005
286	24	2004
286	24	2005
286	24	2006
415	24	2006
415	25	2004
415	36	2005
415	36	2006
415	38	2004
415	38	2006
415	40	2004
415	40	2005
415	40	2006

TourID	TourName	TourType
24	Leeston	Social
25	Kaiapoi	Social
36	WestCoast	Open
38	Canterbury	Open
40	Otago	Open

(Some columns) Member   Entry   Tournament

Figure 4-1. *Member, Entry, and Tournament tables*

We can replace the list of explicit values (36, 38, 40) in Listing 4-2 with the SQL statement (Listing 4-4) that will retrieve the current values for Open tournaments, as shown in Listing 4-5. I've indented the nested part of the query (sometimes called a *subquery*) so you can see it more clearly.

Listing 4-5. *A Nested Query to Find All Entries in Open Tournaments*

```
SELECT e.MemberID
FROM Entry e
WHERE e.TourID IN
     (SELECT t.TourID
     FROM Tournament t
     WHERE t.TourType = 'Open')
```

You can understand a nested query by reading it from the "inside out." The inside SELECT statement retrieves the set of required tournament IDs from the Tournament table, and then the outside SELECT finds us all the entries from the Entry table for tournaments IN that set. To work correctly with the IN keyword, the nested part of the query must return a list of single values.

Have another look at the tables in Figure 4-1. How else might we have retrieved entries for Open tournaments? We did this in the previous chapter using a join. We can join the two tables `Entry` and `Tournament` on their common fields `TourID`. Then select just those rows that are for Open tournaments and retrieve (or project) the `MemberID` column. The SQL statement is in Listing 4-6.

Listing 4-6. *Using a Join to Find All Entries in Open Tournaments*

```
SELECT e.MemberID
FROM Entry e INNER JOIN Tournament t ON e.TourID = t.TourID
WHERE t.TourType = 'Open'
```

The SQL statements in Listings 4-5 and 4-6 retrieve the same information. As I've said a number of times, there are often several different ways to write a query in SQL. The more methods you are familiar with, the more likely you will be able to find a way to express a complicated query.

Being Careful with NOT and <>

As well as asking a question such as "What are the IDs of members who have entered an Open tournament?" it is just as likely that we might want to know "What are the IDs of members who have NOT entered an Open tournament?" They sound very similar, but once we start using negatives in our questions, we have to be very careful about what we really mean. In Chapter 7, we will investigate such questions using set operations, but to keep this chapter complete, I'll talk about how negatives impact the use of nested queries in particular.

Listings 4-5 and 4-6 showed two SQL statements for retrieving member IDs for members who have entered an Open tournament. As a first attempt, novices will often amend these queries slightly by changing = to <> or by changing IN to NOT IN, as in Listing 4-7 and Listing 4-8.

Listing 4-7. *Using NOT IN: What Does This Query Retrieve?*

```
SELECT e.MemberID
FROM Entry e
WHERE e.TourID NOT IN
    (SELECT t.TourID
    FROM Tournament t
    WHERE t.TourType = 'Open')
```

Listing 4-8. *Using <>: What Does This Query Retrieve?*

```
SELECT e.MemberID
FROM Entry e INNER JOIN Tournament t ON e.TourID = t.TourID
WHERE t.TourType <>'Open'
```

Carefully think about which rows will be returned by these two queries. With just a cursory comparison of the statements in Listings 4-5 and 4-6 and those in Listings 4-7 and 4-8, it is not uncommon for someone to think that if the first pair returns those members who have entered an Open tournament, then the second pair will return those who have not. But this is not the case.

The table in Figure 4-2 shows the result of the inner join between Entry and Tournament in Listings 4-6 and 4-8. The bottom set of rows are all for Open tournaments, and these will be retrieved by Listing 4-6, which has the condition WHERE t.TourType = 'Open'. The top set of entries are all for tournaments other than Open and will be retrieved by Listing 4-8, which has the condition WHERE t.TourType <> 'Open'.

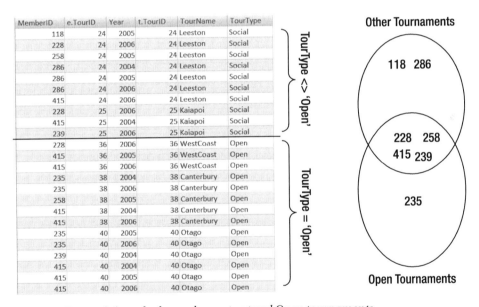

Figure 4-2. *Determining who has or has not entered Open tournaments*

In Figure 4-2 the oval at the bottom represents the people who have entered Open tournaments (those in the bottom part of the table), and the top oval represents those who have entered other types of tournaments (the top part of the table). Some people (in the overlap) have entered both types. Check the numbers in the ovals with those in the table to see where they come from.

It is situations like the one shown in Figure 4-2 that can be potentially confusing when we start looking at negatives. When we ask for "people who have *not* entered an Open tournament," we have to make sure we distinguish the two cases shown in Figure 4-3.

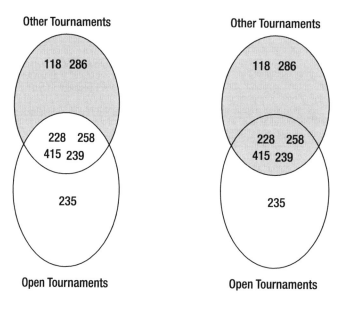

a. Shaded area is people who have not entered an Open tournament

b. Shaded area is people who entered a tournament that is not an Open tournament

Figure 4-3. *It is important to be careful to distinguish the SQL for these two situations.*

Figure 4-3a shows the set of people who have not entered an Open tournament. Figure 4-3b shows those members who have entered something other than an Open tournament (but not excluding those who may have entered an Open tournament as well!).

Now look at Listings 4-7 and 4-8 again, and try to think which set of people we are retrieving.

Listing 4-8 is actually retrieving those members who have entered something other than an Open tournament (but not excluding those who may have entered an Open tournament as well!). This is the set depicted in Figure 4-3b. The same members will be retrieved by the query in Listing 4-7, which uses NOT IN. It will retrieve all entries that are not for Open tournaments as opposed to all members who have not entered an Open tournament. It is a very common mistake to confuse these two different questions.

To decide whether someone has entered an Open competition, we need to find just *one* matching entry. To decide he has *not* entered an Open competition, we need to check *all* the Open entries to make sure there is not one for him.

In terms of our joined tables in Figure 4-2, finding those people who have entered an Open tournament is a simple relational algebra select operation. Remember that for a select operation we look at each row independently and decide whether it should be included in the returned set of rows. However, to find people who have *not* entered an Open tournament, we need to investigate *every* row in the table to ensure that there is not an entry for a particular member. This is a much more complex task than a simple select. We can see from the third row in Figure 4-2 that member 258 has entered a non-Open tournament, but we have to search further down the table to see that he has entered an Open tournament at a different time. In fact, we also need to consider the members who have never entered any tournaments at all. These members' IDs will not appear in the Entry table at all, so we also have to investigate another table, the Member table, to find the complete list.

The type of query described in the previous paragraph can be expressed in the relational algebra using one of the set operations that we will look at in Chapter 7. However, we can also use relational calculus to help us write the SQL statement for this type of query. To do that, we need first to introduce the EXISTS keyword.

EXISTS Keyword

Let's recall some relational calculus from the previous chapter. Our questions about who did or did not enter Open tournaments can be conveniently represented with calculus expressions. This approach allows us to answer the questions involving negatives that we had trouble with in the previous section.

Let's start with a simple question. For example: "What are the names of all members who have ever entered any tournament?" We can start by thinking in terms of which rows of the Member table would satisfy our question. Consider the following sentence and Figure 4-4 together:

> *I'll write out the names from row m, where m comes from the* Member *table, if there exists a row e in the* Entry *table where* m.MemberID = e.MemberID.

Listing 4-9 shows the equivalent calculus expression.

Listing 4-9. *Relational Calculus Expression to Retrieve Members Who Have Entered a Tournament*

```
{m.LastName, m.FirstName | Member(m) and ∃(e) Entry(e) and m.MemberID = e.MemberID}
```

MemberID	LastName	FirstName
118	McKenzie	Melissa
138	Stone	Michael
153	Nolan	Brenda
176	Branch	Helen
178	Beck	Sarah
228	Burton	Sandra
m ☞ 235	Cooper	William
239	Spence	Thomas
258	Olson	Barbara
286	Pollard	Robert
290	Sexton	Thomas
323	Wilcox	Daniel
331	Schmidt	Thomas
332	Bridges	Deborah
339	Young	Betty
414	Gilmore	Jane
415	Taylor	William
461	Reed	Robert
469	Willis	Carolyn
487	Kent	Susan

MemberID	TourID	Year
118	24	2005
228	24	2006
228	25	2006
228	36	2006
e ☞ 235	38	2004
235	38	2006
235	40	2005
235	40	2006
239	40	2004
258	24	2005
258	38	2005
286	24	2004
286	24	2005
286	24	2006
415	25	2005
415	36	2005
415	36	2006
415	38	2004
415	38	2006
415	40	2004
415	40	2005
415	40	2006

a) Member (some columns)   b) Entry

Figure 4-4. *William Cooper has entered a tournament because a matching row exists in the Entry table.*

We can translate this almost directly into SQL with the use of the keyword EXISTS. Have a look at the SQL statement in Listing 4-10.

Listing 4-10. *SQL Statement to Retrieve Members Who Have Entered a Tournament*

```
SELECT m.LastName, m.FirstName
FROM Member m
WHERE EXISTS
    (SELECT * FROM Entry e WHERE e.MemberID = m.MemberID)
```

This is another example of a nested query where we have two SQL SELECT statements, one nested inside the other. This one is a little different from the simpler example in Listing 4-5. The WHERE condition in the inner query refers to part of the row being considered in the outer query, that is, e.MemberID = m.MemberID. I find the easiest way to interpret Listing 4-10 is with reference to Figure 4-4. The inner query is looking for a row in the Entry table with the same value for MemberID as the row under consideration in the Member table. If such a row or several such rows EXIST, then we are in business.

For those of you who are thinking that this seems like a complicated way to get a simple result, you are right (partly). The query in Listing 4-10 retrieves the same members as an inner join (on MemberID) between Member and Entry.

However, what if we want those members who have NOT entered a tournament? This requires only a tiny change to our relational calculus and SQL expressions. Instead of looking for members where a matching row in Entry exists, we now want those where a matching row does NOT exist. Adding the word NOT to Listing 4-10 gives us what we require, as shown in Listing 4-11.

Listing 4-11. *SQL Statement to Retrieve Members Who Have NOT Entered a Tournament*

```
SELECT m.Lastname, m.FirstName
FROM Member m
WHERE NOT EXISTS
        (SELECT * FROM Entry e WHERE e.MemberID = m.MemberID)
```

The NOT EXISTS construction will look through every row in the Entry table checking whether there is a row matching the current row in the Member table. The names of the member will be retrieved only if no matching row is found.

Now we have enough ammunition to tackle the query about members who have not entered an Open tournament. As always, there are several ways we can express the SQL query, and one way appears in Listing 4-12. It is almost the same as Listing 4-11, but instead of looking for members with no matching records in the Entry table, we look for members who do not have a matching record in the bottom section of the table shown in Figure 4-2. That set of rows results from joining Entry and Tournament and selecting just the rows for Open tournaments.

Listing 4-12. *SQL Statement to Retrieve Members Who Have NOT Entered an Open Tournament*

```
SELECT m.Lastname, m.FirstName
FROM Member m
WHERE NOT EXISTS
        (SELECT * FROM Entry e INNER JOIN Tournament t ON e.TourID = t.TourID
         WHERE e.MemberID = m.MemberID and t.TourType = 'Open')
```

We will return to queries like this one when we look at set operations in Chapter 7.

Different Types of Nesting

We saw different types of nested queries in the previous sections. It is useful to review some of the options here.

The inner part of the nested query can return a single value, a set of values, or a set of rows. The inner and outer queries can be independent to some extent, or they can be correlated.

Inner Queries Returning a Single Value

Inner queries that return a single value are often useful in the situation of a simple select operation to retrieve a subset of rows. Let's consider the handicaps of our members, as shown in Figure 4-5.

MemberID	LastName	FirstName	Handicap
118	McKenzie	Melissa	30
138	Stone	Michael	30
153	Nolan	Brenda	11
176	Branch	Helen	
178	Beck	Sarah	
228	Burton	Sandra	26
235	Cooper	William	14
239	Spence	Thomas	10
258	Olson	Barbara	16
286	Pollard	Robert	19
290	Sexton	Thomas	26

Figure 4-5. *Part of the Member table showing names and handicaps*

If we want to find those members with a handicap less than 16, then this can be done simply with the SQL in Listing 4-13.

Listing 4-13. *SQL Statement to Retrieve Members with Handicaps Less Than 16*

```
SELECT *
FROM Member m
WHERE m.Handicap < 16
```

What should we do if we want to find all the members with a handicap less than Barbara Olson's? Listing 4-13 will do that for us but only if Barbara's handicap of 16 doesn't change. We can replace the single value 16 with the result of an inner query that returns Barbara's handicap as in Listing 4-14. Now the query will work for whatever Barbara's current handicap is.

Listing 4-14. *SQL Statement to Retrieve Members with Handicaps Less Than Barbara Olson's*

```
SELECT *
FROM Member m
WHERE Handicap <
      (SELECT Handicap
      FROM Member
      WHERE LastName = 'Olson' AND FirstName = 'Barbara')
```

If, in a situation like this, our inner query returns more than one value (for example, if there were more than one Barbara Olson in the club), then we would get an error when trying to run the query.

An inner query returning a single value is also useful if we want to compare values with an aggregate of some sort. For example, we might want to find all the members who have a handicap less than the average. In this case, we can use the inner query to find the average value, as in Listing 4-15.

Listing 4-15. *SQL Statement to Retrieve Members with Handicaps Less Than the Average*

```
SELECT *
FROM Member m
WHERE m.Handicap <
      (SELECT AVG(Handicap)
      FROM Member)
```

If you take it nice and slowly, you can gradually build up quite complicated queries. Say we want to see whether any junior members have a lower handicap than the average for seniors. The inner query has to return the average value handicap for a senior member, and then we want to select all juniors with a handicap less than that. Both the inner and outer queries have an extra select condition (the inner retrieves just seniors, and the outer retrieves just juniors). Listing 4-16 shows one way of doing this.

Listing 4-16. *SQL Statement to Retrieve Juniors with Handicaps Less Than the Average Senior*

```
SELECT *
FROM Member m
WHERE m.MemberType = 'Junior' AND Handicap <
      (SELECT AVG(Handicap)
      FROM Member
      WHERE MemberType = 'Senior')
```

Inner Queries Returning a Set of Values

This is where we started this chapter. When we use the IN keyword, SQL will expect to find a set of single values. For example, we might ask for rows from the Entry table for members with IDs IN a set of values. In Listing 4-17 the inner query selects the IDs of all senior members, and the outer query returns the entries for those members.

Listing 4-17. *SQL Statement to Retrieve Entries for Senior Members*

```
SELECT *
FROM Entry e
WHERE e.MemberID IN
     (SELECT m.MemberID
      FROM Member m
      WHERE m.MemberType = 'Senior')
```

The inner section in this type of query must return just a single column. IN is expecting a list of single values (in this case a list of MemberIDs). If the inner section returns more than one column (for example, SELECT * FROM Member), then we will get an error.

Many nested queries such as the one in Listing 4-17 can be written in other ways—often by using an inner join as we discussed earlier in the chapter. Some queries will feel more natural to you one way or the other.

Inner Queries Checking for Existence

Another type of inner query is the one we saw working with the EXISTS keyword. A statement using EXISTS just looks to see whether any rows at all are returned by the inner query. The actual values or number of rows returned are not important. Listing 4-18 returns any rows from the Member table where we can find a matching row (with the same value for MemberID) in the Entry table.

Listing 4-18. *SQL Statement to Retrieve Members Who Have Entered a Tournament*

```
SELECT m.Lastname, m.FirstName
FROM Member m
WHERE EXISTS
     (SELECT * FROM Entry e WHERE e.MemberID = m.MemberID)
```

Because the actual values retrieved by the inner query are not important, the inner query usually has the form SELECT * FROM.

Another feature of this type of query is that the inner and outer sections are usually correlated. By this we mean that the WHERE clause in the inner section refers to values in the table in the outer section. This allows us to compare values in two tables at once, and

I find the easiest way to visualize this is as illustrated in Figure 4-4. We write out a member's name (from the outer section) if there is a matching row in the Entry table (inner section).

It is difficult to think of a sensible EXISTS query that doesn't correlate values in the inner and outer sections. Consider Listing 4-19.

Listing 4-19. *What Does This Query Return?*

```
SELECT m.Lastname, m.FirstName
FROM Member m
WHERE EXISTS
    (SELECT * FROM Entry e)
```

Listing 4-19 doesn't really make any sense. It says to write out each member's name if there is a row in the Entry table (any row!). If the Entry table is empty, we will get nothing returned; otherwise, we will get all the names of all the members. I can't think why you'd ever want to do that. EXISTS queries are useful when we are looking for matching values somewhere else, and that is why the select condition needs to compare values from both the inner and outer sections.

Using Nested Queries for Updating

This book is mainly about queries for retrieving data, but many of the same ideas can be used for updating data and adding or deleting records. In Chapter 1 we looked at simple queries such as updating the phone number of a particular member, as in Listing 4-20.

Listing 4-20. *Updating a Single Phone Number*

```
UPDATE Member m
SET m.Phone = '875076'
WHERE m.MemberID = 118
```

We can also update several records at a time; for example, we could update some aspect of all the senior members by changing the WHERE clause in Listing 4-20.

In Chapter 1 we also looked at inserting and deleting rows from a table. Listing 4-21 shows a simple example of inserting a row into the Entry table. We list the columns we are providing values for and then the values.

Listing 4-21. *Inserting a Row into the Entry Table*

```
INSERT INTO Entry (MemberID, TourID, Year)
VALUES (153, 25, 2007)
```

Now let's consider the situation where we want to add an entry for tournament 25 in 2007 for each of the juniors in the club. We want to add a set of rows to the Entry table, as shown in Figure 4-6, where the left column has the member IDs for all the juniors and the next two columns are the specific tournament (25) and year (2007) for each entry.

414	25	2007
286	25	2007
228	25	2007
469	25	2007
118	25	2007

Figure 4-6. *Rows to be added to Entry table*

We can write an SQL query to return a set of rows like those in Figure 4-6, as shown in Listing 4-22. This query is a little different from others we have looked at because it has constants in the SELECT clause. It will construct a row for each junior member with the member's ID and the two constants 25 (for the tournament) and 2007 (for the year).

Listing 4-22. *Constructing New Entry Rows for Junior Members*

```
SELECT MemberID, 25, 2007
FROM Member
WHERE MemberType = 'Junior'
```

Now we can use Listing 4-22 as a subquery in our insert query in Listing 4-21. Rather than provide just one value with the VALUES keyword, we can provide a set of values resulting from the subquery. Listing 4-23 shows how we can do this. The inner SELECT query will produce the set of rows in Figure 4-6, and the outer INSERT query will put them in the table.

Listing 4-23. *Inserting Entries for Juniors into Tournament 25 for 2007*

```
INSERT INTO Entry (MemberID, TourID, Year)
    SELECT MemberID, 25, 2007
    FROM Member
    WHERE MemberType = 'Junior'
```

The same potential for using nested queries applies to other updating issues. Say, for the purpose of finding an example, that after entering data in the Entry table for the 2007 social tournament at Kaiapoi (tournament 25), you realize that only players with handicaps of 20 or more were allowed to enter. You could use a nested query to delete entries for members with handicaps less than 20, as shown in Listing 4-24.

Listing 4-24. *Deleting Entries from Tournament 25, 2007, for Low Handicap Members*

```
DELETE FROM Entry
WHERE TourID = 25 AND Year = 2007 AND
MemberID IN
      (SELECT MemberID FROM Member WHERE Handicap < 20)
```

Summary

We can use nested queries along with the keywords IN and EXISTS in many situations. Many nested queries can be written in alternative ways. In Chapter 9, we will look at performance issues relating to different ways of expressing queries, but in general you should use the way that feels most natural to you when designing a query.

The following are the main types of nested queries:

Nested Query	Example

Replacing a single value with a subquery that returns a single value	`SELECT * FROM Entry e WHERE e.MemberID = 235`
	The previous can be replaced with this:
	`SELECT * FROM Entry e WHERE e.MemberID =`
	`    (SELECT m.MemberID FROM Member m WHERE m.LastName =`
	`    'Cooper')`

Replacing a set of values with a subquery returning a set of single values	`SELECT * FROM Entry e WHERE e.TourID IN (36,38,40)`
	The previous can be replaced with this:
	`SELECT * FROM Entry e WHERE e.TourID in`
	`    (SELECT t.TourID FROM Tournament t WHERE t.TourType =`
	`    'Open')`

Checking for the existence of rows	`SELECT * FROM Member m WHERE EXISTS`
	`    (SELECT * FROM Entry e WHERE e.MemberID = m.MemberID)`
	Show us members who have a corresponding row in the Entry table.

Nested queries can be used in many situations, including the following:

Task	Example

Comparing values with the results of aggregates	`SELECT * FROM Member m WHERE m.Handicap <`
	`    (SELECT AVG(Handicap) FROM Member)`
	Find members with handicaps less than the average.

Constructing queries with negatives	`SELECT * FROM Member m WHERE NOT EXISTS`
	`    (SELECT * FROM Entry e WHERE e.MemberID = m.MemberID)`
	Show us members who have NOT entered a tournament.

Making changes to table data	`INSERT INTO Entry (MemberID, TourID, Year)`
	`    SELECT MemberID, 25, 2007`
	`    FROM Member WHERE MemberType = 'Junior'`
	Add a row in the Entry table for every junior for tournament 25 in 2007.

CHAPTER 5

■ ■ ■

Self Joins

In Chapter 2, we looked at simple queries on a single table. In this chapter, we'll explore more complex queries on a single table—in particular, those requiring us to look at more than one row of the table at a time. The two types of queries we will look at are those where the table is involved in a *self relationship* and queries to answer questions such as "Which members entered *both* these tournaments?"

Self Relationships

Let's add some more information to our Member table. Suppose some members have coaches assigned to them. How do we represent that in the class diagrams we talked about in Chapter 1? We could take the approach shown in Figure 5-1 with two classes: Member and Coach. Recall what the lines and numbers mean. From left to right, a coach might have several members he is training (the 0..n nearest the Member class). From right to left, a particular member might have a single coach or no coach (the 0..1 nearest the Coach class).

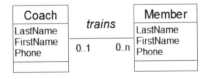

Figure 5-1. *Data model for coaches and members (not recommended!)*

The problem with the model in Figure 5-1 is that coaches, in all probability, are members of the club. When we implement this model with a Coach table and a Member table, some people will have a row recording their details in each table. For example, Brenda Nolan has a row in the Member table. When she takes up a role as coach, we also would need a row about her in the Coach table. The duplicated information (for example, two phone numbers) is likely to become inconsistent. What is really happening here is not that we have two separate classes of people—members and coaches—but that we simply have members, some of whom coach other members. This self relationship is shown in Figure 5-2.

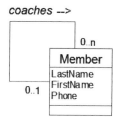

coaches -->

Figure 5-2. *Data model for members coaching members*

The relationship line in Figure 5-2 can be read in a clockwise direction to say that a particular member might coach several other members or none (0..n). In the other direction, we can read that a particular member might have one coach or none (0..1).

Relationships between classes can be represented by foreign keys, as discussed in Chapter 1. We can insert a foreign key column (Coach) in the Member table, as shown in Figure 5-3. In this case, the foreign key doesn't refer to a different table but back to the Member table itself. The values in the Coach column must already exist as a value in the primary key field of the table, MemberID. This ensures that only valid member IDs for existing members are inserted in the Coach column. The first row in the table in Figure 5-3 says that Melissa McKenzie is coached by member 153 (Brenda Nolan).

MemberID	LastName	FirstName	MemberType	Handicap	Gender	Coach
118	McKenzie	Melissa	Junior	30	F	153
138	Stone	Michael	Senior	30	M	
153	Nolan	Brenda	Senior	11	F	
176	Branch	Helen	Social		F	
178	Beck	Sarah	Social		F	
228	Burton	Sandra	Junior	26	F	153
235	Cooper	William	Senior	14	M	153
239	Spence	Thomas	Senior	10	M	
258	Olson	Barbara	Senior	16	F	
286	Pollard	Robert	Junior	19	M	235
290	Sexton	Thomas	Senior	26	M	235
323	Wilcox	Daniel	Senior	3	M	
331	Schmidt	Thomas	Senior	25	M	153
332	Bridges	Deborah	Senior	12	F	235
339	Young	Betty	Senior	21	F	
414	Gilmore	Jane	Junior	5	F	153
415	Taylor	William	Senior	7	M	235
461	Reed	Robert	Senior	3	M	235
469	Willis	Carolyn	Junior	29	F	
487	Kent	Susan	Social		F	

Figure 5-3. *Foreign key column Coach added to the Member table*

With this table, we now can answer several different types of questions, such as:

- What are the names of the coaches?

- Who is Jane Gilmore's coach?

- Is anyone being coached by someone with a higher handicap?

- Are any women being coached by men?

None of these questions can be answered by using simple select or project operations. What we require is a *self join* on the Member table. The easiest way to think of a self join is to see how we make one.

Creating a Self Join

Remember the definition of a join between two tables (from Chapter 3): a Cartesian product (all combination of rows from each table) followed by a select comparing a column in each of the tables. For a self join, we think of two copies of the same table. In Figure 5-4, we see part of the Cartesian product between two copies of the Member table. To distinguish the different bits of the product, I've given the first copy an alias m and the second an alias c (you'll see why in a minute). In the small section of the Cartesian product visible in Figure 5-4, we see the first row (Melissa) from copy m paired with rows from copy c.

Columns from first copy of Member (m)						Columns from second copy of Member (c)				
118 McKenzie	Melissa	Junior	30 F	153	118 McKenzie	Melissa	Junior	30 F	153
118 McKenzie	Melissa	Junior	30 F	153	138 Stone	Michael	Senior	30 M	
118 McKenzie	Melissa	Junior	30 F	153	153 Nolan	Brenda	Senior	11 F	
118 McKenzie	Melissa	Junior	30 F	153	176 Branch	Helen	Social	F	
118 McKenzie	Melissa	Junior	30 F	153	178 Beck	Sarah	Social	F	
118 McKenzie	Melissa	Junior	30 F	153	228 Burton	Sandra	Junior	26 F	153
118 McKenzie	Melissa	Junior	30 F	153	235 Cooper	William	Senior	14 M	153
118 McKenzie	Melissa	Junior	30 F	153	239 Spence	Thomas	Senior	10 M	
118 McKenzie	Melissa	Junior	30 F	153	258 Olson	Barbara	Senior	16 F	
118 McKenzie	Melissa	Junior	30 F	153	286 Pollard	Robert	Junior	19 M	235

m.Coach   c.MemberID

Figure 5-4. *Cartesian product between two copies of the Member table*

For queries about coaching, the interesting rows from the Cartesian product are those where the value of Coach from m is the same as MemberID from c. In Figure 5-4, you can see that the third line contains information about Melissa (from the m copy of Member) and information about her coach (from the c copy of Member). Now you can see why I chose the aliases—m for member and c for coach. Choosing helpful aliases can make understanding self joins much easier. The rows we would like to select from the Cartesian product are those satisfying m.Coach = c.MemberID. This is the join condition required to find information about members and their coaches. The SQL is shown in Listing 5-1.

Listing 5-1. *Self Join on Member Table to Find Information About Members and Their Coaches*

```
SELECT *
FROM Member m INNER JOIN Member c ON m.Coach = c.MemberID
```

The table resulting from the self join is shown in Figure 5-5 (some of the headings of the columns are truncated, as it was getting rather wide).

Information about a member (from m)   Information about a member's coach (from c)

m	m.LastN	m.FirstN	m.Me	m.Hand	m.Gen	m.Coach	c.MemberID	c.LastN	c.FirstN	c.Mer	c.Hand	c.	c.Coach
118	McKenzie	Melissa	Junior	30	F	153	153	Nolan	Brenda	Senior	11	F	
228	Burton	Sandra	Junior	26	F	153	153	Nolan	Brenda	Senior	11	F	
235	Cooper	William	Senior	14	M	153	153	Nolan	Brenda	Senior	11	F	
286	Pollard	Robert	Junior	19	M	235	235	Cooper	William	Senior	14	M	153
290	Sexton	Thomas	Senior	26	M	235	235	Cooper	William	Senior	14	M	153
331	Schmidt	Thomas	Senior	25	M	153	153	Nolan	Brenda	Senior	11	F	
332	Bridges	Deborah	Senior	12	F	235	235	Cooper	William	Senior	14	M	153
414	Gilmore	Jane	Junior	5	F	153	153	Nolan	Brenda	Senior	11	F	
415	Taylor	William	Senior	7	M	235	235	Cooper	William	Senior	14	M	153
461	Reed	Robert	Senior	3	M	235	235	Cooper	William	Senior	14	M	153

Join condition: m.Coach=c.MemberID

Figure 5-5. *Self join on Member table to retrieve information about members and their coaches*

None of these ideas are going to help us if our database has not been designed properly in the first place. However, once we recognize that there is a self relationship involved (members coach other members), and that relationship has been implemented correctly with a foreign key (Coach), then the trickiest part has been done. With this understanding, it is a simple job to create the self join, as shown in Figure 5-5.

Queries Involving a Self Join

With the joined table in Figure 5-5 as our base, we can answer all sorts of questions with quite simple select and project operations. Whenever I need to do queries involving self joins, I usually perform the join first (retaining all the rows and columns as in Figure 5-5), because the answers are usually pretty obvious when I have the joined table (or a quick sketch of the columns) in front of me. Let's see how this works with a few questions.

What Are the Names of the Coaches?

Looking at Figure 5-5, it is clear that the names of the coaches are in the columns coming from the c part of the join. We just want a list of the names in the columns c.LastName and c.FirstName. This is a simple project operation (that is, a subset of the columns). All we need to do is alter the first line of the query in Listing 5-1 to retrieve just those two columns. We don't want the names repeated, so we use the keyword DISTINCT in the SQL statement, as shown in Listing 5-2. For the data in Figure 5-5, this will return Brenda Nolan and William Cooper.

Listing 5-2. *Finding the Names of the Coaches*

```
SELECT DISTINCT c.FirstName, c.LastName
FROM Member m INNER JOIN Member c ON m.Coach = c.MemberID
```

Who Is Being Coached by Someone with a Higher Handicap?

To find out who is being coached by someone with a higher handicap, we need to compare the handicap of the member (m.Handicap) with the handicap of that member's coach (c.Handicap). We want to find the rows where the latter is greater than the former. This is a select operation (that is, retrieving a subset of rows). What is required is a WHERE clause to just retrieve those rows from the result of the join (Listing 5-1, Figure 5-5), as shown in Listing 5-3.

Listing 5-3. *Finding Rows for Members Being Coached by Someone with a Higher Handicap*

```
SELECT *
FROM Member m INNER JOIN Member c ON m.Coach = c.MemberID
WHERE m.Handicap < c.Handicap
```

For the data in Figure 5-5, this will retrieve the data in the last four rows. (You don't have to be a great golfer to be a good coach!) Having done the join and selected the appropriate rows, we can then choose which columns we want to appear in our final result.

List the Names of All the Members and the Names of Their Coaches

Listing the names of members and their coaches sounds pretty trivial, but if we are not careful, we can get it wrong. We have our joined table in Figure 5-5, and a first thought might be just to project the four columns containing the names. However, there are only 10 rows in the joined table, whereas there are 20 members in the Member table. The issue here is that not all the members have coaches. We looked at this in the section on outer joins in Chapter 3.

To recap, let's go back to the Cartesian product of the two copies of the Member table, but look at some rows involving a member with no coach, as shown in Figure 5-6.

Columns from first copy of Member (m)   **Columns from second copy of Member (c)**

m.Member	m.LastN	m.FirstN	m.Me	m.Ha	m.Ge	m.Coach	c.MemberID	c.LastN	c.FirstN	c.Mem	c.Hand	c.Gende	c.Coac
138	Stone	Michael	Senior	30	M		138	Stone	Michael	Senior	30	M	
138	Stone	Michael	Senior	30	M		235	Cooper	William	Senior	14	M	153
138	Stone	Michael	Senior	30	M		153	Nolan	Brenda	Senior	11	F	
138	Stone	Michael	Senior	30	M		414	Gilmore	Jane	Junior	5	F	153
138	Stone	Michael	Senior	30	M		323	Wilcox	Daniel	Senior	3	M	
138	Stone	Michael	Senior	30	M		118	McKenzie	Melissa	Junior	30	F	153
138	Stone	Michael	Senior	30	M		290	Sexton	Thomas	Senior	26	M	235

Join condition is never satisfied for a member with a Null in the Coach field

Figure 5-6. *Part of the Cartesian product between two copies of the Member table*

The join condition (m.Coach = c.MemberID) is never satisfied for a member with a Null in the Coach field, so all those members will be missing from our joined table. We just need to be careful to understand what we really want. Do we want a list of all the members with coaches (10 rows), or a list of all the members along with their coach's name if they have one (20 rows)? If it's the latter, we need an outer join. We need to see the name of each member (from the m copy of the Member table), along with the name of his coach, if any, (from the c copy). The SQL for this outer join is shown in Listing 5-4.

Listing 5-4. *Names of Members Along with the Names of Their Coach (If Any)*

```
SELECT m.FirstName, m.LastName, c.FirstName, c.LastName
FROM Member m LEFT OUTER JOIN Member c ON m.Coach = c.MemberID
```

Recall from Chapter 3 that for a left outer join, where there is no matching row from the right-hand table, those columns will be filled with Nulls. Figure 5-7 shows some of the rows from the left outer join in Listing 5-4.

m.FirstName	m.LastName	c.FirstName	c.LastName
Melissa	McKenzie	Brenda	Nolan
Michael	Stone		
Brenda	Nolan		
Helen	Branch		
Sarah	Beck		
Sandra	Burton	Brenda	Nolan
William	Cooper	Brenda	Nolan
Thomas	Spence		
Barbara	Olson		
Robert	Pollard	William	Cooper
ᵗʰᵒᵐᵃˢ	Sexton	ᵂⁱˡˡⁱ	

Figure 5-7. *Some rows from the left outer join (Listing 5-4)*

Who Coaches the Coaches, or Who Is My Grandmother?

Our self join shows us one level deep of members and coaches. If we look at the rows in Figure 5-7, we can see that Thomas Sexton is coached by William Cooper, who is in turn coached by Brenda Nolan, who doesn't have a coach. The hierarchy isn't all that interesting for this problem, but there are several analogous situations where the hierarchy is of considerable interest. Genealogy is one. Consider the data model and Person table in Figure 5-8. We record information (just a wee bit!) about each person, including who that person's mother is (we'll just consider birth mothers or it will get too complicated).

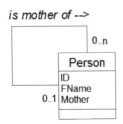

ID	FName	Mother
1001	Agnes	1002
1002	Mary	1006
1003	Linda	1002
1004	Grace	1002
1005	Sue	1001
1006	Brenda	
1007	Bo	1003
1008	Lily	1003

Person

Figure 5-8. *Data model for people and their birth mothers*

The relationship in Figure 5-8 can be read clockwise as "a person can be the mother of several other people" and in the other direction as "a person has at most one mother and might have none." Now in real life, that last statement doesn't sound right—surely everyone has a mother. However, our database is keeping only the data we know about, and unless we trace everyone back to the primeval slime, there will be some people in our table whose mother we do not know. Brenda is one. The table and model in Figure 5-8 are the same as our member and coach example, but a question like "Who is Sue's grandmother?" seems a bit more likely than "Who coaches my coach?"

So how do we get information about people along with information about their mothers? Just as in the previous section, we need to join the Person table to itself. (Don't forget to make the join an outer join so you don't lose Brenda.) The SQL is in Listing 5-5, and the Access diagrammatic interface for the join is shown in Figure 5-9, along with the resulting table. I've given the first copy of the table the alias p for person and the second copy the alias m for mother.

Listing 5-5. *People and Their Mothers*

```
SELECT p.ID, p.FName, p.Mother, m.ID, m.FName, m.Mother
FROM Person p LEFT OUTER JOIN Person m on p.Mother = m.ID
```

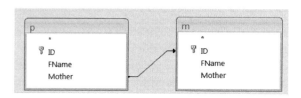

p.ID	p.FName	p.Mother	m.ID	m.FName	m.Mother
1001	Agnes	1002	1002	Mary	1006
1002	Mary	1006	1006	Brenda	
1003	Linda	1002	1002	Mary	1006
1004	Grace	1002	1002	Mary	1006
1005	Sue	1001	1001	Agnes	1002
1006	Brenda				
1007	Bo	1003	1003	Linda	1002
1008	Lily	1003	1003	Linda	1002

Figure 5-9. *Finding people and their mothers: Access diagram for the join (top) and the resulting table (bottom)*

Now what about going back the next generation? For that, we want to take the result table in Figure 5-9 and join that to another copy of the People table (with the alias g for grandmother). The SQL is in Listing 5-6, and the diagram and result table are in Figure 5-10.

Listing 5-6. *People and Their Mothers and Maternal Grandmothers*

```
SELECT p.ID, p.FName, p.Mother, m.ID, m.FName, m.Mother,
       g.ID, g.FName, g.Mother
FROM (Person p LEFT JOIN Person m ON p.Mother = m.ID)
LEFT JOIN Person g ON m.Mother = g.ID
```

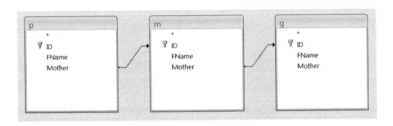

p.ID	p.FName	p.Mother	m.ID	m.FName	m.Mother	g.ID	g.FName	g.Mother
1001	Agnes	1002	1002	Mary	1006	1006	Brenda	
1002	Mary	1006	1006	Brenda				
1003	Linda	1002	1002	Mary	1006	1006	Brenda	
1004	Grace	1002	1002	Mary	1006	1006	Brenda	
1005	Sue	1001	1001	Agnes	1002	1002	Mary	1006
1006	Brenda							
1007	Bo	1003	1003	Linda	1002	1002	Mary	1006
1008	Lily	1003	1003	Linda	1002	1002	Mary	1006

Figure 5-10. *Finding three generations: Access diagram for the joins (top) and the resulting table (bottom)*

Clearly, we can keep making more and more self joins until we run out of generations. These sorts of hierarchical queries are likely to turn up whenever we have self relationships. One small catch is that we must specify the number of joins in each query. Standard SQL doesn't have the notion of a query that automatically keeps doing the self joins until it runs out of generations, such as "Find all my female ancestors."[1]

A Calculus Approach to Self Joins

The questions in the previous sections were all quite easy to answer once we realized we needed a self join. Sometimes, however, these realizations don't always come when you need them. Whenever my mind goes blank when faced with a query, I always resort to a calculus approach.

---

1. Some implementations of SQL do support recursive queries that can track through self relationships. Check your documentation for key phrases like WITH and CONNECT BY.

Let's look at our Member table again and ask a simple question: Who is Melissa's coach? In Figure 5-11, you can see how to figure out the answer, even if you have never heard of a self join (as most people haven't).

	MemberID	LastName	FirstName	MemberType	Coach
m ☞	118	McKenzie	Melissa	Junior	153
	138	Stone	Michael	Senior	
c ☞	153	Nolan	Brenda	Senior	
	176	Branch	Helen	Social	
	178	Beck	Sarah	Social	
	228	Burton	Sandra	Junior	153
	235	Cooper	William	Senior	153
	239	Spence	Thomas	Senior	
	258	Olson	Barbara	Senior	
	286	Pollard	Robert	Junior	235

Figure 5-11. *Finding Melissa's coach*

To find Melissa's coach, we first find the row for Melissa (m in Figure 5-11), and then we find another row (c for coach) that has the MemberID value the same as Melissa's coach. Then we know that Melissa's coach is Brenda. You don't need to know anything about self relationships or foreign keys or joins to figure that out. But once you have that logic clearly in your mind, you can write it down in calculus notation, and then the translation to SQL is pretty straightforward.

Let's write that logic out a bit more clearly:

I need to look at two rows (m and c) in the Member table, and I want to write out c.FirstName, where c.MemberID has the same value as m.Coach and m.FirstName is "Melissa".

Or, you may prefer the more condensed notation in Listing 5-7, where the bit on the left of the bar is what we want to write out and the bit on the right explains the condition.

Listing 5-7. *Calculus Expression to Find the Name of Melissa's Coach*

```
{c.FirstName | Member(c), ∃(m) Member(m)
and c.MemberID = m.Coach and m.FirstName = 'Melissa'}
```

The SQL follows quite easily from these calculus descriptions of the query and is shown in Listing 5-8.

Listing 5-8. *SQL to Find the Name of Melissa's Coach*

```
SELECT c.FirstName
FROM Member m, Member c
WHERE c.MemberID = m.Coach AND m.FirstName = 'Melissa'
```

So how does this calculus approach correspond to the algebra approach? As you might expect, the resulting SQL is just an alternative way of stating the same thing. In Listing 5-8, the middle line is the Cartesian product, and the first part of the WHERE clause is a join condition. The statement FROM Member m, Member c WHERE c.MemberID = m.Coach is just another way of expressing the self join we used in the previous sections.

Let's try one of the other queries using a calculus approach: Who is being coached by someone with a higher handicap? The picture I would need in my head to answer this question is shown in Figure 5-12.

MemberID	LastName	FirstName	MemberType	Coach	Handicap
138	Stone	Michael	Senior		30
153	Nolan	Brenda	Senior		11
176	Branch	Helen	Social		
178	Beck	Sarah	Social		
228	Burton	Sandra	Junior	153	26
235	Cooper	William	Senior	153	14
239	Spence	Thomas	Senior		10
258	Olson	Barbara	Senior		16
286	Pollard	Robert	Junior	235	19
290	Sexton	Thomas	Senior	235	26
323	Wilcox	Daniel	Senior		3
331	Schmidt	Thomas	Senior	153	25
332	Bridges	Deborah	Senior	235	12
339	Young	Betty	Senior		21
414	Gilmore	Jane	Junior	153	5
415	Taylor	William	Senior	235	7
461	Reed	Robert	Senior	235	3
469	Willis	Carolyn	Junior		29
487	Kent	Susan	Social		

Figure 5-12. *Deborah is coached by someone with a higher handicap.*

Here is the informal calculus statement representing the logic depicted in Figure 5-12:

I'm going to look at every row (m) in the Member table and will write out m.LastName if there exists some other row (c) in the Member table where c.MemberID is the same as m.Coach and m.Handicap is less than c.Handicap.

If we start with our finger (labeled m) at the top of the table and check each row, the first row that satisfies our condition is for Deborah Bridges. We can find another row (labeled c in Figure 5-12), which is for Deborah's coach, William Cooper (m.Coach = c.MemberID). Deborah's handicap (m.Handicap) is less than her coach's handicap (c.Handicap). We can carry on with finger m checking the rest of the rows to see if any other rows satisfy the condition (another three do).

The more formal expression for the calculus statement is shown in Listing 5-9.

Listing 5-9. *Calculus Expression to Find the People with a Lower Handicap Than Their Coach*

```
{m.FirstName | Member(m) and ∃(c) Member(c)
and c.MemberID = m.Coach and m.Handicap < c.Handicap}
```

The SQL follows in a straightforward manner, as shown in Listing 5-10.

Listing 5-10. *SQL to Find the People with a Lower Handicap Than Their Coach*

```
SELECT m.FirstName
FROM Member m, Member c
WHERE c.MemberID = m.Coach AND m.Handicap < c.Handicap
```

Once again, you can see the equivalent of the self join in Listing 5-10 (FROM Member m, Member c WHERE c.MemberID = m.Coach). The usefulness of this calculus approach is that you don't need to understand what a self join is, nor must you make the mental leap that you need one. By thinking in terms of virtual fingers and which rows are involved in helping you with your decision, you can sketch a calculus-type statement of the criteria. The SQL usually follows quite easily from that.

Questions Involving "Both"

In the "Avoiding Common Mistakes" section of Chapter 2, we looked at questions such as "Which members have entered *both* tournaments 24 and 36?" To recap, I've reproduced the Entry table in Figure 5-13 and a common first attempt at an SQL statement for this question in Listing 5-11.

Listing 5-11. *SQL to Find Members Who Have Entered Both Tournaments 24 and 36 (Won't Work!)*

```
SELECT e.MemberID
FROM Entry e
WHERE e.TourID = 24 AND e.TourID = 36
```

Listing 5-11 includes a relational algebra select operation (the WHERE clause), which will retrieve a subset of the rows. However, recall that the condition (e.TourID = 24 AND e.TourID = 36) is applied to each row individually. Can we find a single row where the condition is true? From a calculus perspective, our virtual finger (labeled e) will look at each row in turn to see if (e.TourID = 24 AND e.TourID = 36). Because the TourID column will always contain only a single value, the condition will never be satisfied. The query in Listing 5-11 will never return any rows because the value in TourID cannot be two different things (24 and 36) simultaneously. Such a query can be quite dangerous, because the user may interpret the empty result as meaning that no members have entered both tournaments, whereas the query is actually incorrect.

MemberID	TourID	Year
118	24	2005
228	24	2006
228	25	2006
228	36	2006
235	38	2004
235	38	2006
235	40	2005
235	40	2006
239	40	2004
258	24	2005
258	38	2005
286	24	2004
286	24	2005
286	24	2006
415	25	2005
415	36	2005
415	36	2006
415	38	2004
415	38	2006
415	40	2004
415	40	2005
415	40	2006

Figure 5-13. *Entry table*

To answer the question, we need to look at more than one row in the Entry table at the same time. I find a calculus approach the most natural for dealing with questions involving "both."

A Calculus Approach to Questions Involving "Both"

The picture I need in my head to answer "Which members have entered both tournaments 24 and 36?" is shown in Figure 5-14.

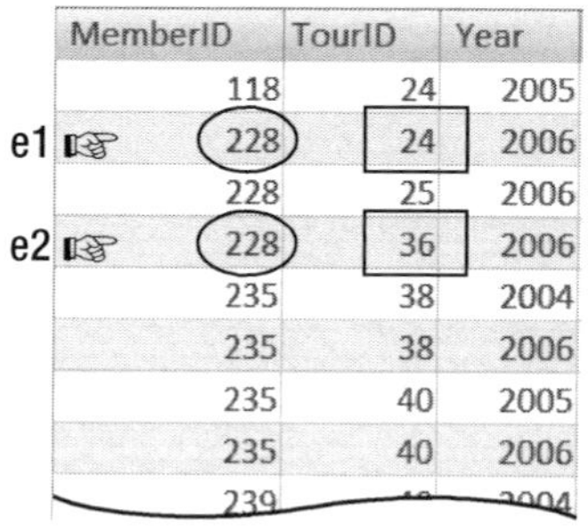

	MemberID	TourID	Year
	118	24	2005
e1	228	24	2006
	228	25	2006
e2	228	36	2006
	235	38	2004
	235	38	2006
	235	40	2005
	235	40	2006

Figure 5-14. *Member 228 has entered both tournaments 24 and 36.*

Looking at Figure 5-14, it is pretty clear that member 228 has entered both the tournaments. We can think of it in informal calculus terms:

> *I'm going to look at every row (e1) in the* `Entry` *table. I'll write out that row's member ID if* `TourID` *has the value 24 and I can also find another row (e2) in the* `Entry` *table with the same value for* `memberID` *and that row has 36 as the value for* `TourID`*.*

Listing 5-12 shows the more formal calculus expression.

Listing 5-12. *Calculus Expression to Find the Members Who Have Entered Both Tournaments 24 and 36*

```
{e1.MemberID| Entry(e1) and ∃(e2) Entry(e2)
and e1.MemberID = e2.MemberID and e1.TourID = 24 and e2.TourID = 36}
```

The SQL follows from here and is shown in Listing 5-13. If you have trouble with it, refer to Figure 5-14.

Listing 5-13. *SQL to Find Members Who Have Entered Both Tournaments 24 and 36 (Will Work!)*

```
SELECT e1.MemberID
FROM Entry e1, Entry e2
WHERE e1.MemberID = e2.MemberID
      AND e1.TourID = 24 AND e2.TourID = 36
```

Questions involving the word "both" often require us to look at more than one row in a table. In our first attempt, Listing 5-11, we were looking at only one row at a time (one finger labeled e). This will never work. We need to investigate at least two rows (two fingers e1 and e2), with matching MemberID values. In more formal calculus terms, we need two tuple variables e1 and e2, which scan all the rows in the Entry table looking for pairs that match our criteria.

An Algebra Approach to Questions Involving "Both"

As always, we have several ways to think about a query. Take a look at the middle two lines of Listing 5-13. FROM Entry e1, Entry e2 is a Cartesian product (which will give us every combination of pairs of rows), followed by a select operation (WHERE e1.MemberID = e2.MemberID). This is a join. In fact, it is a self join between two copies of the Entry table. Part of the join between two copies of the Entry table is shown in Figure 5-15.

Columns from first copy of Entry (e1)   Columns from second copy of Entry (e2)

e1.Member	e1.TourID	e1.Year	e2.Member	e2.TourID	e2.Year
118	24	2005	118	24	2005
228	24	2006	228	24	2006
228	25	2006	228	24	2006
228	36	2006	228	24	2006
228	24	2006	228	25	2006
228	25	2006	228	25	2006
228	36	2006	228	25	2006
228	24	2006	228	36	2006
228	25	2006	228	36	2006
228	36	2006	228	36	2006
235	38	2004	235	38	2004
235	38	2006	235	38	2004
235	40	2005	235	38	2004
235	40	2006	235	38	2004

Join condition: e1.MemberID=e2.MemberID

Figure 5-15. *Part of the self join between two copies of the Entry table*

The self join in Figure 5-15 shows those combinations of rows from the Entry table for the same member. For example, we have every combination or rows involving member 228. We can use this self join to answer the question about members who have entered both tournaments 24 and 36. We just need to find a row that has 24 from the first copy and 36 from the second copy (or vice versa)—that is, e1.TourID = 24 AND e2.TourID = 36.

The SQL for this self join followed by the select condition is shown in Listing 5-14.

Listing 5-14. *SQL to Find Members Who Have Entered Both Tournaments 24 and 36 (Using a Self Join)*

```
SELECT e1.MemberID
FROM Entry e1 INNER JOIN Entry e2 ON e1.MemberID = e2.MemberID
WHERE e1.TourID = 24 AND e2.TourID = 36
```

If you compare Listings 5-13 and 5-14, you will see how similar they are. They will both produce exactly the same result. You will probably find one or other to be more intuitive.

Summary

Many queries require us to obtain information from two rows of a table. This turns up in a number of situations. The main ones are where we have self relationships or questions involving the word "both."

Self Relationships

We have a self relationship when different instances of a class are related to each other. In the example in this chapter, we had that members are coaches of other members. Queries about coaches or coaching relationships require self joins, which take two copies of the table and join them. The self join to provide the names of members and their coaches follows. The copy with the information about the member has the alias m, and the copy with information about the coach has the alias c.

```
SELECT m.LastName, m.FirstName, c.LastName, c.FirstName
FROM Member m INNER JOIN Member c ON m.Coach = c.MemberID
```

Questions Involving the Word "Both"

Questions with the word "both" often mean we need to look at two rows in a table. In our example, we wanted to find the MemberID of members who have entered both tournaments 24 and 36. We needed to find two rows in the Entry table (e1 and e2) for that member: one for tournament 24 and the other for tournament 36. The following is the calculus-based SQL statement:

```
SELECT e1.MemberID
FROM Entry e1, Entry e2
WHERE e1.MemberID = e2.MemberID AND e1.TourID = 24 AND e2.TourID = 36
```

This statement is equivalent to a self join between two copies of the Entry table (on e1.MemberID = e2.MemberID), followed by a select condition to find the rows for the two tournaments.

CHAPTER 6

■■■■

More Than One Relationship Between Tables

In order to get correct information from your database, it is essential that the design is appropriate and you understand it properly. You have already seen simple relationships between tables (for example, each member is associated with one member type), and in Chapter 5, we looked at self relationships (for example, members may coach other members). Another situation that occurs frequently is where there is more than one relationship between two tables.

Representing Multiple Relationships Between Tables

Let's look at the model in Figure 6-1, which shows how we might incorporate the idea of teams into our club database. The top line in Figure 6-1 can be interpreted, from left to right, as that a particular member might manage (at most) one team; and from right to left, as that each team has exactly one manager. The bottom relationship means, from left to right, that a particular member might play in (at most) one team; and from right to left, that a team has at least one member and could have many members playing for it.

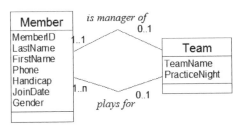

Figure 6-1. *Two relationships between the Member and Team classes*

We can represent this model by introducing a new table, Team, into our database. The top relationship can be represented by including a foreign key field Manager in the Team table, and the bottom relationship can be represented by including a foreign key field Team in the Member table. Some sample rows from the two tables (with some of the columns in Member hidden) are shown in Figure 6-2.

MemberID	LastName	FirstName	Team
118	McKenzie	Melissa	
138	Stone	Michael	
153	Nolan	Brenda	TeamB
176	Branch	Helen	
178	Beck	Sarah	
228	Burton	Sandra	
235	Cooper	William	TeamB
239	Spence	Thomas	
258	Olson	Barbara	
286	Pollard	Robert	TeamB
290	Sexton	Thomas	
323	Wilcox	Daniel	TeamA
331	Schmidt	Thomas	
332	Bridges	Deborah	
339	Young	Betty	TeamB
414	Gilmore	Jane	TeamA
415	Taylor	William	TeamA
461	Reed	Robert	TeamA
469	Willis	Carolyn	
487	Kent	Susan	

TeamName	PracticeNight	Manager
TeamA	Tuesday	239
TeamB	Monday	153

Member   **Team**

Figure 6-2. *Foreign keys Team in Member table and Manager in Team table to represent the relationships in Figure 6-1*

From the Member table, we can see that four people play for TeamB (Brenda Nolan, William Cooper, Robert Pollard, and Betty Young) and from the Team table, we can see that member 153 (Brenda Nolan) is the manager of TeamB. The eagle-eyed will notice that there is nothing in the data model that says whether or not a manager must be a member of the team. TeamB's manager is a member of TeamB, whereas TeamA's manager 239 (Thomas Spence) is not a member of TeamA. The only constraints implied by the foreign keys are that the manager of a team must be in the Member table and a member can belong only to a team that exists in the Team table.

Algebra Approach to Two Relationships Between Tables

We can make a couple of simple joins between the Team table and Member table. If we want to know information about teams and also want to include information about the managers, we can take the Team table and join it with the Member table on the foreign key Manager, as shown in Listing 6-1 and Figure 6-3 (the figure shows the Access join diagram and just some of the columns of the resulting table).

Listing 6-1. *Teams with Additional Information About Their Managers*

```
SELECT *
FROM Member m INNER JOIN Team t on t.Manager = m.MemberID
```

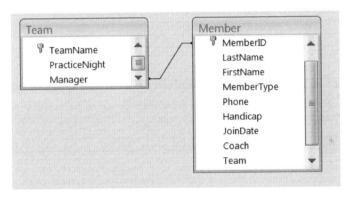

TeamName	PracticeNight	Manager	MemberID	LastName	FirstName
TeamA	Tuesday	239	239	Spence	Thomas
TeamB	Monday	153	153	Nolan	Brenda

Join condition. t.Manager=m.MemberID

Figure 6-3. *Joining Member and Team to get additional information about team managers (Listing 6-1)*

Figure 6-3 shows the information about teams, such as that TeamA practices on Tuesday and the manager has ID 239. By joining the Member table, we get the added information that the manager's name is Thomas Spence.

If we want to find information about team members and include information about their teams, we can take the Member table and join it to the Team table on the foreign key Team, as shown in Listing 6-2 and Figure 6-4.

Listing 6-2. *Members with Additional Information About Their Teams*

```
SELECT * FROM Member m INNER JOIN Team t on m.Team = t.TeamName
```

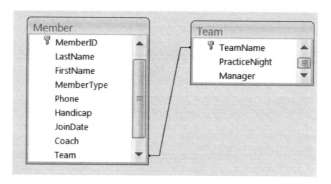

MemberID	LastName	FirstName	Team	TeamName	PracticeNight	Manager
153	Nolan	Brenda	TeamB	TeamB	Monday	153
235	Cooper	William	TeamB	TeamB	Monday	153
286	Pollard	Robert	TeamB	TeamB	Monday	153
323	Wilcox	Daniel	TeamB	TeamA	Tuesday	239
339	Young	Betty	TeamB	TeamB	Monday	153
414	Gilmore	Jane	TeamA	TeamA	Tuesday	239
415	Taylor	William	TeamA	TeamA	Tuesday	239
461	Reed	Robert	TeamA	TeamA	Tuesday	239

Join condition. m.Team=t.TeamName

Figure 6-4. *Joining Member and Team to get additional information about members' teams (Listing 6-2)*

So far, so good. However, a closer look at the result table in Figure 6-4 shows that we might need some more information. For a particular member, we have her team and the number of the team manager. The name of the team manager would be useful to have as well. We need to join the result table in Figure 6-4 to another copy of the Member table to find the name of the manager. Listing 6-3 and Figure 6-5 show how this is done.

Listing 6-3. *Joining an Additional Copy of the Member Table to See Names of Managers*

```
SELECT *
FROM (Member m INNER JOIN Team t ON m.Team = t.TeamName)
INNER JOIN Member m2 ON t.Manager = m2.MemberID
```

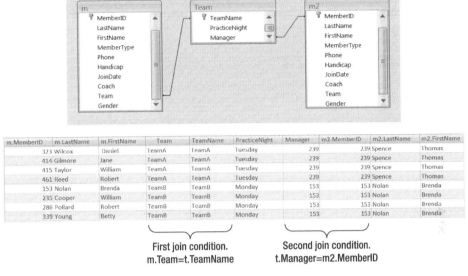

m.MemberID	m.LastName	m.FirstName	Team	TeamName	PracticeNight	Manager	m2.MemberID	m2.LastName	m2.FirstName
323	Wilcox	Daniel	TeamA	TeamA	Tuesday	239	239	Spence	Thomas
414	Gilmore	Jane	TeamA	TeamA	Tuesday	239	239	Spence	Thomas
415	Taylor	William	TeamA	TeamA	Tuesday	239	239	Spence	Thomas
461	Reed	Robert	TeamA	TeamA	Tuesday	239	239	Spence	Thomas
153	Nolan	Brenda	TeamB	TeamB	Monday	153	153	Nolan	Brenda
235	Cooper	William	TeamB	TeamB	Monday	153	153	Nolan	Brenda
286	Pollard	Robert	TeamB	TeamB	Monday	153	153	Nolan	Brenda
339	Young	Betty	TeamB	TeamB	Monday	153	153	Nolan	Brenda

First join condition.
m.Team=t.TeamName

Second join condition.
t.Manager=m2.MemberID

Figure 6-5. *Joining another copy of the Member table to get names of team managers (Listing 6-3)*

The result table in Figure 6-5 is very useful for generating reports about teams and their members. Figure 6-6 shows a report based on the query in Listing 6-3. The report has been grouped by team, with the team and manager information (from the Team table and m2 copy of the Member table) in a group header. The members of the team (from the first copy m of the Member table) are in the detail part of the report.

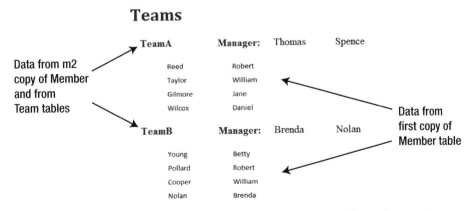

Figure 6-6. *A report based on the query in Listing 6-3 (the result table in Figure 6-5)*

One mistake people sometimes make when trying to get information like that shown in Figure 6-5 is to not recognize that two copies of the Member table are required. This often happens when designing a query in Microsoft Access (2007). Access automatically joins tables in a query on the foreign keys. However, in a situation like this, where each table has a foreign key referencing the other, Access includes only one copy of each table and effectively creates the join shown in Listing 6-4 and Figure 6-7.

Lisitng 6-4. *Just One Join Between the Tables (But with a Complex Condition)*

```
SELECT * FROM Member m INNER JOIN Team t
ON (m.MemberID = t.Manager) AND (m.Team = t.TeamName)
```

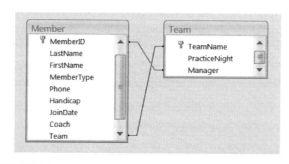

MemberID	LastName	FirstName	Team	TeamName	PracticeNight	Manager
153	Nolan	Brenda	TeamB	TeamB	Monday	153

Just one join with a complex condition.
m.Team=t.TeamName AND t.Manager=m.MemberID

Figure 6-7. *Just one join between the tables but with a complex condition (Listing 6-4)*

To understand what is happening with the join in Listing 6-4 and Figure 6-7, consider first the Cartesian product of Member and Team. The Cartesian product gives us every combination of rows from each table. The join condition says only rows where the MemberID is the same as the Manager and Team and TeamName are the same. In everyday language, this amounts to "Show me the members who manage the team they are in." For our data, that is just the single row for Brenda Nolan we see in Figure 6-7. This can be disconcerting for beginners, who quite rightly wonder what happened to all the other team members. In Access, you must manually remove one of the join conditions and add another copy of the Member table, as in Figure 6-5.

Calculus Approach to Two Relationships Between Tables

You can use different ways to construct the query to retrieve all the information about a team (members' names, team name, and manager's name) for a report like the one in Figure 6-6. I find the idea of two joins quite intuitive, but other people prefer to take a calculus approach.

I have reproduced the two tables in Figure 6-8. Now let's see how we can pick a member and find out what team he is in and who the manager is for that team.

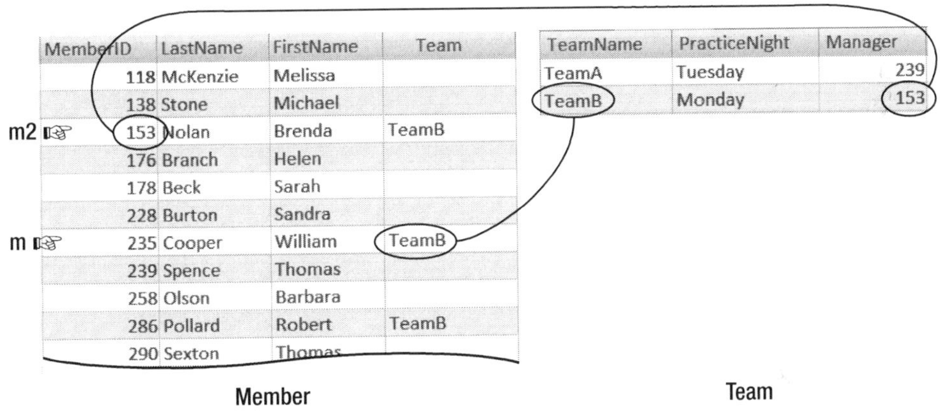

Figure 6-8. *Finding a team member (William Cooper), his team's name, and the name of the team's manager*

Without needing to think about joins, we can find the information we require. We need information from three rows. Let's look at one specific case. One row (m) from the Member table will give us the name of a member (William Cooper in Figure 6-8). We need to find the row (t) in the Team table for that member's team (m.Team = t.TeamName). Then we need another row in the Member table (m2) for the manager of the team (t.Manager = m2.MemberID). The calculus expression to find all such rows is shown in Listing 6-5.

Listing 6-5. *Calculus Expression for Information About Members, Their Team, and Their Team's Manager*

```
{m,t,m2 | Member(m), Team(t), Member(m2)
AND m.Team = t.TeamName AND t.Manager = m2.MemberID}
```

The SQL equivalent is in Listing 6-6.

Listing 6-6. *SQL Statement for Information About Members, Their Team, and Their Team's Manager*

```
SELECT * FROM Member m, Team t, Member m2
WHERE m.Team = t.TeamName AND t.Manager = m2.MemberID
```

Listing 6-6 is equivalent to the SQL in Listing 6-3. The WHERE clause is the equivalent of a join between Member (m) and Team (t) on m.Team = t.TeamName, and another join between Team and another copy of Member (m2) on t.Manager = m2.MemberID.

Business Rules

The data model in Figure 6-1 shows the two relationships between members and teams: members can belong to teams, and members can manage teams. When we implement these relationships with foreign keys, the constraints that are placed on the data are quite simple. A member can be in only a team that exists in the Team table, and a team can be managed only by someone in the Member table.

Other constraints are likely to apply in various situations. For example, we might have the additional constraints that a team can have no more than four members and/or the manager must be a member of the team (or not). Referential integrity alone cannot address these rules.

Relational database products will usually provide some way to enforce such constraints. Large systems such as SQL Server and Oracle provide *triggers*. Triggers are actions that take place at a specified time (for example, when inserting or updating a record). The trigger will check and reject any changes that do not obey the rules. In Access and other products, it is not possible to apply such constraints to the tables themselves. However, you can attach macros, which can do some sort of checking, to input forms.

We won't look in detail at how such constraints are implemented in various products, but we will look at how queries can help find any instances where the constraints are not satisfied. Although this is finding the problem after it has occurred, variations of these queries would form a basis for any trigger or macro that you would need to write to enforce the constraints.

Let's look at finding teams whose managers are not members of the team. My mind often goes blank when faced with a query like this, and in that case, I always take a calculus approach. This means picturing the tables involved and imagining the type of instance I am seeking. Take a look at Figure 6-9.

In Figure 6-9, TeamA's manager is 239, and we can see from the Member table that member 239 is not a member of any team. If we had a constraint that managers must belong to the team, TeamA would not obey it.

TeamName	PracticeNight	Manager
t ☞ TeamA	Tuesday	(239)
TeamB	Monday	153

MemberID	LastName	FirstName	Team
118	McKenzie	Melissa	
138	Stone	Michael	
153	Nolan	Brenda	TeamB
176	Branch	Helen	
178	Beck	Sarah	
228	Burton	Sandra	
235	Cooper	William	TeamB
m ☞ (239)	Spence	Thomas	(??)
258	Olson	Barbara	
286	Pollard	Robert	TeamB
290	Sexton	Thomas	
323	Wilcox	Daniel	TeamA
331	Schmidt	Thomas	
332	Bridges	Deborah	
339	Young	Betty	TeamB
414	Gilmore	Jane	TeamA
415	Taylor	William	TeamA
461	Reed	Robert	TeamA
469	Willis	Carolyn	
487	Kent	Susan	

Team   **Member**

Figure 6-9. *Finding teams whose managers do not play for the team*

To find all teams like this, we would say:

Find the team names from all the rows (t) in the Team *table where the matching row (m) in the* Member *table for the team manager (i.e.,* t.Manager = m.MemberID*) has a team (*m.team*) that is either empty or different from the team in the* Team *table (*m.Team <> t.TeamName*).*

The slightly more formal calculus notation representing this situation (and illustrated in Figure 6-9) is shown in Listing 6-7.

Listing 6-7. *Calculus Expression to Find Teams Where the Manager Is Not a Member of the Team*

```
{t.TeamName | Team(t) and ∃(m) Member(m) AND t.Manager = m.MemberID
AND (m.Team IS NULL OR m.Team <> t.Team)}
```

The equivalent SQL is shown in Listing 6-8. The middle two lines are equivalent to a join between the two tables on m.MemberID = t.Manager.

Listing 6-8. *SQL to Find Teams Where the Manager Is Not a Member of the Team (Based on Calculus)*

```
SELECT t.teamname
FROM Member m, Team t
WHERE m.MemberID = t.Manager
AND (m.Team <> t.Teamname OR m.Team IS NULL)
```

The query could also be constructed from an algebra perspective, as shown in Listing 6-9, if you prefer this approach.

Listing 6-9. *SQL to Find Teams Where the Manager Is Not a Member of the Team (Based on Algebra)*

```
SELECT t.teamname
FROM Member m INNER JOIN Team t ON m.MemberID = t.Manager
WHERE m.Team <> t.Teamname OR m.Team IS NULL
```

Why have we included the IS NULL condition in Listings 6-8 and 6-9? You might remember from Chapter 2 that if we make a comparison with a Null value, the result is false in SQL. If we want to find managers who aren't in a team, we need to specifically include that possibility in our query. Had the requirement been just that a manager must not belong to a different team, we could have left out the checking of Null values, because a manager with no team would have been OK. As always, clearly understanding what you are actually trying to find can be the most difficult part of formulating any query.

The queries in Listings 6-8 and 6-9 will find teams with incorrect managers, but only after they have been added to the database. How do we prevent them from being added in the first place? The solution depends on which database product you are using. Before changes to data are finally committed to a database, they are usually recorded in a buffer of some sort. For example, in SQL Server, the records being updated or added are kept in a temporary table called inserted. If we add or update some records to the Team table, a temporary table (inserted) that has the same structure as the Team table is created to hold the new records temporarily. We want to perform a query similar to that in Listing 6-10 to check if any of the new records have managers who don't obey the constraint. However, instead of looking at the Team table, we want to look at the records in the temporary inserted table and count how many of those are invalid.

Listing 6-10. *Part of a SQL Server Trigger to Prevent Adding Invalid Team Managers*

```
IF
    (SELECT COUNT(*)
     FROM Member m INNER JOIN inserted i ON m.MemberID = i.Manager
     WHERE m.Team <> i.Teamname OR m.Team IS NULL)
    <> 0)
BEGIN
```

```
    Rollback Tran
END
```

The two innermost lines in Listing 6-10 are almost exactly the same as the query in Listing 6-8, except we have replaced Team with inserted. Rather than selecting each of the rows with incorrect managers, we have just counted how many of these rows exist. The IF statement says if there are any invalid records (COUNT() <> 0), then don't add the records to the database (that is, roll back the whole transaction).

This is a bit of a crude approach, because if any of the new records are incorrect, the whole lot gets rejected. You will need to consult the documentation for your database product to see how to develop triggers that work efficiently, but the idea of using a query to check the validity of new records is a common one.

In Access, the checking is done at the interface level, usually on a form. Instead of checking the inserted table as in Listing 6-9, we would create a macro to investigate the values of fields on the form before committing them to the database.

Whatever the product, for a constraint of this type, we will always need to look at the new Team values and compare them with the existing information in the Member table, so a query like the one in Listing 6-8 or Listing 6-9 provides a good starting place.

Summary

There can be more than one relationship between tables. For example, "a member may belong to a team" is one relationship. "A team has a club member who is the manager" is another relationship. To find the information about a member's team (including the manager's ID) requires a join between Member and Team. If we want to also find the name of the manager, we need to join that result to another copy of the Member table, like this:

```
SELECT * FROM
(Member m INNER JOIN Team t ON m.Team = t.TeamName)
INNER JOIN Member m2 ON t.Manager = m2.MemberID
```

When we have two relationships between tables, there can be quite complex business rules or constraints involving the relationship, such as that the manager must be a member of the team she captains, a manager should not be a member of any team, and so on. These often require the use of triggers. The types of queries discussed in this chapter will be helpful in formulating the code required in triggers.

CHAPTER 7

■ ■ ■

Set Operations

One of the great strengths of relational database theory is that the tables (or more formally, the relations) are made up of *distinct* rows and so can be considered a *set*. You can then use all the power of mathematical set theory to help you with combining and extracting specific information. Don't be alarmed by the words "mathematical" and "theory," as the ideas presented are both simple and elegant.

The algebra notation introduced in Chapters 1 and 2 is a useful way of expressing queries, especially as they become more complex. I will use the algebra notation in this chapter, but will always give you an SQL equivalent so you can choose which representation you find the most helpful. In this chapter, we will look at four set operations:

- Union

- Intersection

- Difference

- Division

Many implementations of SQL (but not all) have keywords that support the first three of these operations directly. We will look at how to use these keywords, as well as alternative ways to achieve the same result when the keywords are not available.

Overview of Basic Set Operations

We will look at each of the set operations in turn, but so that you know where we are heading, I'll begin with a very quick overview of the three most common operations: union ($\cup$), intersection ($\cap$), and difference ($-$). Imagine we have membership tables from two golf clubs. We might want to do the following:

- Determine who is in both clubs.

- Form a large list that combines all the members.

- Find out who is in one club but not the other.

The basic set operations allow us to carry out all these tasks.

Let's assume that the two clubs keep the names of their members in two tables that have exactly the same columns (more about this in the next section). Let's say the two tables are those shown in Figure 7-1. (OK, they are very small clubs!)

LastName	FirstName
Cooper	William
Gilmore	Jane
Kent	Susan
McKenzie	Melissa
Olson	Barbara
Pollard	Robert

ClubA

LastName	FirstName
Olson	Barbara
Pollard	Robert
Reed	Robert
Schmidt	Thomas
Sexton	Thomas

ClubB

Figure 7-1. *Two tables of member names*

The basic set operations on these two tables are summarized in Figure 7-2. The two club tables have been overlaid so that the members in common are superimposed. ClubA is the top table in each picture.

The union operator (top left in Figure 7-2) shows all the names from each table (with duplicates removed). The intersect operator (top right) returns the two rows that appear in both tables. The difference operators (bottom) return those rows that are found in one club but not the other.

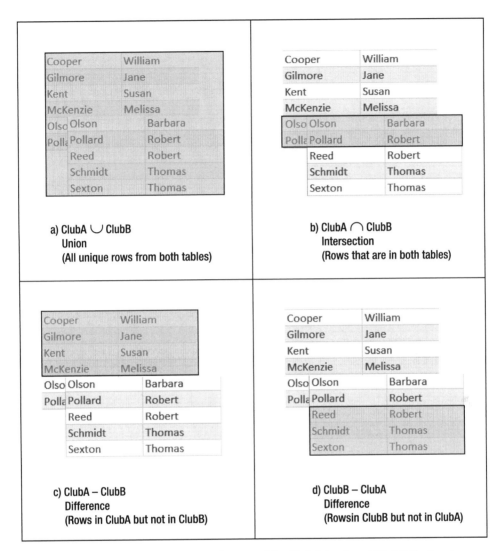

Figure 7-2. *The basic set operations on the two tables ClubA (top) and ClubB (bottom)*

Union-Compatible Tables

The set operations union, intersection, and difference operate between two sets of rows. It does not make any sense to try to compare rows in sets that have very different structures, such as those in Figure 7-3.

MemberID	Lastname	FirstName	Handicap	MemberType
235	Cooper	William	14	Senior
414	Gilmore	Jane	5	Junior
487	Kent	Susan		Social
118	McKenzie	Melissa	30	Junior
153	Nolan	Brenda	11	Senior
258	Olson	Barbara	16	Senior
286	Pollard	Robert	19	Junior

MemberID	TourID	Year
118	24	2005
228	24	2006
228	25	2006
228	36	2006
235	38	2004
235	38	2006
235	40	2005
235	40	2006
239	25	2006
239	40	2004

Member table   Entry table

Figure 7-3. *It makes no sense to try to compare rows with different structures.*

So what determines whether two sets of rows can be compared using the set operations union, intersection, and difference? Formally, the two sets must have the same number of columns, and each column must have the same domain. Strictly speaking, a *domain* is a set of possible values. However, in practice, the requirement for set operations is that the corresponding columns in each set of rows have the same types—both character, both integer, and so on. The names of the columns do not need to be the same. Sets or tables that meet these requirements are referred to as being *union compatible*, although the requirement is necessary for the intersection and difference operations as well.

Figure 7-4 shows pairs of membership tables from different clubs. The two tables on the left are union compatible. Even though the names of the columns are different, they have the same number of columns, and corresponding columns have the same types. The two tables on the right are not union compatible. Even though they have columns with the same names, the order is such that the fourth column has a character type in the top table and a number type in the bottom, and vice versa for the last column.

Different implementations of SQL may interpret the strictness of this "sameness" of domains or types differently. Strictly speaking, two fields defined as CHAR(10) and CHAR(12) have different domains, but many implementations of SQL will allow these to be regarded as the same for the purposes of set operations. Some implementations will also convert numbers into characters to enable set operations to be carried out. I find this particularly scary and don't recommend you let your application make these sorts of decisions for you. The following sections demonstrate how you can use SQL to make your tables union compatible.

ID	FamilyName	Name	MemberType	Handicap
235 Cooper		William	Senior	14
414 Gilmore		Jane	Junior	5
487 Kent		Susan	Social	
118 McKenzie		Melissa	Junior	30
153 Nolan		Brenda	Senior	11
258 Olson		Barbara	Senior	16
286 Pollard		Robert	Junior	19

ClubA

MemberID	Lastname	FirstName	Handicap	MemberType
235	Cooper	William	14	Senior
414	Gilmore	Jane	5	Junior
487	Kent	Susan		Social
118	McKenzie	Melissa	30	Junior
153	Nolan	Brenda	11	Senior
258	Olson	Barbara	16	Senior
286	Pollard	Robert	19	Junior

ClubC

MemberID	Lastname	FirstName	MemberType	Handicap
258	Olson	Barbara	Senior	16
286	Pollard	Robert	Junior	19
461	Reed	Robert	Senior	3
331	Schmidt	Thomas	Senior	25
290	Sexton	Thomas	Senior	26

ClubB

MemberID	Lastname	FirstName	MemberType	Handicap
258	Olson	Barbara	Senior	16
286	Pollard	Robert	Junior	19
461	Reed	Robert	Senior	3
331	Schmidt	Thomas	Senior	25
290	Sexton	Thomas	Senior	26

ClubD

a) Union compatible   b) Not union compatible

Figure 7-4. *Union compatiblity of tables*

Union

Union allows you to combine all the rows in two union-compatible tables (or two sets of rows), as in the top left of Figure 7-2. Listing 7-1 shows the algebra expression for the union of the two tables ClubA and ClubB.

Listing 7-1. *Algebra Expresion for the Union of Two Compatible Tables*

ClubA ∪ ClubB

The order of the tables in the expression does not matter, because the resulting rows in the union will be the same; that is, ClubA ∪ ClubB = ClubB ∪ ClubA.

To carry out a union in SQL, we need to first retrieve two sets of rows using two SELECT clauses. We can then combine the two sets with the UNION keyword. Listing 7-2 shows the SQL for performing a union between the pair of tables on the left side of Figure 7-4.

Listing 7-2. *SQL for the Union of Two Compatible Tables*

```
SELECT * FROM ClubA
UNION
SELECT * FROM ClubB
```

The resulting table will include all the rows from both tables with no duplicates, so you will see only one row each for Barbara Olson and Robert Pollard, as shown in Figure 7-5. If you wish to retain the duplicates for some reason, you can use the key phrase UNION ALL.

ID	FamilyName	Name	MemberType	Handicap
235	Cooper	William	Senior	14
414	Gilmore	Jane	Junior	5
487	Kent	Susan	Social	
118	McKenzie	Melissa	Junior	30
153	Nolan	Brenda	Senior	11
258	Olson	Barbara	Senior	16
286	Pollard	Robert	Junior	19
461	Reed	Robert	Senior	3
331	Schmidt	Thomas	Senior	25
290	Sexton	Thomas	Senior	26

Figure 7-5. *Union of ClubA and ClubB*

Union-compatible tables do not need to have the same column names. The names of the columns in the resulting virtual table will usually be from one of the tables. In the example in Figure 7-5, the column names are the same as the first table mentioned in the union query in Listing 7-2.

Ensuring Union Compatibility

When tables are not union compatible, you can often remedy the incompatibility in the SELECT clauses. For example, the two tables on the right side of Figure 7-4 have the columns in different orders. We can alter that order in the query, as shown in Listing 7-3.

Listing 7-3. *Ensuring the Tables Have Columns in the Same Order*

```
SELECT MemberID, LastName, FirstName, Handicap, MemberType FROM ClubC
UNION
SELECT MemberID, LastName, FirstName, Handicap, MemberType FROM ClubD
```

Another incompatibility problem occurs when the types of the columns have been defined differently. For example, the ClubC table may have the Handicap field declared as an INT, whereas the ClubD table may have (unwisely) stored the Handicap values in a CHAR field. As I mentioned earlier, different implementations of SQL will treat these inconsistencies in a variety of ways. Many will try to convert the numbers to strings or vice versa. You can take control of these conversions yourself (which is probably a good idea) by using type-conversion functions.

For example, in SQL Server, the expression CONVERT(INT, Handicap) would take the value in the Handicap field and convert it to an integer value. If the Handicap field in the ClubD table were a CHAR type, then Listing 7-4 would ensure that the types were integers in both tables. Of course, if any of the values in the ClubD table's Handicap column could not be converted to integers, you would get an error, and you would need to fix the data.

Listing 7-4. *Ensuring the Tables Have Columns of the Same Type*

```
SELECT MemberID, LastName, FirstName, Handicap, MemberType FROM ClubC
UNION
SELECT MemberID, LastName, FirstName, CONVERT(INT, Handicap), MemberType FROM ClubD
```

Selecting the Appropriate Columns

When combining data from two tables, you need to think about what it is you actually want. The examples with the clubs are rather contrived (as you have no doubt noticed). It is very unlikely that two clubs would have members with the same ID numbers and identical membership types. For example, a more likely scenario is that if Barbara Olson did belong to two clubs, she would have different data in each club table. In the ClubA table, she might be a "Senior" with ID 258. In the ClubB table, she might be an "Associate" member with an ID of 4573. If we do the union in Listing 7-2, where we select all the columns from each table, the two rows for Barbara will be different, and so both will appear in the result of the union, as in Figure 7-6.

ID	FamilyName	Name	Handicap	MemberType
235	Cooper	William	14	Senior
414	Gilmore	Jane	5	Junior
487	Kent	Susan		Social
118	McKenzie	Melissa	30	Junior
153	Nolan	Brenda	11	Senior
4573	Olson	Barbara		Associate
258	Olson	Barbara	16	Senior
286	Pollard	Robert	19	Junior

Figure 7-6. *Two records appear for Barbara Olson in the union because the rows are different.*

We need to consider what we really want from such a union. If we need a list of names for a joint Christmas party for the two clubs, then we don't want anyone listed twice. The way to avoid duplicates is to project just the names from each table. The algebra expression is shown in Listing 7-5 and the SQL in Listing 7-6.

Listing 7-5. *Relational Algebra to Project the Appropriate Columns Before the Union*

$\pi_{FamilyName,Name}(\text{ClubA}) \cup \pi_{LastName,FirstName}(\text{ClubB})$

Listing 7-6. *SQL to Project the Appropriate Columns Before the Union*

```
SELECT FamilyName, Name FROM ClubA
UNION
SELECT LastName, FirstName FROM ClubB
```

With the query in Listing 7-6, we will now get just one row for Barbara in the union. This will, of course, depend on her name being spelled the same in both clubs. And what if there are actually two different people named Barbara Olson? Sadly, real data is fraught with these sorts of problems, and there is little you can do other than be aware of them.

Uses for Union

The main use for union is combining data from two or more tables, as we have been doing in the previous sections. For example, if data for different months had been stored in separate tables (not necessarily a great design decision!), you could use several union operations to combine the data for the whole year.

It is also possible to combine two sets of rows from the one table. Say we wanted to find the IDs of all the people who have entered either tournament 24 or tournament 40 from the Entry table in Figure 7-7.

MemberID	TourID	Year
118	24	2005
228	24	2006
228	25	2006
228	36	2006
235	38	2004
235	38	2006
235	40	2005
235	40	2006
239	25	2006
239	40	2004

Figure 7-7. *Entry table*

We could get a list of all the IDs of members entering tournament 24 and a list of IDs of members entering tournament 40, and take the union. To get the list of IDs for tournament 24, we need to select the rows for that tournament (`TourID = 24`), and then project just the `MemberID` column. Similarly for tournament 40, we need to select the rows where the value of `TourID` is 40. The algebra and the SQL for the union are shown in Listings 7-7 and 7-8.

Listing 7-7. *Relational Algebra for Finding IDs of Members Who Have Entered Either Tournament 24 or 40*

$$\pi_{\text{MemberID}}(\sigma_{\text{TourID}=24}(\text{Entry})) \cup \pi_{\text{MemberID}}(\sigma_{\text{TourID}=40}(\text{Entry}))$$

Listing 7-8. *SQL for Finding IDs of Members Who Have Entered Either Tournament 24 or 40*

```
SELECT MemberID FROM Entry
WHERE TourID = 24

UNION

SELECT MemberID FROM Entry
WHERE TourID = 40
```

While Listing 7-8 will find the correct IDs, most people would use the more straightforward query in Listing 7-9 to achieve the same result.

Listing 7-9. *Finding IDs of Members Who Have Entered Either Tournament 24 or 40*

```
SELECT MemberID FROM Tournament
WHERE TourID = 24 OR TourID = 40
```

Another use for union is to perform the equivalent of a full outer join in products that don't support the FULL OUTER JOIN key phrase. Microsoft Access 2007 is one product that does not implement full outer joins explicitly. Let's recap the different types of outer joins that we discussed in Chapter 3. Figure 7-8 shows the different types of joins between the `Member` table (just a very little one!) and the `Type` table. All the joins are on `MemberType = Type`. The inner join would have just three rows. We would not get a row for William Cooper, as he does not have a value in `MemberType`, and we would not get a row for the "Associate" type, as no row in the `Member` has this value in the `MemberType` field. The left outer join ensures that we see all the rows from the left-hand table (`Member`); the right outer join gives us all rows from the right-hand table (`Type`); and the full outer join gives us all rows from both tables. Figure 7-8 illustrates these joins.

MemberID	LastName	FirstName	MemberType
118	McKenzie	Melissa	Junior
178	Beck	Sarah	Social
235	Cooper	William	
239	Spence	Thomas	Senior

Member

Type	Fee
Junior	150
Senior	300
Social	50
Associate	60

Type

MemberID	LastName	FirstName	MemberType	Type	Fee
118	McKenzie	Melissa	Junior	Junior	150
178	Beck	Sarah	Social	Social	50
239	Spence	Thomas	Senior	Senior	300

Member inner join Type

MemberID	LastName	FirstName	MemberType	Type	Fee
118	McKenzie	Melissa	Junior	Junior	150
178	Beck	Sarah	Social	Social	50
235	Cooper	William			
239	Spence	Thomas	Senior	Senior	300

Member left join Type

MemberID	LastName	FirstName	MemberType	Type	Fee
118	McKenzie	Melissa	Junior	Junior	150
239	Spence	Thomas	Senior	Senior	300
178	Beck	Sarah	Social	Social	50
				Associate	60

Member right join Type

MemberID	LastName	FirstName	MemberType	Type	Fee
				Associate	60
118	McKenzie	Melissa	Junior	Junior	150
178	Beck	Sarah	Social	Social	50
235	Cooper	William			
239	Spence	Thomas	Senior	Senior	300

Member full join Type

Figure 7-8. *The different joins between Member and Type (on MemberType = Type)*

Figure 7-8 shows that, in this case, the full outer join consists of the unique rows from each of the other two outer joins—that is, a union. So if your SQL implementation does not explicitly support a full outer join, you can always achieve the same result with the code in Listing 7-10.

Listing 7-10. *A Full Outer Join Expressed As the Union Between a Left and Right Outer Join*

```
SELECT * FROM Member LEFT JOIN Type ON MemberType = Type
UNION
SELECT * FROM Member RIGHT JOIN Type ON MemberType = Type
```

Intersection

If you take the intersection of two compatible tables, you will retrieve those rows that are found in both tables. The intersection of our two tables, ClubA and ClubB, is reproduced in Figure 7-9, and the algebra expression is in Listing 7-11.

Listing 7-11. *Algebra to Retrieve Names That Are in Both ClubA and ClubB*

$\pi_{FamilyName,Name}(ClubA) \cap \pi_{LastName,FirstName}(ClubB)$

Cooper	William
Gilmore	Jane
Kent	Susan
McKenzie	Melissa
Olso Olson	Barbara
Polla Pollard	Robert
Reed	Robert
Schmidt	Thomas
Sexton	Thomas

Figure 7-9. *Intersection of ClubA and ClubB returns rows common to both tables.*

The keyword for the intersection operator in SQL is INTERSECT. The expression to retrieve the two rows (for Barbara Olson and Robert Pollard) is shown in Listing 7-12.

Listing 7-12. *Finding the Names That Are in Both ClubA and ClubB*

```
SELECT FamilyName, Name FROM ClubA
INTERSECT
SELECT LastName, FirstName FROM ClubB
```

As with the union operator, the two sets of rows must be union compatible; that is, they must have the same number of columns, and the corresponding columns must have the same domains. This may mean projecting the appropriate columns from the base tables, in the same way as described in the "Selecting the Appropriate Columns" section earlier in this chapter. It makes no difference which of the tables we mention first in the query, as the intersection will be the same regardless of the order.

Uses of Intersection

A common use of the intersection operation is the one shown in Figure 7-9: finding common rows in two tables with similar information. Another very common use of intersection is answering questions that include the word "both." A typical example is "Which members have entered *both* tournaments 25 and 36?" The Entry table is reproduced in Figure 7-10.

MemberID	TourID	Year
118	24	2005
228	24	2006
228	25	2006
228	36	2006
235	38	2004
235	38	2006
235	40	2005
235	40	2006
239	25	2006
239	40	2004
258	24	2005
258	38	2005
286	24	2004
286	24	2005
286	24	2006
415	24	2006
415	25	2004
415	36	2005
415	36	2006
415	38	2004
415	38	2006
415	40	2004
415	40	2005
415	40	2006

Figure 7-10. *Entry table*

We can retrieve the member IDs for each tournament (by selecting the appropriate rows and retaining just the IDs), and then taking the intersection, as illustrated in Figure 7-11. As with a union, the result of the intersection operation just returns unique rows.

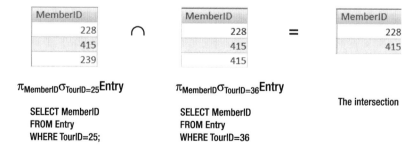

MemberID
228
415
239

$\cap$

MemberID
228
415
415

=

MemberID
228
415

$\pi_{MemberID}\sigma_{TourID=25}$Entry

SELECT MemberID
FROM Entry
WHERE TourID=25;

$\pi_{MemberID}\sigma_{TourID=36}$Entry

SELECT MemberID
FROM Entry
WHERE TourID=36

The intersection

Figure 7-11. *Using intersection to find members entered in both tournaments 25 and 36*

The complete algebra expression and the equivalent SQL are shown in Listings 7-13 and 7-14.

Listing 7-13. *Algebra to Retrieve IDs of Members Entered in Both Tournaments 25 and 36*

$$\pi_{\text{MemberID}}(\sigma_{\text{TourID}=25}(\text{Entry})) \cap \pi_{\text{MemberID}}(\sigma_{\text{TourID}=36}(\text{Entry}))$$

Listing 7-14. *SQL to Retrieve IDs of Members Entered in Both Tournaments 25 and 36*

```
SELECT MemberID FROM Entry WHERE TourID = 25
INTERSECT
SELECT MemberID FROM Entry WHERE TourID = 36
```

Suppose we now want to find the names of the members. From an algebra point of view, we could take the result of the intersection and join it with the `Member` table to get the names, as shown in Figure 7-12.

MemberID	LastName	FirstName
118	McKenzie	Melissa
138	Stone	Michael
153	Nolan	Brenda
176	Branch	Helen
178	Beck	Sarah
228	Burton	Sandra
235	Cooper	William
239	Spence	Thomas
258	Olson	Barbara
286	Pollard	Robert
290	Sexton	Thomas
323	Wilcox	Daniel
331	Schmidt	Thomas
332	Bridges	Deborah
339	Young	Betty
414	Gilmore	Jane
415	Taylor	William
461	Reed	Robert
469	Willis	Carolyn
487	Kent	Susan

Member Table (just some columns)

$\bowtie$

MemberID
228
415

Intersection

=

MemberID	LastName	FirstName
228	Burton	Sandra
415	Taylor	William

Member $\bowtie_{\text{MemberID=MemberID}}$ Intersection

Figure 7-12. *Joining the intersection with the Member table to find the names*

I always feel I should be able to just take the SQL in Listing 7-14 and join the result with the `Member` table, as shown in Listing 7-15. However, standard SQL doesn't like having a nested query as part of the join.

Listing 7-15. *SQL to Retrieve Names by Joining the Member Table to Intersection (Doesn't Work)*

```
SELECT LastName, FirstName
FROM Member m INNER JOIN
     (SELECT e1.MemberID FROM Entry e1 WHERE e1.TourID = 25
      INTERSECT
      SELECT e2.MemberID FROM Entry e2 WHERE e2.TourID = 36)
ON m.MemberID = e1.MemberID
```

However, a very tiny change makes this work. Most implementations of SQL have the idea of a *derived table*. This essentially takes the subquery and thinks of it as a new, virtual table. All we need to do is give it a name, or alias. The name is placed just after the closing parenthesis of the subquery. In Listing 7-16, I've given the virtual table produced by the subquery the alias NewTable. You need to use the alias in the join condition.

Listing 7-16. *Giving the Subquery an Alias, for a Derived Table (Does Work!)*

```
SELECT LastName, FirstName
FROM Member m INNER JOIN
     (SELECT e1.MemberID FROM Entry e1 WHERE e1.TourID = 25
      INTERSECT
      SELECT e2.MemberID FROM Entry e2 WHERE e2.TourID = 36)NewTable
ON m.MemberID = NewTable.MemberID
```

Another way to retrieve the names is to use a nested query, as in Listing 7-17. Here, the inner query retrieves the IDs that are in the intersection, and the outer query finds the corresponding names from the Member table.

Listing 7-17. *Using a Nested Query to Find Names Associated with the Intersection*

```
SELECT LastName, FirstName
FROM Member
WHERE MemberID IN
     (SELECT MemberID FROM Entry WHERE TourID = 25
      INTERSECT
      SELECT MemberID FROM Entry WHERE TourID = 36)
```

The Importance of Projecting Appropriate Columns

You must be very careful to think about which columns you include in the tables you are using in an intersect operation. Figure 7-13 shows what happens if we include all the columns as in Listing 7-18, instead of just projecting the MemberIDs.

Listing 7-18. *This Intersection Will Not Return Anything*

```
SELECT * FROM Entry WHERE TourID = 25
INTERSECT
SELECT * FROM Entry WHERE TourID = 36
```

MemberID	TourID	Year
228	25	2006
415	25	2004
239	25	2006

∩

MemberID	TourID	Year
228	36	2006
415	36	2005
415	36	2006

=

MemberID	TourID	Year

SELECT*
FROM Entry
WHERE TourID=25;

SELECT*
FROM Entry
WHERE TourID=36

The intersection is empty

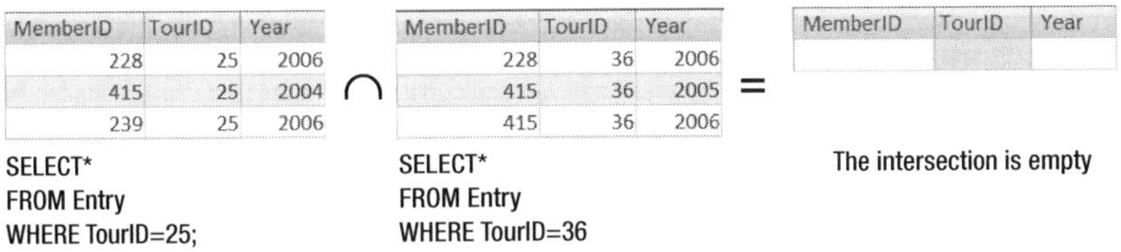

Figure 7-13. *With all the columns projected, no rows appear in both tables.*

With all the columns projected, we get an empty set as the result of the intersection. Because of the WHERE clause producing each of the tables, all the values for TourID are 25 in the first table, and all the values for TourID are 36 in the second table. There will never be any rows that are common to both tables. In the previous example, Listing 7-14 and Figure 7-11, the columns with the tournament ID and year had been removed before the intersection.

Projecting different columns can provide answers to different questions. Take a look at Listing 7-19 and Figure 7-14. What is the intersection finding in this case?

Listing 7-19. *What Will the Intersection Return with These Columns Projected?*

```
SELECT MemberID, Year FROM Entry WHERE TourID = 25
INTERSECT
SELECT MemberID, Year FROM Entry WHERE TourID = 36
```

MemberID	year
228	2006
415	2004
239	2006

∩

MemberID	Year
228	2006
415	2005
415	2006

=

MemberID	Year
228	2006

SELECT MemberID, Year
FROM Entry
WHERE TourID=25;

SELECT MemberID, Year
FROM Entry
WHERE TourID=36

What does the
intersection mean?

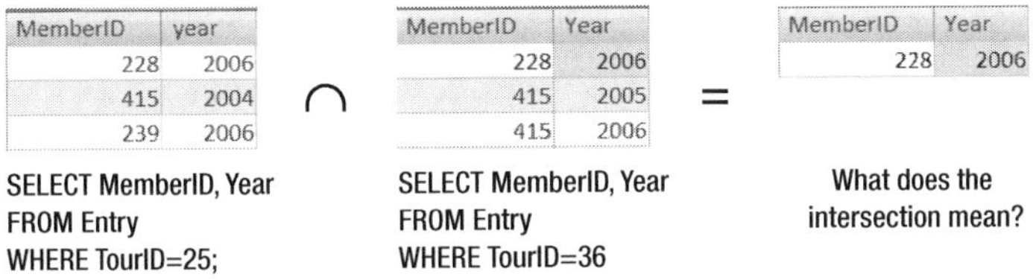

Figure 7-14. *What does the intersection mean?*

In Figure 7-14, we are finding all the members who entered tournaments 25 and 36 in the same year. This is why there is no entry for member 415 in the intersection: he entered tournament 25 in 2004, and tournament 36 in 2005 and 2006. Although his member ID appears in the two contributing tables, the corresponding rows are for different years. There is no row for member 415 that is the same in both tables.

As you can see, the choice of columns that are projected for the contributing tables is fundamental to what will appear in the intersection. It means there are many different questions that can be answered very elegantly, but it also means that you can easily get incorrect answers if you don't think the query through carefully.

Managing Without the INTERSECT Keyword

Not all implementations of SQL support intersection explicitly. However, we have other ways to perform the queries involving "both." In Chapter 5, you saw how to do these queries using relational calculus. To recap, we imagine we have two fingers traversing each row of the Entry table, as in Figure 7-15. To find members who have entered both tournaments 25 and 36, we need to find two rows with the same MemberID: one with TourID = 25 and one with TourID = 36.

MemberID	TourID	Year
118	24	2005
228	24	2006
228	25	2006
228	36	2006
235	38	2004
235	38	2006
235	40	2005
235	40	2006
239	25	2006
239	40	2004

Figure 7-15. *Picturing the relational calculus method of finding members who have entered both tournaments 25 and 36*

The SQL expression equivalent to Listing 7-14 is shown in Listing 7-20.

Listing 7-20. *Finding Members Who Have Entered Both Tournaments 25 and 36 Without the INTERSECT Keyword*

```
SELECT DISTINCT e1.MemberID
FROM Entry e1, Entry e2
WHERE e1.MemberID=e2.MemberID
AND e1.TourID=25 AND e2.TourID=36
```

Listing 7-21 shows the equivalent of Listing 7-12 to find the names of people who are members of both ClubA and ClubB. We need to explicitly compare each column that we want to be the same in the two contributing tables.

Listing 7-21. *Finding People in Both ClubA and ClubB Without the INTERSECT Keyword*

```
SELECT DISTINCT a.MemberID
FROM ClubA a, ClubB b
WHERE a.FamilyName=b.LastName
AND a.Name=b.FirstName
```

Difference

Taking the difference between two tables finds those rows that are in the first but not the second and vice versa. For our two tiny clubs, I have reproduced the results of the difference operator in Figure 7-16.

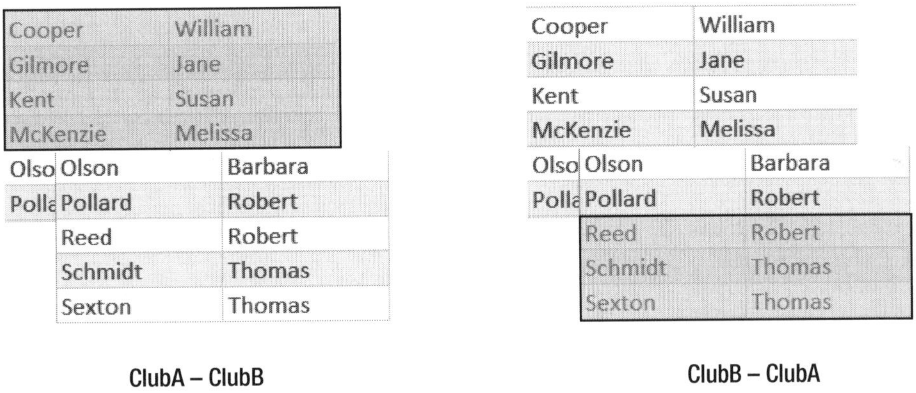

ClubA – ClubB   ClubB – ClubA

Figure 7-16. *The difference operator finds rows in one table but not the other.*

The keyword in standard SQL for the difference operator is EXCEPT. Oracle differs from the ISO SQL standard, and from most other database systems, in its use of the keyword MINUS, rather than EXCEPT.

Unlike with the union and intersection operators, the order of the tables is important for the difference operator; the results for ClubA-ClubB are different from those for ClubB-ClubA (as shown in Figure 7-16). Listing 7-22 shows the SQL for finding those people in the ClubA table but not in the ClubB table.

Listing 7-22. *Finding the Names That Are in ClubA But Not ClubB*

```
SELECT FamilyName, Name FROM ClubA
EXCEPT
SELECT LastName, FirstName FROM ClubB
```

Uses of Difference

Whenever you have a query that has the word "not," you should consider the possibility that the difference operator will be useful. For example, how do we find members who have not entered tournament 25? Recall from Chapter 5 why the query in Listing 7-23 does not give us the correct rows from the Entry table.

Listing 7-23. *Members Who Have Not Entered Tournament 25 (Incorrect)*

```
SELECT MemberID FROM Entry
WHERE TourID <> 25
```

Listing 7-23 selects all the rows in the Entry table that are not for tournament 25. Looking at Figure 7-15, we can see that the query would return the row marked e2 for member 228 entering tournament 36. However, in the row above, we see that member 228 has also entered tournament 25. This is not what we might naively have expected from Listing 7-23 (before reading Chapter 5, of course!). What we need is a list of all members, a list of all the members entering tournament 25, and then to take the difference between them, as in Figure 7-17.

The set of rows on the left in Figure 7-17—all member IDs—is retrieved by projecting the MemberID column from the Member table. The rows in the middle of Figure 7-17—IDs of all members entering tournament 25—are found by selecting the rows from the Entry table for tournament 25 and then projecting just the MemberID column. We then need the difference between these two sets of rows to find the IDs of members who have not entered tournament 25.

The complete algebra and SQL expressions to retrieve the IDs of members who have not entered tournament 25 are in Listings 7-24 and 7-25.

Listing 7-24. *Algebra to Retrieve IDs of Members Who Have Not Entered Tournament 25*

$$\pi_{MemberID}(Member) - \pi_{MemberID}\sigma_{TourID=25}(Entry)$$

Listing 7-25. *SQL to Retrieve IDs of Members Who Have Not Entered Tournament 25*

```
SELECT MemberID FROM Member
EXCEPT
SELECT MemberID FROM Entry WHERE TourID = 25
```

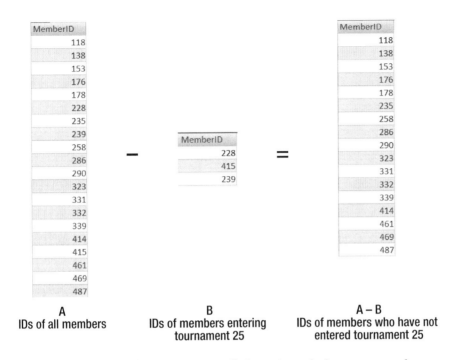

Figure 7-17. *Using the difference operator to find members who have not entered tournament 25*

As with intersection and union operations, it is important that we project the appropriate columns before we use the difference operator. In Figure 7-17, we have retrieved the IDs from the Member and Entry tables. If we want to include the names of the members, we can use one of the methods explained in the "Uses of Intersection" section earlier in this chapter. However, in this difference example, we already had the names of the members in the Member table before we removed them to get the set of rows on the left side of Figure 7-17. It seems a bit perverse to remove the names and then put them back later. What is important is that the two sets of rows involved in the difference are union compatible; that is, the corresponding columns must have the same domains. Either both sets have just IDs or both sets have IDs and names. In the operation on the left side of Figure 7-17, we took the first option and removed the names from Member. We could have left the names in the Member table and added the names to the rows in the middle of Figure 7-17 by joining the Entry and Member tables, as shown in Figure 7-18. We can then take the difference between these two sets of rows.

MemberID	LastName	FirstName
118	McKenzie	Melissa
138	Stone	Michael
153	Nolan	Brenda
176	Branch	Helen
178	Beck	Sarah
228	Burton	Sandra
235	Cooper	William
239	Spence	Thomas
258	Olson	Barbara
286	Pollard	Robert
290	Sexton	Thomas
323	Wilcox	Daniel
331	Schmidt	Thomas
332	Bridges	Deborah
339	Young	Betty
414	Gilmore	Jane
415	Taylor	William
461	Reed	Robert
469	Willis	Carolyn
487	Kent	Susan

MemberID	LastName	FirstName
228	Burton	Sandra
239	Spence	Thomas
415	Taylor	William

a) IDs and names from Member

$\pi_{\text{MemberID,LastName,FirstName}}$ Member

b) Entry table first joined with Member table to include names of members entering tournament 25

$\pi_{\text{MemberID,LastName,FirstName}}$ $\sigma_{\text{TourID=25}}$
(Member $\bowtie_{\text{MemberID=MemberID}}$ Entry)

Figure 7-18. *Including names of members in both sets of rows before taking the difference*

The SQL equivalent of the operations shown in Figure 7-18 is given in Listing 7-26.

Listing 7-26. *Including the Names Before Taking the Difference*

```
SELECT MemberID, LastName, FirstName FROM Member
EXCEPT
SELECT m.MemberID, m.LastName, m.FirstName
FROM Entry e inner join Member m on e.MemberID = m.MemberID
WHERE TourID = 25
```

Another use for the difference operation is in checking or validating data from different sources. By using the difference operation, and with appropriate projecting of columns, you can check if any instances have been added or deleted during translation.

Managing Without the EXCEPT Keyword

Not all versions of SQL support the EXCEPT (or MINUS) keyword. As always, there is usually another way to formulate a query. In Chapter 4, we looked at relational calculus ways to answer queries to do the equivalent of the difference operation. Listing 7-27 shows how we can use the NOT EXISTS keyword to find members who have not entered tournament 25. It essentially says this:

> *Write out the names of each member from the* Member *table where there does not exist a row in the* Entry *table for that member (i.e., with the same* MemberID*) for tournament 25.*

Listing 7-27. *SQL to Find Members Who Have Not Entered Tournament 25 (Without Using EXCEPT)*

```
SELECT m.LastName, m.FirstName
FROM Member m
WHERE NOT EXISTS
    (SELECT * FROM Entry e
     WHERE e.MemberID = m.MemberID
     AND e.TourID = 25)
```

Which type of query should you use: the ones based on algebra with the keyword EXCEPT or the ones based on calculus with the keywords NOT EXISTS or NOT IN? Usually, I say it doesn't really matter, as your database engine will probably be smart enough to recognize them as being the same. However, the version of SQL Server I am using at the moment (2005) performs the calculus-based queries that return the names (as in Listing 7-27) much more efficiently than corresponding algebra-based ones using EXCEPT (as in Listing 7-26). You have to ask yourself whether you care! Queries on small databases are usually so quick that it really doesn't matter if they run a bit slower. However, if you have a lot of data, then everything changes. The efficiency of queries can become extremely important, and in that case, you will need to also consider other aspects of your database design, such as indexes. I'll talk a little more about this in Chapter 9.

Division

The last set operator we will look at in this chapter is division. Division is useful for queries that involve the word "all" or "every." An example is "Which members have entered *every* tournament?" Standard SQL doesn't have a keyword for the divide operation, but you can construct alternative statements to carry out queries involving "all" or "every." Here, we will look at how the division operation is defined and how to use it to construct algebraic queries. In Chapter 8, we'll look at aggregates, and I'll show you what I think is the simplest way of writing an SQL equivalent of the division operator.

The easiest way to understand the division operation is with an example. If we want to know which members have entered every tournament, we need two bits of information. First, we need information about the members and the tournaments they have entered, which we can get from the Entry table. We also need a list of all the tournaments, which needs to come from the `Tournament` table, as not all tournaments may be represented in the `Entry` table.

In Figure 7-19, you can see how division works. I've projected just the `MemberID` and `TourID` columns from the `Entry` table, and the `TourID` column from the `Tournament` table. It is important which columns you project, and I'll come back to that in a moment.

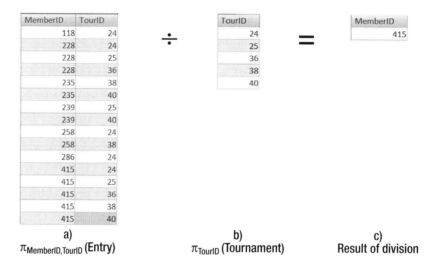

a)
$\pi_{MemberID,TourID}$ (Entry)

b)
π_{TourID} (Tournament)

c)
Result of division

Figure 7-19. *Using division to find members who have entered all tournaments*

The division has found those `MemberID` values in the table on the left-hand side of the operator (the far left in Figure 7-19) that has a row for each `TourID` in the table on the right-hand side of the operator (the middle of Figure 7-19). Member 415 can be found paired with each of the five tournaments in the `Entry` table, and so appears in the result of the division. Member 228 does not appear in the result because there are no rows in the `Entry` table with 228 paired with 38 or 40. The algebra expression is shown in Listing 7-28.

Listing 7-28. *Algebra for Finding Members Who Have Entered All Tournaments*

$$\pi_{MemberID,TourID}(Entry) \div \pi_{TourID}(Tournament)$$

As a small aside, many people wonder why this operation is called *division*, as it doesn't seem to relate particularly well to something like $4 \div 2$. Division is the inverse (or undoing) of multiplication in normal arithmetic. In relational algebra, division is like the inverse of the Cartesian product. If you think of taking the Cartesian product of the two tables in the middle and far right of Figure 7-19, you will get a table with the same columns (but not rows), as on the far left of Figure 7-19.

I like to think of setting up the division operation like this:

- Decide which attribute I want to find out about. Let's call this "Answer." In this case, I want to find MemberIDs, so our "Answer" attribute is MemberID.

- On the right-hand side of the division operator, the attribute(s) in the table should be the thing I want to check against, Let's call this attribute "Check." In this case, the "Check" attribute is TourID. We can get all the values for TourID from the Tournament table.

- On the left-hand side of the division, I want a table containing those two sets of attributes "Answer" and "Check"; that is, the MemberID and the TourID (in this case, which members have entered which tournament from the Entry table).

We can answer a number of questions by changing what is on the right-hand side of the division operator. For example, if we wanted to know who had entered all the Open tournaments, we would replace the table in the middle of Figure 7-19 with a list that selected just the rows for Open tournaments before projecting the tournament IDs. The algebra is shown in Listing 7-29.

Listing 7-29. *Algebra for Finding Members Who Have Entered All Open Tournaments*

$$\pi_{\text{MemberID,TourID}}(\text{Entry}) \div \pi_{\text{TourID}}\sigma_{\text{TourType='Open'}}(\text{Tournament})$$

Projecting Appropriate Columns

As with intersection and difference operations, projecting different columns in division operations will give you answers to different questions. Once again, an example is the easiest way to understand this. In Figure 7-20, I have included an extra column from the Entry table. Can you understand what this query is finding?

The division is looking for a set of "Answer" attributes in the left-hand table that are paired with every attribute from the "Check" table. In this case, the operation looks for a pair MemberID and Year in the left-hand table that appears with each of the tournaments. There is no such pair. The pair 415, 2006 nearly makes it into the answer, but we are missing a row where it is associated with tournament 25. This division example is finding those members who have entered all tournaments in the same year.

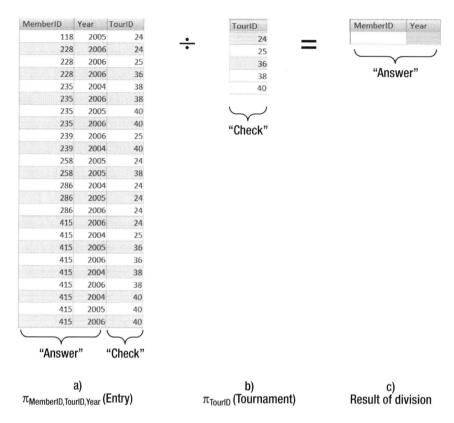

a)

$\pi_{MemberID,TourID,Year}$ (Entry)

b)

π_{TourID} (Tournament)

c)

Result of division

Figure 7-20. *What is the division operation finding?*

SQL for Division

There is no algebra operator for division in standard SQL. In Chapter 8, I'll describe a reasonably straightforward way to do the equivalent. In the meantime, we'll look at a calculus expression. This can be a bit hard to follow, so you may want to skip this section and wait for the next chapter. For the brave, if we want to find the names of members who have entered every tournament, we are saying something like this (take your time):

> *Write out the value of* m.LastName, m.FirstName *from rows (m) in the* Member *table where for every row (t) in the* Tournament *table there exists a row (e) in the* Entry *table with* e.MemberID = m.MemberID *and* e.TourID = t.TourID*.*

The equivalent expression in calculus notation is shown in Listing 7-30. The symbol ∃ stands for "there exists" (as in Chapter 4), and the new symbol ∀ means "for every."

Listing 7-30. *Calculus Expression to Find Members Who Have Entered Every Tournament*

```
{ m.LastName, m.FirstName | Member (m) AND
∀(t) Tournament(t)
(∃(e) Entry(e) AND e.MemberID = m.MemberID AND e.TourID = t.TourID) }
```

Chapter 4 showed that SQL has an EXISTS keyword that corresponds to ∃. There is no similar word in SQL to represent the ∀ in Listing 7-30. However, it is possible to rephrase statements containing "every." The phrase "every tournament has a corresponding row in the Entry table" is the same as "there is no tournament without a corresponding row in the Entry table." (I did say this could be a bit hard on the brain.) We can use this to rephrase our description of the values we want to retrieve:

> Write out the value of m.LastName, m.FirstName from rows (m) in the Member table where ~~for every row~~ **there does not exist** a row (t) in the Tournament table ~~there exists~~ **for which there does not exist** a row (e) in the Entry table with e.MemberID = m.MemberID and e.TourID = t.TourID.

The equivalent expression in calculus notation for this alternative is shown in Listing 7-31.

Listing 7-31. *Alternative Calculus Expression to Find Members Who Have Entered Every Tournament*

```
{m.LastName, m.FirstName | Member (m) AND
NOT ∃(t) Tournament(t)
(NOT ∃(e) Entry(e) AND e.MemberID = m.MemberID AND e.TourID = t.TourID) }
```

Now that we have removed the ∀, we can transcribe this into SQL, as in Listing 7-32. I've indented the different bits to make it easier to read. The essential structure of the query is "return all the members where there is no tournament for which there is not a corresponding entry."

Listing 7-32. *SQL to Find the Names of Members Who Have Entered Every Tournament*

```sql
SELECT m.LastName, m.FirstName FROM Member m
WHERE NOT EXISTS
    (
     SELECT * FROM Tournament t
     WHERE NOT EXISTS
         (
          SELECT * FROM Entry e
          WHERE e.MemberID = m.MemberID AND e.TourID = t.TourID
         )
    )
```

The double negatives can be a bit daunting, but as I've said, I promise a conceptually easier method in the next chapter.

Summary

Because tables in a relational database have unique rows (if they are properly keyed!), they can be treated like mathematical sets. This allows us to use the set operations union, intersection, difference, and division.

Union, intersection, and difference are operations that act between union-compatible tables. This means the table on each side of the operator must have the same number of columns, and the columns must have the same domains (commonly interpreted as the same types). You can get union-compatible tables by sensibly projecting columns.

SQL has keywords to represent union, intersection, and difference, although not every implementation supports the keywords for all of these operations. If your SQL product does not support keywords for intersection or difference, you can find other ways to express the query. You should formulate your queries in the way you find most natural. Where you have very large amounts of data and speed is important, you may need to investigate the efficiencies of the different ways of formulating some queries.

Table 7-1 summarizes union, intersection, and difference. A and B are two union-compatible tables with (for simplicity) just one column called attribute.

Table 7-1. *Basic Set Operations and Their SQL Representation*

Operator	Description	SQL	Alternative

Union	A ∪ B finds all the rows that are in either table A or table B	`SELECT attribute FROM A`
		`UNION`
		`SELECT attribute FROM B`	

Intersection	A ∩ B finds all rows that are in both table A and table B	`SELECT attribute FROM A`
		`INTERSECT`
		`SELECT attribute FROM B`
			`SELECT A.attribute`
			`FROM A`
			`WHERE EXISTS`
			`(SELECT B.attribute`
			`FROM B`
			`WHERE A.attribute =`
			`B.attribute)`

Difference	A - B finds all rows that are in table A and not in table B	`SELECT attribute FROM A`
		`EXCEPT`
		`SELECT attribute FROM B`
			`SELECT A.attribute`
			`FROM A`
			`WHERE NOT EXISTS`
			`(SELECT B.attribute`
			`FROM B`
			`WHERE A.attribute =`
			`B.attribute)`

The division operation helps with queries with the word "every" or "all." Current versions of SQL do not support division directly, but there are ways to formulate the queries.

CHAPTER 8

■ ■ ■

Aggregate Operations

SQL has many functions for manipulating numbers and text. In this chapter, we will look at some of the functions for summarizing data—for example, to count all the senior members in the club—and how to make the best use of them. We will also explore how to group data before doing your aggregates or summaries.

Simple Aggregates

Simple aggregates include averages, totals, and counts. These are straightforward ideas, but as always, you need to be sure you understand how they work when things like Nulls and duplicates are involved.

The COUNT Function

In its simplest manifestation, the COUNT function calculates the number of rows being returned from a query. To do this, use the expression `SELECT COUNT(*)`. Listings 8-1, 8-2, and 8-3 show some examples. The AS phrase—AS NumMembers and AS NumWomen in Listings 8-1 and 8-2, for example—formats the output to include that name as the column header. This phrase can be omitted, as in Listing 8-3.

Listing 8-1. *Return the Number of Members in the Club*

```
SELECT COUNT(*) AS NumMembers
FROM Member
```

Listing 8-2. *Return the Number of Women in the Club*

```
SELECT COUNT(*) AS NumWomen
FROM Member
WHERE Gender = 'F'
```

Listing 8-3. *Return the Number of Members Who Are Not Women*

```
SELECT COUNT(*)
FROM Member
WHERE Gender <> 'F'
```

All is well and good. But we need to be careful. In Chapter 2, we looked at how WHERE conditions operate when we make comparisons with a Null (or empty) value. In a WHERE clause, if the value we are comparing is a Null, then the answer will always be false. Therefore, if there is a row in our table with a Null value in the Gender column, it won't be included in either of the queries in Listings 8-2 and 8-3. That means that our counts of members who have Gender = 'F' plus the count of members who have Gender <> 'F' will not add up to the count of all members.

We can explicitly find how many of the rows do not have a value for Gender with the query in Listing 8-4. Queries like the one in Listing 8-4 can be very useful for checking the validity of your data before doing any queries involving counts or other statistics.

Listing 8-4. *Return the Number of Members with No Value for Gender*

```
SELECT COUNT(*)
FROM Member
WHERE Gender IS NULL
```

The COUNT function can also return the number of values in a particular column of a table or query. Let's look at a few of the columns in the Member table, as shown in Figure 8-1.

Say we want to find the number of members who have a coach. We have two options. One way is to formulate a query to return just those members who do not have a Null value for Coach and count those, as in Listing 8-5.

Listing 8-5. *Return the Number of Members Who Have a Coach (One Method)*

```
SELECT COUNT(*)
FROM Member
WHERE Coach IS NOT NULL
```

The other option is to ask the COUNT function to specifically count the number of values in the Coach column, using COUNT(Coach). Listing 8-6 will return the same result as Listing 8-5.

Listing 8-6. *Return the Number of Members Who Have a Coach (Another Method)*

```
SELECT COUNT(Coach)
    FROM Member
```

MemberID	LastName	FirstName	Gender	Handicap	Coach
118	McKenzie	Melissa	F	30	153
138	Stone	Michael	M	30	
153	Nolan	Brenda	F	11	
176	Branch	Helen	F		
178	Beck	Sarah	F		
228	Burton	Sandra	F	26	153
235	Cooper	William	M	14	153
239	Spence	Thomas	M	10	
258	Olson	Barbara	F	16	
286	Pollard	Robert	M	19	235
290	Sexton	Thomas	M	26	235
323	Wilcox	Daniel	M	3	
331	Schmidt	Thomas	M	25	153
332	Bridges	Deborah	F	12	235
339	Young	Betty	F	21	
414	Gilmore	Jane	F	5	153
415	Taylor	William	M	7	235
461	Reed	Robert	M	3	235
469	Willis	Carolyn	F	29	
487	Kent	Susan	F		

Figure 8-1. *Some columns of the Member table*

So if we just want to find the number of rows returned from a query (or a whole table), we use SELECT COUNT(*). If we want to find the number of rows that have a value in a particular column, we use SELECT COUNT(<*Column_Name*>). The COUNT(*) and COUNT(<*Column_Name*>) options allow us to be specific about how we want Null values to be treated. But what about duplicate values?

The values in the Coach column of the Member table (Figure 8-1) are duplicated. There are only two distinct values (153 and 235). We therefore have two quite different questions that can be answered by counting: "How many people have coaches?" and "How many coaches are there?" The answer to the first question requires us to include all the values, as in Listing 8-6. The answer to the second question requires us to count just the distinct values. This can be done by including the DISTINCT keyword, as in Listing 8-7.

Listing 8-7. *Return the Number of Different Coaches*

```
SELECT COUNT(DISTINCT Coach)
FROM Member
```

While I am trying not to be product-specific in this book, I feel obliged (given how many copies of Access are out in the world) to point out that Access does not currently support COUNT(DISTINCT). However, you can get the equivalent result with a nested query, as in Listing 8-8.

Listing 8-8. *Alternative SQL for Access Where COUNT(DISTINCT) Is Not Supported*

```
SELECT COUNT(*)
FROM (SELECT DISTINCT Coach FROM Member WHERE Coach IS NOT NULL)
```

You can also use the keyword ALL. This just reinforces that you want to count all values, rather than just distinct values. If you do not include either DISTINCT or ALL (as in Listing 8-6), all values are included by default. Similar sorts of queries can be applied to other columns. For example, we might want to know how many people have handicaps (COUNT (Handicap)), or we might want to know how many different handicaps are represented by our club members (COUNT (DISTINCT Handicap)).

With all these examples, we can include a WHERE clause as well, so we can find out how many women have coaches, how many junior members have handicaps, and so on. If no rows are returned by the query, the count will be 0.

The AVG Function

To find averages, we use the AVG function. The parameter for the function—that is, what goes in the parentheses (. . .)—is the expression you want to average. The expression must have a numeric value. The expression could be just the name of one of the numeric-valued columns or some function of a value, such as the length of a piece of text or the number of days between two dates. For example, we can find the average handicap for members of our club by averaging the values in the Handicap column, as in Listing 8-9.

Listing 8-9. *Return the Average Handicap*

```
SELECT AVG(Handicap)
FROM Member
```

As with the COUNT function, the AVG function includes only non-Null values for the handicap. We have 20 members in total, and 17 members with handicaps. If we sum all the handicaps, we get 287. The AVG function will take the total of the handicaps (287) and divide by the number of rows that have a value in the Handicap column (17). This is what we want. If we included the members without handicaps (by dividing by the total number of rows, 20), we would essentially be saying that these members have a handicap of 0 by default, which is not at all what we want in this case.

It is not always so obvious whether you want the Null values considered. For example, say we have another database with a table called Student and a column called TestScore. If we enter test scores for students, and some of the students do not take the test, then we will have a Null in the TestScore column for that student. What do we mean by the average score? We could take the average over all the students (divide the total score by the count of all students), which means the students who missed the test are effectively being counted as having scored 0. On the other hand, we might take the average of just those who participated in the test (divide by the number who took the test). People (especially academics!) will argue about such things. AVG(TestScore) will always give us just the average for those who took the test (which is what I personally think we want). If we want the average over all the students, including those with a Null mark (counted as 0), we can calculate the average by hand— totaling the marks (using the SUM function) and dividing by the full count. This computed average is shown in Listing 8-10.

Listing 8-10. *Calculate an Average Where Null Values Are Counted As Zero*

```
SELECT SUM(TestMark)/COUNT(*)
FROM Student
```

The query in Listing 8-10 is preferable to entering a mark of 0 for students who missed the test. If we do that, then we can no longer distinguish students who took the test and got 0 from students who missed the test (and even academics will agree this distinction is useful).

As with the COUNT function, the AVG function can also incorporate the keywords ALL and DISTINCT. Just be aware that ALL means all the non-Null values, as opposed to distinct non-Null values. It doesn't mean take an average over all the rows (including those with Nulls), as in our discussion about test scores. I find it quite hard to come up with examples of when you would want to just average over distinct values—certainly none that apply to our club database.

How do the different types of the fields used as a parameter to the AVG function affect the result? The AVG function will accept only numeric types. We can't attempt to average FirstName or JoinDate (although we could use functions to average the length of members' first names or the number of days since their join date). What result do we expect to get when we average the handicaps of our members? The total of the handicaps is 287, and the number of people with handicaps is 17. If you divide these two numbers with a calculator, you get something like 16.88235. What will SQL give us? That depends. When I try this in Access 2007, I get 16.88235. In SQL Server 2005, I get 16. In SQL Server (and some other implementations of SQL), the average function returns the same type as the numbers being averaged. In this case, the Handicap column is an INT type, and so AVG(Handicap) in SQL Server returns an integer. It also does an integer division (which means the result is truncated to 16 rather than rounded to 17).

We do have control over how the result is calculated. If we want to get a noninteger result for our average, we can convert the Handicap value to a floating-point number before we do the average. To do this we can use the CONVERT function, described in Chapter 7.[1] Another way to do this is just to multiply the handicap by 1.0: AVG(Handicap * 1.0). The SQL Server syntax using the CONVERT function is shown in Listing 8-11.

---

1. Different versions of SQL will have different functions to do this. In Oracle, you might consider using the CAST function.

Listing 8-11. *Convert Integers to Floating-Point Numbers to Get a Floating-Point Average*

```
SELECT AVG(CONVERT(FLOAT,Handicap))
FROM Member
```

Listing 8-11 will give us a result with a lot of decimal places. We can also use a rounding function to specify the number of decimal places we would like included in the output. To round the result to two decimal places, as in 16.88, we would use the statement in Listing 8-12.

Listing 8-12. *Round the Result to Two Decimal Places*

```
SELECT ROUND ( AVG (CONVERT (FLOAT,Handicap) ), 2 )
FROM Member
```

In both Listings 8-11 and 8-12, we are averaging an expression, rather than just the values directly from the column of our table. We might want to do this for many reasons. Say in another database we have an Order table, which includes the columns Price and Quantity. The net value of each order can be found by multiplying the Price and Quantity. If we want to find the average value for all our orders, we can put the expression Price * Quantity in the parentheses, as in Listing 8-13.

Listing 8-13. *Find the Average Cost*

```
SELECT AVG (Price * Quantity)
FROM Order
```

The examples so far have shown the aggregate functions applied to a whole table, but they can also be applied to the result of a query. For example, we could find the average handicap of women or of junior members by adding an appropriate WHERE clause, as in Listing 8-14.

Listing 8-14. *Return the Average Handicap of Junior Members*

```
SELECT AVG(Handicap)
FROM Member
WHERE MemberType = 'Junior'
```

If the WHERE clause returns no rows, or no rows with a value in Handicap, then the value returned by the average function is Null.

Other Aggregate Functions

Depending on your version of SQL, you might have dozens of other aggregate functions to explore. All versions will provide the common SQL aggregate functions SUM, MAX, and MIN, which are very straightforward to use. The arguments to the SUM function must be a numeric expression (either a number column or some expression with a numeric result, such as `Price * Quantity`). The arguments to MAX and MIN can be numeric, text, or date types. For text types, the order is alphabetical. For dates, the order is chronological. For example, `MIN(LastName)` would return the first value of `LastName` alphabetically.

It is possible to combine several aggregate functions in one query. For example, Listing 8-15 shows how to find the maximum, minimum, and average values for `Handicap`. The AS clause after each function is just saying, "Call the resulting column by this name." Without such a label, it can be quite hard to remember which order you are expecting the numbers. Figure 8-2 shows some typical output.

Listing 8-15. *Return the Maximum, Minimum, and Average Handicaps of Members*

```
SELECT MAX(Handicap) AS maximum, MIN(Handicap) AS minimum, AVG(Handicap) AS average
FROM Member
```

	maximum	minimum	average
1	30	3	16

Figure 8-2. *Typical output from a query with several aggregate functions*

Grouping

Say we want to know how many times a particular member has entered tournaments. We would need to look at the `Entry` table. For example, if we wanted to find how many times member 235 had entered tournaments, we could select all the rows in the `Entry` table for that member and count them. Listing 8-16 shows the SQL for doing this.

Listing 8-16. *Find How Many Tournaments Member 235 Has Entered*

```
SELECT COUNT(*) AS NumEntries
FROM Entry
WHERE MemberID = 235
```

If we wanted to find the number of entries for a different member, we would need to rewrite the statement in Listing 8-16 with a different WHERE clause. If we wanted to find the counts for all members, that would get very tedious.

Grouping allows us to find the counts for all members using one SQL statement. The key phrase GROUP BY is used to do this. Look at the SQL in Listing 8-17.

Listing 8-17. *Find How Many Tournaments Each Member Has Entered*

```
SELECT COUNT(*) AS NumEntries
FROM Entry
GROUP BY MemberID
```

The extra GROUP BY clause says, "Rather than just count all the rows in the Entry table, count all the subsets with the same MemberID." Figure 8-3 depicts this. In Figure 8-3, the rows in the Entry table have been ordered by MemberID to make it clear what is happening.

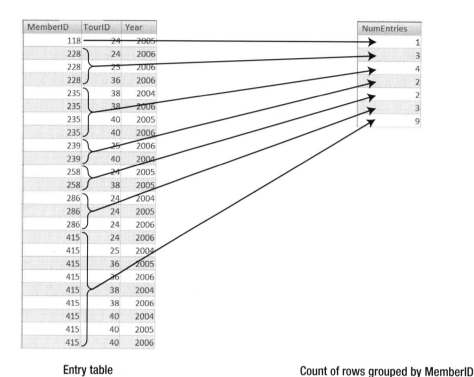

Entry table   Count of rows grouped by MemberID

Figure 8-3. *Counting the rows in the Entry table grouped by MemberID*

We can include the fields we are grouping by in the SELECT clause so we can see which counts belong to which entries. This is shown in Listing 8-18, and the output is shown in Figure 8-4.

Listing 8-18. *Include the MemberID (the Grouping Field) in the Output*

```
SELECT MemberID, COUNT(*) AS NumEntries
FROM Entry
GROUP BY MemberID
```

MemberID	NumEntries
118	1
228	3
235	4
239	2
258	2
286	3
415	9

Figure 8-4. *Including the MemberID in the output*

We might prefer to see the names of the members in the output of Listing 8-18 and Figure 8-4. In this case, we need to join the Entry table with the Member table first, and then group and count. Listing 8-19 shows the SQL, and Figure 8-5 shows the output. In Listing 8-19, you might wonder if you can group just by MemberID as we did in Listing 8-17. That would indeed give us the same counts. However, when you are using GROUP BY, you can include in the SELECT clause only the fields you are grouping by or the aggregates. If we want to see the names in the output, we need to include them in the fields we are grouping by.

Listing 8-19. *Join Entry and Member Tables First to Show the Names of Members*

```
SELECT m.MemberID, m.LastName, m.FirstName, COUNT(*) AS NumEntries
FROM Entry e INNER JOIN Member m on m.MemberID = e.MemberID
GROUP BY m.MemberID, m.LastName, m.FirstName
```

MemberID	LastName	FirstName	NumEntries
118	McKenzie	Melissa	1
228	Burton	Sandra	3
235	Cooper	William	4
239	Spence	Thomas	2
258	Olson	Barbara	2
286	Pollard	Robert	3
415	Taylor	William	9

Figure 8-5. *Joining the Entry and Member tables and grouping by the IDs and names*

We can get a wealth of information from our tables using GROUP BY. Just considering the Entry table, we can find the number of entries for each member, as in the preceding examples, or we can find the number of entries for each tournament. If we would like to find the number of entries for each tournament, we want to imagine grouping all the rows with the same TourID together and then counting the rows in each set. Listing 8-20 and Figure 8-6 show how to find the number of entries in each tournament.

Listing 8-20. *Find the Number of Entries in Each Tournament*

```
SELECT TourID, COUNT(*) AS NumEntries
FROM Entry
GROUP BY TourID
```

TourID	NumEntries
24	7
25	3
36	3
38	5
40	6

Figure 8-6. *Counting the number of entries in each tournament*

We do not need to count all the rows in the table. We might like to select a subset of the rows first. For example, we might just want to gather our statistics for the year 2006. Listing 8-21 shows the SQL to do this. Notice that the WHERE clause (which finds the subset of the rows we want to consider) must come before the GROUP BY clause.

Listing 8-21. *Find the Number of Entries in Each Tournament for the Year 2006*

```
SELECT TourID, COUNT(*) AS NumEntries
FROM Entry
WHERE Year = 2006
GROUP BY TourID
```

By adding more fields in the GROUP BY clause, we can get more detailed information. If we wanted to find the equivalent of Listing 8-21 for each year, we could remove the WHERE clause and group by both year and tournament ID. Listing 8-22 shows the SQL, and Figure 8-7 shows how the grouping on both fields works. In Figure 8-7, I've ordered the rows in the Entry table by TourID and Year so that it is easier to see the grouping.

Listing 8-22. *Find the Number of Entries in Each Tournament for Each Year*

```
SELECT TourID, Year, COUNT(*) AS NumEntries
FROM Entry
GROUP BY TourID, Year
```

We can use grouping with the other aggregate functions. For example, if we wanted to see the average handicap for women and men, we could use a query like the one in Listing 8-23.

Listing 8-23. *Find the Average Handicaps of Members Grouped by Gender*

```
SELECT Gender, AVG(Handicap) AS AverageHandicap
FROM Member
GROUP BY Gender
```

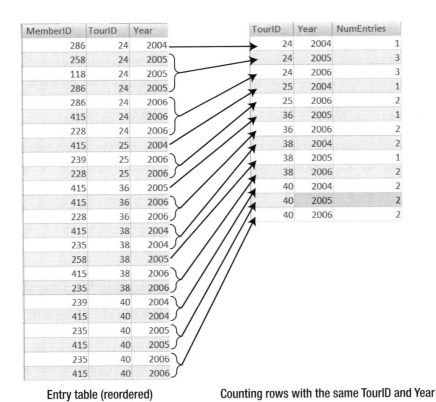

Entry table (reordered)   Counting rows with the same TourID and Year

Figure 8-7. *Grouping by TourID and Year*

Filtering the Result of an Aggregate Query

Once we have calculated some aggregates for groups of rows, we may want to ask some
questions about the results. For example, in Figure 8-7, we have found the number of
entries in each tournament in each year. A likely question is "Which tournaments had
three or more entries?" Looking at the result table in Figure 8-7, we want to select just
those rows with the count greater or equal to 3. We can do this with the HAVING keyword.
Take a look at Listing 8-24.

Listing 8-24. *Find Tournaments with Three or More Entries*

```
SELECT TourID, Year, COUNT(*) AS NumEntries
FROM Entry
GROUP BY TourID, Year
HAVING COUNT(*) >= 3
```

The HAVING clause always comes after a GROUP BY clause. It selects rows matching some condition (in this case, COUNT(*) >= 3) from the result of the grouping. It is like having a WHERE clause that acts on the aggregated numbers. As a little aside, we must use COUNT(*) in the HAVING clause; we can't use the alias NumEntries from the first line of the statement. This alias is just used at the end of the query to label the output column.

Let's look at another example. Say we want to find those members who have entered four or more tournaments. First, construct a set of rows with the members and the counts of the tournaments they have entered, as in the first three lines of Listing 8-25. Then use the HAVING clause to select just those rows from the result with COUNT(*) >= 4.

Listing 8-25. *Find Members Who Have Entered More Than Four Tournaments*

```
SELECT MemberID, COUNT(*) AS NumEntries
FROM Entry
GROUP BY MemberID
HAVING COUNT(*) >= 4
```

We have two opportunities to select a subset of rows in queries involving aggregates. If we take the subset *before* we do the aggregation, we use a WHERE clause. When we want to select just some rows *after* the aggregation, we use a HAVING clause. For example, let's change the query in Listing 8-25 to find out which members have entered more than four Open tournaments. We need to do the following:

- Join the Entry table with the Tournament table.

- Take just the subset of entries for Open tournaments (with a WHERE clause).

- Group the entries for each member and count them.

- Take the resulting aggregate table and retrieve just those rows with a count greater than 4 (with a HAVING clause).

The process is depicted in Figure 8-8, and the complete SQL is in Listing 8-26.

Listing 8-26. *Find Members Who Have Entered More Than Four Open Tournaments*

```
SELECT MemberID, COUNT(*) AS NumEntries
FROM Entry e INNER JOIN Tournament t ON e.TourID = t.TourID
WHERE t.TourType = 'Open'
GROUP BY MemberID
HAVING COUNT(*) > 4
```

We can also sort the output by the aggregate. If we wanted to see results in descending order of the number of tournaments entered, we could add an `ORDER BY COUNT(*) DESC` clause at the end of Listing 8-26.

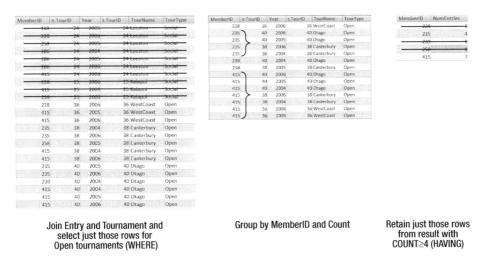

| | | Join Entry and Tournament and select just those rows for Open tournaments (WHERE) | | Group by MemberID and Count | | Retain just those rows from result with COUNT≥4 (HAVING) |

Figure 8-8. *Finding members who have entered more than four Open tournaments*

Using Aggregates to Perform Division Operations

In Chapter 7, we looked at the algebra operation division. To recap, division allows us to answer many questions containing the words "all" or "every." For example, say we want to find those members who have entered *every* tournament. Figure 8-9 show how we can use division to do this. On the right side of the division operator, we have the set of things we are checking against (in this case, a list of all the `TourID` values projected from the `Tournament` table). On the left side of the division operator is a table that connects members with the tournaments they have entered (in this case, we project the columns `MemberID` and `TourID` from the `Entry` table). The results of the division are the `MemberID` values that appear with every tournament (in this case, just the one member with ID 415).

Currently, standard implementations of SQL do not have a keyword for the division operation, so we need to find other ways to express a query like that depicted in Figure 8-9. We looked at one way in Chapter 7. Here, we will look at another way that uses aggregates.

The `Tournament` table lists five different tournaments. If we can find a member who has entered five different tournaments, then he must have entered all of them. We now have the ability to use aggregates and grouping to construct the equivalent of a division operation.

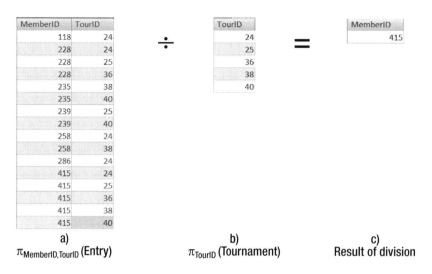

a)
$\pi_{\text{MemberID,TourID}}$ (Entry)

b)
π_{TourID} (Tournament)

c)
Result of division

Figure 8-9. *Using division to find the members who have entered every tournament*

We have already counted how many tournaments each member has entered (Listing 8-18). However, we want to count only the *different* tournaments entered by each member. We want to count the distinct TourIDs in the Entry table for each member. Listing 8-27 shows how to do that, and the result is in Figure 8-10.

Listing 8-27. *Count the Distinct Tournaments Entered by Each Member*

```
SELECT MemberID, COUNT(DISTINCT TourID) AS NumTours
FROM Entry e
GROUP BY MemberID
```

MemberID	NumTours
118	1
228	3
235	2
239	2
258	2
286	1
415	5

Figure 8-10. *Finding the number of distinct tournaments entered by each member*

From the resulting table in Figure 8-10, we now want just those rows where the count (NumTours) is equal to the number of distinct tournaments, which is 5 in this case. Listing 8-28 shows how the HAVING clause can be used to find those members who have entered five different tournaments, and Listing 8-29 shows the more general statement that replaces 5 with an expression to find the number of distinct tournaments directly.

Listing 8-28. *Find Members Who Have Entered Five Different Tournaments*

```
SELECT MemberID
FROM Entry e
GROUP BY MemberID
HAVING COUNT(DISTINCT TourID) = 5
```

Listing 8-29. *Find Members Who Have Entered All the Different Tournaments in the Tournament Table*

```
SELECT MemberID
FROM Entry e
GROUP BY MemberID
HAVING COUNT(DISTINCT TourID) =
     (SELECT COUNT(DISTINCT TourID) FROM Tournament)
```

Listing 8-29 is equivalent to the algebra division operation as depicted in Figure 8-9. It returns the IDs of members who have entered every tournament. To summarize, we count the number of distinct tournaments each member has entered, and then using the HAVING clause, retain just those whose count equals the number of possible tournaments (a distinct count from the Tournament table). I find this method of doing a division conceptually more straightforward than the one I suggested in Chapter 7. However, both methods accomplish the same goal.

Nested Queries and Aggregates

We have already covered a little about nested queries and aggregates in Chapter 4. It is useful to revisit this idea here. In this chapter, we've looked at how to find averages, totals, counts, and so on. Now we can use these aggregate results in other queries. For example, we might want to find everyone with a handicap greater than the average handicap. We can do this as shown in Listing 8-30. The inner part of the query returns the average, and the outer part of the query compares the handicap of each member with that average.

Listing 8-30. *Return Members with a Handicap Greater Than Average*

```
SELECT * FROM Member
WHERE Handicap >
     (SELECT AVG (Handicap)
      FROM Member)
```

Let's try something else. What about finding members who have entered more than three tournaments? If your mind goes blank, you can revert to the calculus approach of picturing the tables and figuring out what the rows you want returned will look like. Figure 8-11 shows how I think of this query.

MemberID	LastName	FirstName	Gender
118	McKenzie	Melissa	F
138	Stone	Michael	M
153	Nolan	Brenda	F
176	Branch	Helen	F
178	Beck	Sarah	F
228	Burton	Sandra	F
235	Cooper	William	M
239	Spence	Thomas	M
258	Olson	Barbara	F
286	Pollard		

MemberID	TourID	Year
118	24	2005
228	24	2006
228	25	2006
228	36	2006
235	38	2004
235	38	2006
235	40	2005
235	40	2006
239	25	2006
239	40	2004
258	24	2005
258	38	2005
286	24	2004
286	24	2005
286	24	2006
415	24	2006

Figure 8-11. *Which members have more than three entries in tournaments?*

We can describe the members we want returned like this:

Find all the rows (m) from the Member table where if we count the number of rows (e) from the Entry table for that member (m.MemberID = e.MemberID) the count is > 3.

This turns into SQL in a straightforward way, as shown in Listing 8-31.

Listing 8-31. *Find Members Who Have Entered More Than Three Tournaments*

```
SELECT * FROM Member m
WHERE
        (SELECT COUNT (*)
        FROM Entry e
        WHERE e.MemberID = m.MemberID) > 3
```

What about something a bit more complex? How do we find the average number of tournaments entered by members? Your first thought might be to use the AVG function, but what are we trying to average? We want to count the number of tournaments for each member and then average those counts.

We can use grouping, as described in the previous section, to find the numbers of tournaments entered by each member. The SQL is shown in Listing 8-32, and the result is in Figure 8-12. I have included an AS clause so we can refer to the column with the counts in it.

Listing 8-32. *Find the Number of Entries for Each Member*

```
SELECT MemberID, COUNT (*) AS CountEntries FROM Entry
GROUP BY MemberID
```

MemberID	CountEntries
118	1
228	3
235	4
239	2
258	2
286	3
415	9

Figure 8-12. *Finding the number of entries for each member*

Now we want to find the average of the column CountEntries. As a first try, it seems reasonable to use the SQL statement in Listing 8-33. We put the grouped count (Listing 8-32) as the inner part of a nested query, and then attempt to find the average. However, many versions of SQL do not support a nested query in a FROM clause. Listing 8-33 works fine in Access 2007 but not in some other implementations of SQL.

Listing 8-33. *Find the Average Number of Tournaments Entered by Members (Doesn't Always Work)*

```
SELECT AVG (CountEntries) FROM
     (SELECT MemberID, COUNT (*) AS CountEntries FROM Entry
     GROUP BY MemberID)
```

We can use derived tables in this situation. We encountered derived tables in the previous chapter, when we wanted to join a table with the result of a union. We would like to consider SELECT MemberID, COUNT (*) AS CountEntries FROM Entry GROUP BY MemberID as a new table. We could create this as a separate view, but if we want to use it only in this context, we can use a derived table. We do this simply by adding a name for this virtual table after the parentheses. In Listing 8-34, I have called the derived table CountTable (for want of a better name). It appears in bold in the listing.

Listing 8-34. *Using a Derived Table to Find the Average of Counts*

```
SELECT AVG (CountEntries) FROM
     (SELECT MemberID, COUNT (*) AS CountEntries FROM Entry
      GROUP BY MemberID) CountTable
```

We consider the SELECT clause in the parentheses as if it were creating a temporary table called CountTable (but, in fact, no actual table is ever made). We can then quite happily find the average of the counts in our new virtual table.

Summary

Aggregate functions provide us with the means to answer a huge range of questions about our data. Here is a summary of some of the main points in this chapter.

Regarding simple aggregate functions:

- Most versions of SQL will offer the simple aggregate functions MIN, MAX, COUNT, SUM, and AVG.

- For COUNT, you often just want to count rows, which can be done by including an asterisk in the parentheses: COUNT(*).

- For COUNT and other aggregates, you can include a field name or some other numeric expression, such as AVG(Handicap).

Regarding Nulls and duplicates:

- Null values are not included when calculating aggregates. For example, AVG(Handicap) is the sum of the handicaps divided by the number of rows that have a non-Null value for Handicap. COUNT(Handicap) will count only those rows with a non-Null value in the Handicap column.

- By default, all non-Null values are included in the aggregates. You can include the keyword DISTINCT to remove duplicates. For example, COUNT(DISTINCT Handicap) will count the number of different values appearing in the Handicap column.

Regarding grouping:

- The key phrase GROUP BY can be used to collect rows together and then apply the aggregates to the groups. For example, we can find the number of tournaments each member has entered with SELECT MemberID, COUNT(*) FROM Entry GROUP BY MemberID.

- After you have grouped and performed an aggregate, you can select rows from the resulting table using the keyword HAVING. For example, we can find members who have entered three or more tournaments by adding the clause HAVING COUNT(*) >= 3 to the expression in the previous item.

- Use WHERE to select a subset of rows *before* the grouping and aggregating. Use HAVING to select a subset of rows *after* the grouping and aggregating.

Regarding more complex aggregates:

- Use derived tables where you want to nest aggregates, such as to find the average of counts.

- Compare counts of rows to do the equivalent of relational division.

CHAPTER 9

■ ■ ■

Efficiency Considerations

You may not need to read this chapter! Most database management systems are very efficient, and if you have a modest amount of data, most of your queries will probably be carried out in the blink of an eye. Complicating your life to make those queries a little faster does not make a great deal of sense. On the other hand, if you have (or might have) vast amounts of data, and speed is absolutely critical, you will need more skill and experience than you are likely to get from reading one chapter in a beginners' book. Having said that, you are likely to have people tell you that it matters how you express your queries or that you should be indexing your tables, so it is handy to have some idea about what is going on behind the scenes.

Throughout this book, I have emphasized that there are often many ways to phrase a query in SQL. The implementation of SQL you are using may not support some constructions, so your choices may be limited. Even then, you usually have alternatives for most queries. Does it matter which one you use? One consideration is the transportability of your queries. For example, some implementations of SQL support the INTERSECT keyword, but many do not. If you are unsure where your query may be used, you might choose to avoid keywords and operations that are not widely supported (yet). However, typically, you will be writing queries for a specific database with a specific implementation of SQL. In that case, your main questions are "How will the different constructions of a query affect the performance?" and "Is there anything I can do to improve performance?"

In this chapter, we will take a brief look at what goes on when a query is performed, how to determine if the phrasing of the query matters, and how indexes might help with the efficiency of some queries.

Indexes

Queries involve finding particular rows in tables and combining or comparing them in different ways. Being able to find rows quickly is therefore important for the efficiency of your queries. Depending on the type of query, the criteria for finding the row will be different. Let's just think about the Member table:

- We might want to find a row with a particular `MemberID` to match with a row in the `Entry` table.

- We might want to find a row with a particular `LastName` because we are interested in a particular member.

- We might want rows with particular values in the `Handicap` column because we want to find all members that have a certain handicap.

Indexes can help us access tables in different ways to speed up finding rows.

Types of Indexes

Let's start by thinking about some simple queries on a single table such as the `Member` table, shown in Figure 9-1. Recall that in relational theory, a table (relation) is a set of rows, and so there is no prescribed order to the rows.

MemberID	LastName	FirstName	Handicap
415	Taylor	William	7
178	Beck	Sarah	
228	Burton	Sandra	26
290	Sexton	Thomas	26
332	Bridges	Deborah	12
258	Olson	Barbara	16
153	Nolan	Brenda	11
414	Gilmore	Jane	5
339	Young	Betty	21
176	Branch	Helen	
286	Pollard	Robert	19
323	Wilcox	Daniel	3
469	Willis	Carolyn	29
239	Spence	Thomas	10
487	Kent	Susan	
235	Cooper	William	14
331	Schmidt	Thomas	25
118	McKenzie	Melissa	30
138	Stone	Michael	30
461	Reed	Robert	3

Figure 9-1. *Member table*

If we want to select a particular row or rows in the `Member` table (such as the row for member 323 or rows for members with a handicap less than 10), the database software must scan through every row in the table to check if it meets the condition. Indexes can help make finding particular rows much more efficient.

When we create a primary key on a table, most database systems will automatically create an index on the key field(s). This means that it will keep a list of every value in the key fields in order, so you can find the value you are looking for quickly. Imagine several thousand names in no particular order, and then think of them ordered as in a telephone book. The sorted list is clearly much more efficient when looking for a name.

Indexes on primary keys are a special type called a *unique index*, in which each value can appear only once. This is how the database system ensures that primary key values are never duplicated in your tables.

Many large, full-featured database systems support two different types of indexes: clustered and nonclustered. (In Oracle, the equivalent of a clustered index is a feature called an *index-organized table*.) Smaller products may not support both; for example, Access has only nonclustered indexes.

Let's think about an index to keep the values of the MemberID field in numerical order. You can think of a clustered index as keeping all the data for each row in the index, essentially maintaining the table in order sorted by MemberID. This is a bit simplified, but it does as a start. A clustered index is like a telephone book or a dictionary. You find the entry you are looking for, and all the information you require is right there. A nonclustered index keeps just the values of the MemberID field in order, along with a pointer or reference to the full row. A nonclustered index is like the index in the back of a book. You can quickly search the index for the topic you want, and then you get a reference to a page that you must look up to find the rest of the information. Figure 9-2 shows the two types of indexes on MemberID for the Member table.

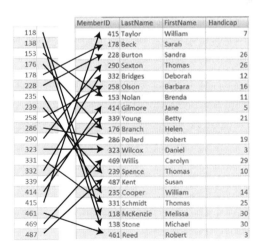

Clustered index on MemberID   Nonclustered index on MemberID

Figure 9-2. *Clustered and nonclustered indexes on MemberID*

If you want to find all the information about Member 228, with the clustered index, you can quickly find the entry 228, which has the whole row there. With the nonclustered index, you can search for 228 in the index, and then follow the reference (the arrow in Figure 9-2) to find the rest of the information about the member.

You can have only one clustered index on a table, because the set of rows can be maintained in only one order at a time. However, you can have several nonclustered indexes. Old hymnbooks are a good example. The actual hymns are in the book in just one order (clustered index), but there may be several (nonclustered) indexes in the back: composer, first line, name, and so on.

Let's look at the Entry table, shown in Figure 9-3. We might want to find out two things from this table:

- Which tournaments has a particular member, such as 235, entered?

- Who has entered a particular tournament, such as tournament 40?

For the first question, we want to quickly find all the rows with MemberID = 235. For the second question, we want to quickly find all the records with TourID = 40. The two nonclustered indexes in Figure 9-3 can help speed up both these searches.

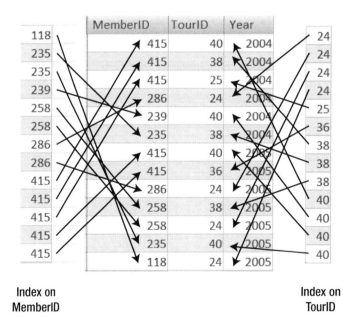

Index on   Index on
MemberID   TourID

Figure 9-3. *Two nonclustered indexes on the Entry table*

If we want to find all the entries for tournament 40, the system can quickly search the index on TourID to find the entries for 40. The index also contains a reference to the full row in the Entry table, so the system can quickly locate the rest of the information. Alternatively, if we want to find the tournaments entered by member 235, we can use the MemberID index to quickly access the appropriate records for that member.

Listing 9-1 shows the SQL statements to create two indexes on the Entry table: one on MemberID and the other on TourID. The syntax requires that you give the index a name (I've called them idx_Member and idx_Tournament), specify which table the index is to be created on, and provide the field that is to be indexed.

Listing 9-1. *Creating Two Indexes on the Entry Table*

```
CREATE INDEX idx_Member ON Entry (MemberID)
CREATE INDEX idx_Tournament ON Entry (TourID)
```

Once you have created indexes, the database management system will use them if it decides the index will make certain queries more efficient. We'll talk about this in the "Query Optimizer" section later in this chapter.

The most usual way that you are likely to want to access a table is through a primary key field. The index on the primary key can be clustered or nonclustered. In SQL Server, it defaults to being a clustered index. The SQL Server syntax for manually creating a clustered index on the primary key fields of the Entry table is shown in Listing 9-2.

Listing 9-2. *Creating a Clustered Index on the Primary Key Fields of the Entry Table*

```
CREATE CLUSTERED INDEX idx_PK ON Entry (MemberID, TourID, Year)
```

The index in Listing 9-2 is a compound index involving three fields. The index will contain all three values. They will be sorted first by the first value, MemberID. Where there are two or more entries for the same MemberID, they will be sorted by the value of TourID and then Year.

Indexes for Efficiently Ordering Output

If we wanted to get member information in alphabetical order by name, we would use a query with the ORDER BY clause, as in Listing 9-3.

Listing 9-3. *Retrieving Member Information in Alphabetical Order*

```
SELECT *
FROM Member
ORDER BY LastName
```

If the Member table did not have an index on the names, this would require the rows to be retrieved and then sorted. Will it help to provide an index on LastName (or better still, a compound index on LastName, FirstName)? Not necessarily.

If the name index is a clustered index, it will definitely help speed up the process, because all the information we are seeking is contained in the required order in the index. If it is a nonclustered index, we can find the names in the correct order, but then we need to follow the reference to the whole row to look up the rest of the information. The lookup operation can be quite costly, and often the database system will choose to scan the unsorted table and then sort the records later.

How does the database software know what to do and, more important, how do we know what it is going to do? We will come back to these questions in the "Query Optimizer" section later in this chapter.

Indexes and Joins

Very few queries involve just a single table, and one of the most common operations in a query is the join. Making joins efficient is certainly worthwhile. Joins involve comparing the values of fields in each of the tables involved in the join. While a join can be on any field, a very common situation is joining the foreign key in one table to the primary key in the table it is referencing.

Figure 9-4 shows the Entry table and some columns from the Member table. In the Entry table, MemberID is a foreign key referring to the Member table, which means that any value in MemberID in the Entry table must already exist in the Member table. The data was split into these two separate tables to avoid the updating problems discussed in Chapter 1. However, many queries involving the Entry table will also require information from the Member table (for example, a member's name), so we need to join the tables as shown in Listing 9-4. A similar join between the Entry and Tournament tables is also likely to be carried out often.

Listing 9-4. *Joining the Entry and Member Tables*

```
SELECT *
FROM Member m INNER JOIN Entry e
ON m.MemberID = e.MemberID
```

How does a database management system carry out a join between the Entry and Member tables? Well, it can take many approaches. You don't need to specify which approach to take, as the query optimizer in your database software will choose the most efficient one, as discussed shortly. However, it is useful to have a bit of an idea of what may happen, so you can make some informed decisions about adding indexes.

One approach to joining tables is called *nested loops*. This means that you scan down the rows in one table, and for each row, you look through all the rows in the other table to find matches for the join condition. The nested-loop approach is depicted in Figure 9-5.

MemberID	LastName	FirstName	Handicap	Gender
178	Beck	Sarah		F
176	Branch	Helen		F
332	Bridges	Deborah	12	F
228	Burton	Sandra	26	F
235	Cooper	William	14	M
414	Gilmore	Jane	5	F
487	Kent	Susan		F
118	McKenzie	Melissa	30	F
153	Nolan	Brenda	11	F
258	Olson	Barbara	16	F
286	Pollard	Robert	19	M
461	Reed	Robert	3	M
331	Schmidt	Thomas	25	M
290	Sexton	Thomas	26	M
239	Spence	Thomas	10	M
138	Stone	Michael	30	M
415	Taylor	William	7	M
323	Wilcox	Daniel	3	M
469	Willis	Carolyn	29	F
339	Young	Betty	21	F

Part of Member table

MemberID	TourID	Year
286	24	2004
235	38	2004
239	40	2004
415	40	2004
415	38	2004
415	25	2004
235	40	2005
258	24	2005
118	24	2005
286	24	2005
415	36	2005
415	40	2005
258	38	2005

Part of Entry table

Figure 9-4. *A join will often occur on the two MemberID fields in the Member and Entry tables.*

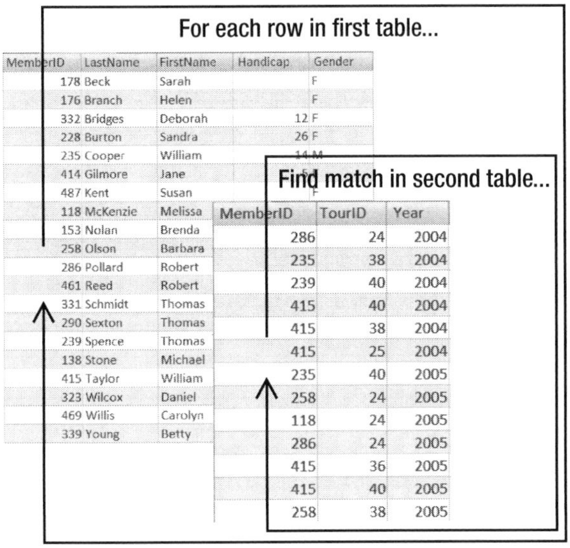

Figure 9-5. *Nested-loops approach to finding rows with matching MemberIDs*

Obviously, which table is in the outside loop will make a difference. If we start scanning the Entry table, we need to be able to quickly find the row with the matching MemberID in the Member table. If we start by choosing rows in the Member table, we need to quickly find the matching MemberID in the Entry table. Because there will always be an index on the primary key MemberID in the Member table, the first option will always be quite efficient.

The picture in Figure 9-5 shows the outside loop being around the Member table. For each row, the database system will need to search for the matching row in the Entry (inner) table. If there is an index on the foreign key MemberID in the Entry table, this option will also be a possible choice. Your query optimizer software will do all the sums and figure out the best way.

Another approach to doing a join is to first sort both tables by the join field. It is then very easy to find matching rows. This is called a *merge join* and is shown in Figure 9-6.

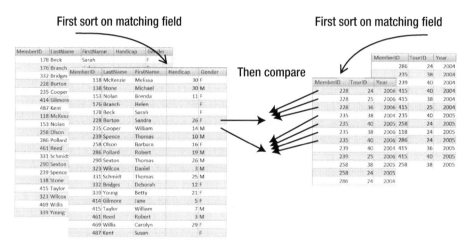

Figure 9-6. *A merge-join approach first sorts each table by the field being compared.*

Sorting each table as in Figure 9-6 is an expensive operation. However, if the tables are already sorted (they both have a clustered index on the join field MemberID), then this merging operation is very efficient.

What Should We Index?

We have two types of indexes, clustered and nonclustered, and as you saw in the previous section, it can make quite a difference which you use. Clustered indexes provide rapid access to all the information in a row via the field on which you have indexed. For this reason, you need very good reasons not to have the primary key as the clustered index on a table.

What about nonclustered indexes? You can have as many of those as you like. Appropriate indexes will certainly help with finding rows quickly, and therefore make many queries more efficient. There is a downside to having many indexes, however.

If you have a lot of indexes, then every time you add, delete, or amend a row in a table, all the indexes must be updated. Database systems are very smart about how they manage indexes, but it still takes time. So while indexes can speed up retrieval, they may slow some maintenance operations. Indexes also take up room on your storage device, although this is not often a huge problem these days.

Most large database systems provide analysis tools that allow you to experiment with placing different indexes on your tables and estimate how the performance might be affected for various queries and maintenance processes. The only way to really see how the performance will vary is to use these tools and try some experiments.

Query Optimizer

In the previous sections, we looked at a couple ways the database system could carry out a join: with nested loops or with a sort and merge. Which one will occur? Fortunately, we don't have to worry about this, as good relational database products have a query optimizer to figure out the most efficient way.

What Does the Query Optimizer Consider?

The query optimizer will take into account a number of things, such as which indexes are present, the number of rows in the tables, the length of the rows, and which fields are required in the output. An optimizer will look at all the possible steps for completing the task and assign time costs to each. It then comes up with the most efficient plan.

In the previous section, we looked at just a single join, but queries usually involve a number of steps. Consider finding the tournaments that member 235 has entered. This will require us to join the Entry and Member tables, to perform a select operation to find the rows for member 235, and then to project the required columns. In what order should we do the join and the select operations? Listing 9-5 shows two possibilities.

Listing 9-5. *Two Algebra Expressions to Find the Tournaments That Member 235 Has Entered*

$\pi_{TourID,Year} (\sigma_{MemberID=235} (Entry \bowtie_{MemberID=MemberID} Member))$

$\pi_{TourID,Year} (Entry \bowtie_{MemberID=MemberID} (\sigma_{MemberID=235} Member))$

In the first of the two expressions in Listing 9-5, we first do the complete join of Entry and Member (the innermost set of parentheses). This involves comparing all the rows from each table. In the second expression, we first select the single row for member 235, and then join just that single row with the Entry table. Clearly, the second option involves less work looking up matching rows. Remember that algebra expressions tell us *how* to carry out the query, whereas calculus expressions describe *what* rows we want. The rows we want can be described like this:

> Retrieve TourID and Year from rows (e) in the Entry table where there is a matching row (m) in the Member table and m.MemberID = t.TourID and m.MemberID = 235.

The SQL equivalent to this calculus-like description is in Listing 9-6.

Listing 9-6. *SQL to Find the Tournaments That Member 235 Has Entered*

```
SELECT e.TourID, e.Year
FROM Entry e , Member m
WHERE e.MemberID = m.MemberID AND m.MemberID = 235
```

The SQL in Listing 9-6 is calculus-based and so gives no indication of what order to carry out the relevant operations. The query optimizer will sort out the best way. However, other equivalent SQL expressions will return the same result as returned by the SQL in Listing 9-6. Does it matter which we choose? It might. The answer depends on how smart your database product is. Most good relational databases provide tools that allow you to see the query plan your optimizer has chosen.

Does the Way We Express the Query Matter?

As you've seen in this book, you often have many equivalent ways of expressing a query in SQL. Some are based on the relational calculus; others use explicit algebra operators such as inner join and intersect. Listings 9-7, 9-8, and 9-9 show three different ways to express the same simple join and select operations to find the tournaments entered by senior members.

Listing 9-7. *A Join Expressed with a Calculus-like Expression*

```
SELECT m.LastName, e.TourID
FROM Entry e, Member m
WHERE e.MemberID = m.MemberID AND m.MemberType = 'Senior'
```

Listing 9-8. *A Join Expressed with an Inner Join Operation*

```
SELECT m.LastName, e.TourID
FROM Entry e INNER JOIN Member m
ON e.MemberID = m.MemberID
WHERE m.MemberType = 'Senior'
```

Listing 9-9. *A Join Expressed with a Nested Query*

```
SELECT m.LastName, e.TourID
FROM Entry e
WHERE e.MemberID IN
    (SELECT m.MemberID FROM Member m
     WHERE m.MemberType = 'Senior')
```

So does it make a difference which of these we use? The answer is not simple. It very much depends on the query optimizer in your database product. Most full-featured relational database products have tools that allow you to make comparisons between different query plans.

Figure 9-7 shows some output from the query analyzer in SQL Server 2005. I've given it the three queries and asked to see its intended plan for each. It shows that each time the join is done with a nested loop, and it also shows the estimated relative costs. There is no way you could have predicted this result without using the analyzer or having a very detailed understanding of how the particular optimizer works in the current version of the product.

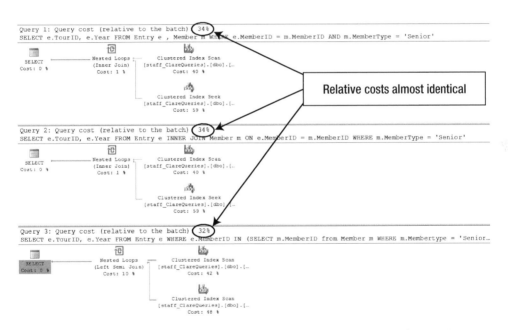

Figure 9-7. *SQL Server query analyzer showing relative costs for three ways of expressing a join and select*

In some cases, the way you express the query can make quite a difference. Consider a query to find members who have never entered tournament 25. Three different ways of expressing this query are shown in Listings 9-10, 9-11, and 9-12.

Listing 9-10. *Using NOT EXISTS*

```
SELECT m.Lastname, m.FirstName
FROM Member m
WHERE NOT EXISTS
      (SELECT * FROM Entry e
      WHERE e.MemberID = m.MemberID
      AND e.TourID = 25)
```

Listing 9-11. *Using a Join and Then a Difference Operator (EXCEPT)*

```
SELECT LastName, FirstName FROM Member
EXCEPT
SELECT m.LastName, m.FirstName
FROM Entry e INNER JOIN Member m ON e.MemberID = m.MemberID
WHERE TourID = 25
```

Listing 9-12. *Using a Nested Query and a Difference Operator*

```
SELECT LastName FirstName FROM Member
WHERE MemberID IN
      (SELECT MemberID FROM Member
      EXCEPT
      SELECT MemberID
      FROM Entry
      WHERE TourID = 25)
```

Figure 9-8 shows the estimated plans for each of the three versions of the query. You can see that they are very different. The versions using the EXCEPT keyword are significantly slower. This is the first version of SQL Server to support the EXCEPT keyword, and I suspect that in future versions, the optimizer will change to make these queries more efficient.

Before you get too bothered about differences in efficiency, you need to make sure that it actually matters to you. When you run these queries, each appears to be carried out in an instant. With bigger tables, the difference may become noticeable (or it may not). You can try to future-proof your queries for when your tables get bigger, but as the optimizers improve, the differences may well disappear. I'm inclined to not worry too much about the efficiency of different versions of queries unless it is absolutely crucial. And if it is absolutely crucial, get some expert advice for your situation!

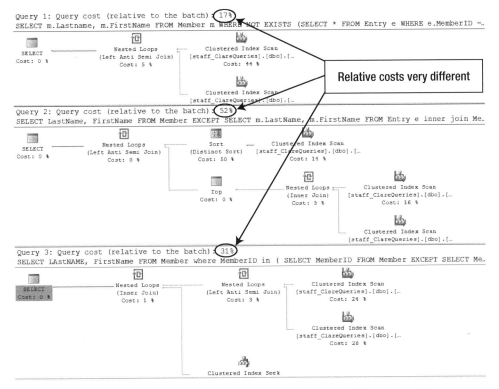

Figure 9-8. *SQL Server query analyzer shows that how you express this query makes a significant difference to the efficiency.*

You can also use query plan analysis tools to investigate the effect of adding indexes to your tables. Consider the query in Listing 9-13, which projects the LastName field from the Member table and then orders the names.

Listing 9-13. *Selecting a Field from a Table*

```
SELECT LastName FROM Member
ORDER BY LastName
```

What will be the impact of adding a nonclustered index on LastName to the Member table? To illustrate the difference, I've used the SQL Server query analyzer to compare the query on two identical tables: one, renamed MemberIndex, with an index on LastName, and one without an index on that column. Figure 9-9 shows the result. As you can see, the index speeds up this query significantly. This is because all the last names are kept in order in the index.

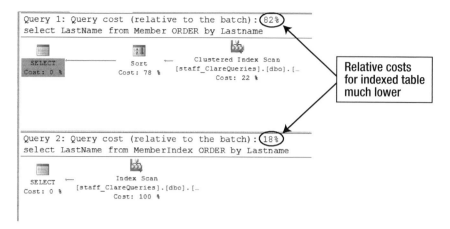

Figure 9-9. *An index improves the query by retrieving just the fields in the index.*

However, if we ask for extra fields to be retrieved by the query, as in Listing 9-14, the additional cost of having to look up the values of the other fields must be taken into account.

Listing 9-14. *Selecting All the Fields from a Table*

```
SELECT * FROM Member
ORDER BY LastName
```

Figure 9-10 shows that the optimizer has decided that it is better to just retrieve whole records and then sort them.

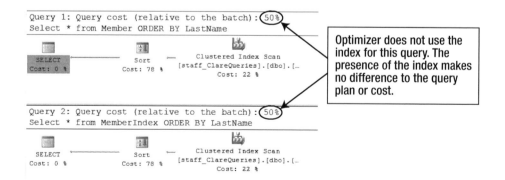

Figure 9-10. *The index is not used for retrieving all the fields.*

The two examples in Figures 9-9 and 9-10 illustrate that it is not sensible to try to guess what your optimizer will do. A good optimizer will take into account all manner of statistics about your tables before it arrives at its decision. You might think an index will help speed up a query, but you should check with some analysis tools. You also need to remember that indexes will affect different queries in different ways. Having a clustered index on LastName would certainly make both the queries in Listings 9-13 and 9-14 more efficient, but might make queries involving a join between Member and Entry less efficient.

For most small databases, these deliberations are not necessary. Where you have very large tables and speed is critical, it becomes a job for an expert to determine which combinations of indexes and other factors will make your database most efficient overall.

Summary

You can access the tables in a query to find the required rows in many different ways. The query optimizer in your database will check the different options and choose the approach it thinks is the most efficient. Optimizers vary in how good they are at doing this and are constantly being improved.

Here are two of the most obvious things that you can do to try to improve the efficiency of your queries:

- Check the efficiency of different ways of expressing queries.

- Add appropriate indexes.

Query optimizers are pretty clever! They can usually work out the most efficient query plan, regardless of how you express the query. But this is not always the case. The only way to tell is to use query analysis tools to check the different query plans. Be aware that as the optimizers improve, the plans might change with each new version of your database product, so you need to keep checking.

Adding appropriate indexes can often make quite significant improvements to some queries. Indexes are usually automatically added for primary key fields. Indexes on fields that you want to order by or use in a select condition can also be useful. It is always worth checking the usefulness of adding an index to foreign key fields, as these are often used in join conditions.

However, indexes come at a cost because they need to be updated every time a row in the table is added, deleted, or altered. This can slow some updating operations while speeding some retrieval operations. You need to decide how important the various efficiencies are for your particular situation. For small databases, you probably don't need to worry about efficiency at all, but bear in mind that small databases have a habit of growing.

CHAPTER 10

∎∎∎

How to Approach a Query

In the previous chapters, you have seen how to use relational algebra operations to combine tables and extract subsets of information. You've also seen how to express many different types of queries in terms of the relational calculus and how to translate these to SQL statements using a number of keywords and phrases.

However, when you are presented with a complicated, natural-language description of a query, it is not uncommon to find that your mind goes blank. You have a lot of ammunition at hand, but for a moment or two, you have no idea which weapons to choose.

Usually, it is just a matter of being confident and relaxing. Large, complicated queries can always be broken down into a series of smaller, simpler queries that can be combined later. This chapter describes how to do just that.

Understanding the Data

It may sound like stating the obvious, but you can't retrieve information from a database without understanding where all the different bits of data are stored and how the relevant tables are interrelated. Most of the time, you will be querying a database designed by someone else, and probably maintained and altered over time by various people. You need to understand their model. You also must be alert to the unfortunate reality that the database may have been badly designed.[1] This might mean that you are not able to retrieve the required information accurately. We will consider this problem of working against bad design a bit more in Chapter 11.

Determine the Relationships Between Tables

The best way to get an overview of a database is to look at a schematic of the relationships between the tables. Most database management software provides a way of viewing the fields in the tables and the relationships between the tables. Figures 10-1 and 10-2 show the relationship diagrams for our club database as depicted by SQL Server and Microsoft Access.

---

1. See my design book, *Beginning Database Design: From Novice to Professional* (Apress, 2007).

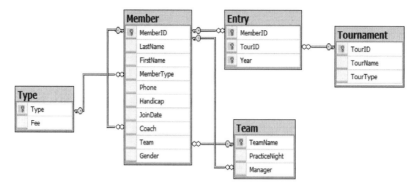

Figure 10-1. *The database diagram from SQL Server*

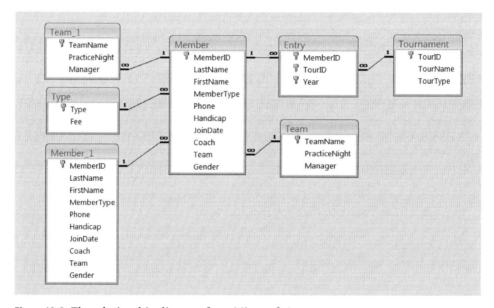

Figure 10-2. *The relationship diagram from Microsoft Access*

On the surface, the diagrams in Figures 10-1 and 10-2 look a bit different, but they are representing exactly the same database. The Access schematic in Figure 10-2 displays an additional copy of the Member and Team tables. The two copies of the Member table arise from the self relationship between members (that is, a member can coach other members). The additional copy of the Team table is because of the two relationships between Member and Team: a member can be the *manager* of a team, and a member can *belong* to a team. These relationships are depicted in the SQL Server diagram in Figure 10-1 without needing to display the tables twice. The different diagrammatic representations are just a quirk of the different management systems. Both schematics represent the same set of tables and relationships.

The lines in the two diagrams in Figures 10-1 and 10-2 represent the foreign keys that were set up when the tables were created. If your database management software does not have a useful way of depicting the relationships graphically, you can sketch your own diagram from the SQL statements that created the tables. For example, the statement for creating the Member table is shown in Listing 10-1. It contains two foreign key constraints.

Listing 10-1. *SQL for Creating the Member Table*

```
CREATE TABLE Member(
MemberID Int Primary Key,
LastName Char(20),
FirstName Char(20),
MemberType Char(20) Foreign Key References Type,
Phone Char(20),
Handicap Int,
JoinDate Datetime,
Coach Int Foreign Key References Member,
Team Char(20),
Gender Char(1))
```

Recall from Chapter 1 that this line of code:

```
MemberType Char(20) Foreign Key References Type
```

means that the values in the MemberType field must exist in the primary key field in the Type table; that is, there is a relationship between the Member table and the Type table.

This line of code:

```
Coach Int Foreign Key References Member
```

means that the values in the Coach field must already exist in the primary key field in the Member table; that is, there is a self relationship on the Member table.

You can see the resulting lines in the diagrams in Figures 10-1 and 10-2. You can investigate all the foreign key statements in the SQL that created the tables in your database and create your own diagram, if necessary.

The Conceptual Model vs. the Implementation

One word of caution: there are two models you need to understand. First is the *conceptual* data model that describes how the data for a particular problem is interrelated. A number of methods exist for representing a conceptual model, such as entity-relationship (ER) diagrams and Unified Modeling Language (UML) class diagrams. In addition to the conceptual model is the *real* database that has been implemented. The conceptual model and actual implementation may be different!

The schematics that your database management software shows you depict the foreign keys that have actually been set up. However, the developer may not have implemented the foreign key constraint on the Coach field (for example) for many reasons. He may not have realized the constraint was necessary; he may not have known how to define it; or he may have decided to enforce the constraint that a coach must be an existing member some other way (with a trigger or via the interface).

The CREATE statements and the relationship schematics show you what relationships have actually been implemented in the database. However, even if there is no foreign key constraint on the Coach field in the Member table, we still need to understand that members coach other members if we want to design reliable queries about coaching.

It is often a good idea to sketch a conceptual model, as in Figure 10-3. Refer back to Chapter 1 if you need to refresh your understanding of how to read the lines and numbers.

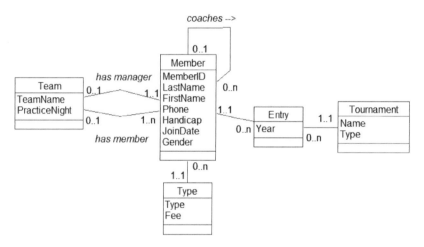

Figure 10-3. *Conceptual model of the data*

The conceptual model depicts how the various bits of data actually interrelate in the real world. The database diagrams show us which foreign keys have been implemented in the database to represent the relationships. The conceptual model in Figure 10-3 and the SQL Server diagram in Figure 10-1 are just about identical (because I designed the database according to the model!). Real problems arise when the database has been designed badly (or not at all), and the implementation bears little resemblance to the reality.

If we had a set of tables as in Figure 10-1 but the developer had, for some reason, chosen not to set up the foreign keys, the two models would be much the same but with a few lines missing. In that case, we could still answer questions about the data reasonably effectively (although the data values may not be very accurate or consistent).

In some cases, the actual database may not have much in common with the conceptual model. For example, if the database contained additional tables for coaches and managers or did not have a separate table for entries, the two models would look quite different. The likelihood of getting reliable information would be low. Chapter 11 looks at these kinds of problems, although short of a major redesign, there is not much you can do in many cases.

What Tables Are Involved?

Once you have an understanding of the tables in the database and how they are related, you can look at which tables you will need in order to extract the subset of data you require. Consider a query like "Find all the men who have entered a Leeston tournament." This sentence contains a few key words. Nouns are often a clue to which tables or fields we are going to need. Verbs often help us find relationships. Let's look at the nouns. "Tournament" is a big clue, and we have a Tournament table, so that is a start. The word "men" is another noun in the query description. We don't have a Men table, but we do have a Member table.

It is fairly clear then that the Member and Tournament tables are going to play a part in our query. Now we need to get a feel for how these two tables are related. Figure 10-4 shows the part of the SQL Server database diagram containing these two tables. We see that that they are not directly related but are connected via the Entry table. That makes sense, because the verb "enter" is in our query description.

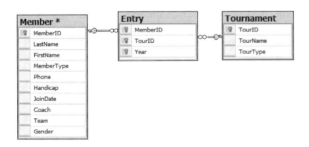

Figure 10-4. *Part of the database diagram showing the Member and Tournament tables*

So it looks like at least three tables will be involved in our query: Member, Tournament, and Entry. We then use our understanding of the relational algebra to decide how these tables need to be combined. Do we need a join or a union, or some combination of these and other relational operators? We'll look at ways to help decide on the appropriate operations in later sections in this chapter.

Look at Some Data Values

Requests for information from a database are usually couched in rather informal and imprecise natural language. Even a simple request, such as "Find all the men who have entered a Leeston tournament," has a few things we need to clarify. Having a look at the actual data in the tables can sometimes help.

Our query does not actually "find" the men, but returns some information about them. Looking at the data values in the table will help us decide what information might be helpful. Presumably, the questioner would like to see the names of the men. Do we need the IDs as well? We will need IDs if we want to distinguish two members with the same name.

It may not always be clear what some of the words in the question refer to. What is a *Leeston* tournament? Is Leeston the name of a tournament, a type of tournament, or a location? Looking at a few rows of the `Tournament` table (as shown later in Figure 10-5) can help us. We see that the `TourName` field has the value "Leeston" here and there. Sometimes it might not be so easy to determine what imprecise words in the query description refer to. It may be necessary to talk to the developer or users to get a better understanding of what information they are trying to retrieve.

How do we determine which members are men? Fortunately, the `Member` table has a `Gender` column, and it looks like we want "M" values. Is selecting rows with values of "M" going to be enough? Might there be some rows that have "m" or "male" as the values? We'll look at how to deal with issues of inconsistent data in the next chapter. For now, let's assume that men are denoted by "M" values.

For the simple query in this example, we now have a more precise description. It is something like "Retrieve the `MemberID`, `LastName`, and `FirstName` of the men (`Gender = 'M'`) who have entered the tournament where the value of `TourName` is Leeston."

If you are on the ball, you might think of some other particulars that need clearing up. It is often a good idea to ask why this information is required. Do we just want to find which men have ever been to Leeston, or do we want to know how many times our male club members have entered Leeston tournaments? These questions can have different answers, as you will see in the "Retain the Appropriate Columns" section coming up soon.

Big Picture Approach

My first attempt at a query is seldom elegant or complete. For a simple query like "Find all the men who have entered a Leeston tournament," there are two ways I might tackle it, depending how my muses are working. One way is the big picture. I do this if I have a bit of an idea of how to combine the tables. I will cover the other way in the section "No Idea Where to Start?" which I use when I have no idea how to start!

In the big picture approach, I like to combine all the tables I'll need and retain all the columns, so I can see what is happening. I usually find it easiest to have an SQL window of some sort open, so I can try small queries to see if the intermediate results look promising for answering the overall question.

Let's look at the big picture approach to the query "Find all the men who have entered the Leeston tournament." We decided we needed three tables: Member, Entry, and Tournament. These tables are all connected by foreign keys, and this often suggests that joins will be useful. If it isn't clear to you that a join is what is required for the query, then resort to the methods in the "No Idea Where to Start?" section later in this chapter.

Combine the Tables

Having established which tables are likely to be useful for the query, we need to combine them. We'll talk about how to decide on the relevant operations for combining the tables in the "Spotting Key Words in Questions" section later in this chapter. For now, let's assume that you think joins look promising for the query about men entering the Leeston tournament. You don't have to do everything at once. Start slowly with some small queries to see how things shape up.

To carry out a join, we need to find the fields on which to join. Review Chapter 3 if you need to refresh your understanding of join-compatible fields. The Entry table is critical to this query, as it connects the Member and Tournament tables. The Entry table has a foreign key field TourID, which we can join with the primary key of the Tournament table. Do that much first. Listing 10-2 shows the SQL, and Figure 10-5 shows a few rows of the resulting virtual table.

Listing 10-2. *Joining the Tournament and Entry Tables*

```
SELECT * FROM
Tournament t INNER JOIN Entry e ON t.TourID=e.TourID
```

t.TourID	TourName	TourType	e.MemberID	e.TourID	Year
24	Leeston	Social	118	24	2005
24	Leeston	Social	228	24	2006
25	Kaiapoi	Social	228	25	2006
36	WestCoast	Open	228	36	2006
38	Canterbury	Open	235	38	2004
38	Canterbury	Open	235	38	2006
40	Otago	Open	235	40	2005
40	Otago	Open	235	40	2006
40	Otago	Open	239	40	2004
24	Leeston	Social	258	24	2005
38	Canterbury	Open	258	38	2005
24	Leeston	Social			2004

Figure 10-5. *Part of the result of joining the Tournament and Entry tables*

The result shown in Figure 10-5 is certainly helpful. We can see the entries and the names of the corresponding tournaments. We can see from the first two rows that members 118 and 228 have entered a Leeston tournament. Now we need to find out whether 118, 228, and other members, entering the tournament are men and find their names. We can get this additional information by joining the virtual table in Figure 10-5 to the Member table on the MemberID fields. Listing 10-3 shows the SQL, and Figure 10-6 shows the result. I haven't included all the columns in Figure 10-6 because there are a lot of them. You will see shortly why I like to leave all the columns in as long as possible.

Listing 10-3. *Joining the Tournament and Entry Tables and Then Joining the Member Table*

```
SELECT * FROM
(Tournament t INNER JOIN Entry e ON t.TourID=e.TourID)
INNER JOIN Member m ON m.MemberID = e.MemberID
```

t.TourID	TourName	TourType	e.MemberID	e.TourID	Year	m.Member	LastName	FirstName	Gender
24	Leeston	Social	118	24	2005	118	McKenzie	Melissa	F
24	Leeston	Social	228	24	2006	228	Burton	Sandra	F
25	Kaiapoi	Social	228	25	2006	228	Burton	Sandra	F
36	WestCoast	Open	228	36	2006	228	Burton	Sandra	F
38	Canterbury	Open	235	38	2004	235	Cooper	William	M
38	Canterbury	Open	235	38	2006	235	Cooper	William	M
40	Otago	Open	235	40	2005	235	Cooper	William	M
40	Otago	Open	235	40	2006	235	Cooper	William	M
40	Otago	Open	239	40	2004	239	Spence	Thomas	M
24	Leeston	Social	258	24	2005	258	Olson	Barbara	F
38	Canterbury	Open	258	38	2005	258	Olson	Barbara	F
24	Leeston	Social	286	24	2004	286	Pollard	Robert	M
24	Leeston	Social	286	24	2005	286	Pollard	Robert	M
24	Leeston	Social	286	24	2007	286			M

Figure 10-6. *Part of the result of joining the Tournament, Entry, and Member tables (just some columns)*

The virtual table resulting from Listing 10-3 has all the information we need to find the required data. The first two rows show that members 118 and 228 are women. The row for member 286 (circled) looks more promising. How do we amend the query to find the appropriate subset of rows and columns?

Find the Subset of Rows

To fix the query to obtain the subset of rows we need, first look at which rows we want to retain. We just want the subset of rows where the Gender field has the value "M" and the TourName field has the value "Leeston" as shown in Figure 10-6. This is a relational algebra select operation, similar to the operations described in Chapter 2. In SQL, a subset of rows is retrieved by using a WHERE clause with the appropriate condition. In Listing 10-4, we have added the WHERE clause.

Listing 10-4. *Retrieving the Rows for Men and Leeston Tournament*

```
SELECT * FROM
(Entry e INNER JOIN Tournament t ON t.TourID=e.TourID)
INNER JOIN Member m ON m.MemberID = e.MemberID
WHERE m.Gender = 'M' AND t.TourName = 'Leeston'
```

Figure 10-7 shows just some of the columns from the result of the query in Listing 10-4. It has four rows: three for Robert Pollard and one for William Taylor.

t.TourID	TourName	TourType	e.MemberID	e.TourID	Year	m.Member	LastName	FirstName	Gender
24	Leeston	Social	286	24	2004	286	Pollard	Robert	M
24	Leeston	Social	286	24	2005	286	Pollard	Robert	M
24	Leeston	Social	286	24	2006	286	Pollard	Robert	M
24	Leeston	Social	415	24	2006	415	Taylor	William	M

Figure 10-7. *Men who have entered Leeston tournaments (just some columns)*

Why do we have three rows for Robert Pollard? The rows are identical except for the value of the Year field. Robert has entered the Leeston tournament in three different years. We can see this quite clearly from Figure 10-7 because we have left the Year column in the output. Had we retained only the name columns, we might initially be a bit puzzled at having Robert Pollard repeated three times. What we do about the repetition of Robert Pollard depends on understanding the initial question a bit more clearly, as you will see in the next section.

Retain the Appropriate Columns

We have the appropriate subset of rows from our large join. Now we need to retain just the columns we require. This is not as simple as it first sounds. The three rows for Robert Pollard give us a bit of a clue that things may not be as straightforward as we might think. We have two possibilities:

- If we only want to know who has entered the tournament at some time, then we want just the distinct names Robert Pollard and William Taylor.

- If the objective of the question is to find out how often men enter Leeston tournaments, then we want to retain all the entries. In that case, it might be useful to retain the year as well.

Listings 10-5 and 10-6 show two options for the SELECT clause reflecting these two scenarios.

Listing 10-5. *The Names and IDs of Men Who Have Entered Leeston Tournaments*

```
SELECT DISTINCT m.MemberID, m.LastName, m.FirstName
FROM ...
```

Listing 10-6. *Information About Entries of Men in Leeston Tournaments*

```
SELECT m.MemberID, m.LastName, m.FirstName, e.Year
FROM ...
```

Consider an Intermediate View

The SQL in Listing 10-3 is likely to be the basis of many queries about entries in tournaments. For example, the following questions will all require a join of the Member, Entry, and Tournament tables:

- Do junior members enter Open tournaments?

- Which tournaments did William Taylor enter in 2005?

- What is the average number of Social tournaments that members entered in 2006?

As we are likely to use this large join many times, it can be convenient to make a view. Listing 10-7 shows a first attempt at the SQL for creating a view that retains all the fields from the joins.

Listing 10-7. *Creating a View for the Join of the Tournament, Entry, and Member Tables (First Attempt)*

```
CREATE VIEW AllTourInfo AS
SELECT * FROM
(Entry e INNER JOIN Tournament t ON t.TourID=e.TourID)
INNER JOIN Member m ON m.MemberID = e.MemberID
```

As it stands, this query will not run in most versions of SQL. This is because the view would have fields with the same name; for example, there will be two fields called MemberID: one from the Entry table and one from the Member table.

When you create a view, all the field names must be distinct. The view will not use the aliases to differentiate the columns in the resulting table. The * in the SELECT clause needs to be altered to list all the field names. We need to either delete the duplicate names or rename those that are duplicated—SELECT m.MemberID AS MMember, e.MemberID AS EMember, and so on and on and on. This is a bit tedious, but if you are creating a view that you are likely to use many times, it is worth the effort.

Once we have the view `AllTourInfo`, it can be used in the same way as any other table in our queries. To find the names of men who have entered a Leeston tournament, we can use the view as shown in Listing 10-8.

Listing 10-8. *Retrieving the Names of Men Who Have Entered a Leeston Tournament Using a View*

```
SELECT DISTINCT LastName, FirstName
FROM AllTourInfo
WHERE Gender = 'M' AND TourName = 'Leeston'
```

Spotting Key Words in Questions

The big picture approach assumes that you have decided how to combine the tables that will contribute to the query. Sometimes, you will think it is obvious that, for example, you need to join the tables. Other times, it may not be at all clear initially. In this section, we will look at some key words that often appear in questions and that can provide a clue about which relational operations you will need. If none of these help, remember that we still have the "No Idea Where to Start?" section coming up!

And, Both, Also

"And" and "also" can be tricky words when it comes to interpreting queries, and we will consider this further in the next chapter. In this section, we will look at queries that have the idea of two conditions needing to be met simultaneously. Queries that require two conditions to be met fall into two sorts: those that can be carried out with a simple WHERE clause containing AND and those that require an intersection or self join.

To decide if a query really needs two conditions to be met, I usually look at a natural-language statement and see if I can reword it with the word "both" connecting the conditions. Consider these examples:

- Find the junior boys. (*Both* a male and a junior? Yes.)

- Find those members who entered tournaments 24 and 38. (*Both* tournaments? Yes.)

- Find the women and children. (*Both* a female and a child? No.)

The last query is the one that can trick you. Although it contains the word "and," the common interpretation of "women and children" doesn't mean someone who is *both* a female and a child (that is, a girl). Rather, the phrase means anyone who is *either* a female *or* a child (especially when populating lifeboats).

The diagram in Figure 10-8 is a way of visualizing whether a query needs two conditions to be met. It portrays the example about woman and children. It shows both the union (only one condition must be satisfied) and the intersection (both conditions must be satisfied) of the set of women and the set of children. It is worth thinking like this about your data to decide what you actually need to answer your query accurately.

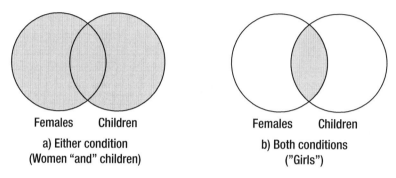

Figures:

Females   Children
a) Either condition
(Women "and" children)

Females   Children
b) Both conditions
("Girls")

Figure 10-8. *Visualizing if two conditions both need to be met*

When two conditions must be met, we are looking at the intersection of two groups of data, as in the diagram in Figure 10-8b. If we have a query that requires an intersection, that doesn't necessarily mean we must use the INTERSECT keyword. I find the following question helpful in deciding what to do next:

Do I need to look at more than one row to decide if both conditions are satisfied?

Consider the query to find junior boys. This is going to need the Member table. Can we look at a single row and determine if the member is *both* a junior and a boy? As we can see in Figure 10-9, it is possible to determine both these conditions from a single row.

MemberID	LastName	FirstName	Handicap	Gender	MemberType
178	Beck	Sarah		F	Social
228	Burton	Sandra	26	F	Junior
235	Cooper	William	14	M	Senior
239	Spence	Thomas	10	M	Senior
258	Olson	Barbara	16	F	Senior
286	Pollard	Robert	19	M	Junior
290	Sexton	Thomas	26	M	Senior
323	Wilcox	Daniel			

Figure 10-9. *We can investigate both conditions by looking at a single row.*

In this situation, we can use a simple select operation with the Boolean AND to check for both conditions. This is discussed in Chapter 2, and the SQL is shown in Listing 10-9.

Listing 10-9. *Both Conditions Can Be Checked in a Single WHERE Clause*

```
SELECT * FROM Member m
WHERE m.Gender = 'M' AND m.MemberType = 'Junior'
```

Now consider a different type of query. What about finding the members who have entered *both* tournaments 24 and 36? To do this, we need to look at the Entry table (probably joined with the Member table if we want the names). As we can see in Figure 10-10, we cannot check that a member has entered both tournaments by looking at a single row.

MemberID	TourID	Year
118	24	2005
228	24	2006
228	25	2006
228	36	2006
235	38	2004
235	38	2006
235	40	2005
235	40	2006
239	25	2006
239	40	2004

Figure 10-10. *We need to investigate more than one row to check both tournaments.*

Where we have a question needing to satisfy both of two conditions *and* we need to look at more than one row in the table, we can use a self join (discussed in Chapter 5) or an intersection (discussed in Chapter 7), as in Listings 10-10 and 10-11.

Listing 10-10. *Finding Members Who Have Entered Both Tournaments Using a Self Join*

```
SELECT e1.MemberID
FROM Entry e1 INNER JOIN Entry e2 ON e1.MemberID = e2.MemberID
WHERE e1.TourID = 24 AND e2.TourID = 36
```

Listing 10-11. *Finding Members Who Have Entered Both Tournaments Using an Intersection*

```
SELECT MemberID FROM Entry WHERE TourID = 24
INTERSECT
SELECT MemberID FROM Entry WHERE TourID = 36
```

Not, Never

Here are some examples of queries involving the word "not" or "never":

- Find the members who are *not* seniors.

- Find members who are *not* in a team.

- Find members who have *never* played in a tournament.

Often when people see "not" in a description of a query, they immediately think of using a Boolean NOT or a <> operator in a WHERE clause. This is fine for some queries, but not for all of them. As in the previous section, I find the following test helpful to determine the type of *not* query:

Do I need to look at more than one row to decide if a condition is not true?

For the first two queries, we can look at a single row in the Member table and decide whether that member satisfies the condition. In the first query, the condition in the WHERE clause would be NOT MemberType = 'Senior' or MemberType <> 'Senior'. To find members who are not in a team, we want the Team field to be empty, so a clause like WHERE Team IS NULL would do the trick.

To find the members who have not entered a tournament, what tables do we need? We are certainly going to need the Entry table. We can decide if a member has entered a tournament by finding just one row with his member ID. To see if he has *not* entered a tournament, we need to look at every row. We also must look at the Member table to find a list of all our members. In situations like this, we need to think about the relational algebra difference operator. We can do this are by using the keyword EXCEPT (discussed in Chapter 7) or by using a nested query (discussed in Chapter 4). Two examples to retrieve the member IDs of members who have never entered a tournament are shown in Listings 10-12 and 10-13. Once we have the IDs, we can perform another join to get the names. Chapter 7 shows many examples of how to carry out difference operations.

Listing 10-12. *Finding Members Who Have Never Entered a Tournament Using EXCEPT*

```
SELECT MemberID FROM Member
EXCEPT
SELECT MemberID FROM Entry
```

Listing 10-13. *Finding Members Who Have Never Entered a Tournament Using a Nested Query*

```
SELECT m.MemberID FROM Member m
WHERE m.MemberID NOT IN
    (SELECT e.MemberID FROM Entry e)
```

All, Every

Wherever you see the word "all" or "every" in a description of a query, you should immediately think of the division operator (discussed in Chapter 7). Here are some examples of such queries:

- Find members who have entered every open tournament.

- Has anyone coached all the juniors?

No Idea Where to Start?

So you have looked at the query and decided which tables you think will be involved. You're not sure if a join is the right path. You've checked for some key words, but you still feel confused. Now what? This is not uncommon (it happens to me regularly), so just relax.

When I have no idea where to start, I forget all about set operations and SQL. I stop thinking about tables, foreign keys, joins, and so on. Instead, I open the tables I think I will need to answer the question and look at some of the data. I try to find examples that should be retrieved by the query. Then I try to write down the conditions that make that particular data acceptable. This is the relational calculus approach. Relational calculus is describing *what* the rows returned by the query are like. I've been using this approach all the way through the book, alongside the algebra approach of deciding *how* to manipulate the tables.

Let's try a query that stumped me a bit when I first thought of it: "Which teams have a coach as a manager?" The steps described here can really help.

Find Some Helpful Tables

Let's look at the key words in the query "Which teams have a coach as a manager?" We have the nouns "team," "coach," and "manager." We have a table called Team. Coach and Manager are fields in the Member and Team tables, respectively. So the Team and Member tables look like a good place to start.

Try to Answer the Question by Hand

Next, take a look at the data in the tables and see how you would decide if a team had a coach as a manager. Figure 10-11 shows the relevant columns of the two tables.

TeamName	PracticeNight	Manager
TeamA	Tuesday	239
TeamB	Monday	153

MemberID	LastName	FirstName	Coach
118	McKenzie	Melissa	153
138	Stone	Michael	
153	Nolan	Brenda	
176	Branch	Helen	
178	Beck	Sarah	
228	Burton	Sandra	153
235	Cooper	William	153
239	Spence	Thomas	
258	Olson	Barbara	
286	Pollard	Robert	235
290	Sexton	Thomas	235
323	Wilcox	Daniel	
331	Schmidt	Thomas	153
332	Bridges	Deborah	235
339	Young	Betty	
414	Gilmore	Jane	153
415	Taylor	William	235
461	Reed	Robert	235
469	Willis	Carolyn	
487	Kent	Susan	

Team   **Member**

Figure 10-11. *How do we tell if a team has a coach as a manager?*

We can find the IDs of the two team managers easily enough. They are the values in the Manager column of the Team table (239 and 153). Now, how do we check if these members are coaches? Looking at the Member table, we see that the coaches are in the Coach column. We need to check if either of our two managers appears in the Coach column. Member 239 doesn't appear, so his team (TeamA) is not managed by a coach. Member 153 does appear somewhere in the Coach column, so his team (TeamB) is managed by a coach. So we have answered our query. TeamB is managed by a coach.

Write Down a Description of the Retrieved Result

Our query is "Which teams have a coach as a manager?" So following what we did in the previous section, we can write a description of what the rows we retrieve should be like. This is where I like to have imaginary fingers pointing to the relevant rows to make it easier to describe the query, as in Figure 10-12.

We are going to check every team to decide if it should be retrieved. The condition that would allow us to decide is something like this (we'll look at a different way shortly):

> *I'll write out the TeamName from row t, where t comes from the Team table, if there exists a row (m) in the Member table where the value of coach (m.Coach) is the manager of the team (t.Manager).*

TeamName	PracticeNight	Manager
TeamA	Tuesday	239
TeamB	Monday	153

MemberID	LastName	FirstName	Coach
118	McKenzie	Melissa	153
138	Stone	Michael	
153	Nolan	Brenda	
176	Branch	Helen	
178	Beck	Sarah	
228	Burton	Sandra	153
235	Cooper	William	153
239	Spence	Thomas	
258	Olson	Barbara	
286	Pollard	Robert	235
290	Sexton	Thomas	235
323	Wilcox	Daniel	
331	Schmidt	Thomas	153
332	Bridges	Deborah	235
339	Young	Betty	
414	Gilmore	Jane	153
415	Taylor	William	235
461	Reed	Robert	235
469	Willis	Carolyn	
487	Kent	Susan	

Team   Member

Figure 10-12. *Naming the rows to help describe what the retrieved data should be like*

In a slightly more formal way (if you prefer), we can write this as the relational calculus expression in Listing 10-14.

Listing 10-14. *Relational Calculus Expression for Finding Teams with a Coach As a Manager*

{t.TeamName | Team(t) and ∃ (m) Member(m) and t.Manager = m.Coach}

We can now translate this almost directly into SQL using a nested query (discussed in Chapter 4). One possibility is shown in Listing 10-15.

Listing 10-15. *Finding Teams with Coaches As Managers (One Way)*

```
SELECT t.TeamName FROM Team t
WHERE EXISTS
    (SELECT * FROM Member m WHERE m.Coach = t.Manager)
```

Is There Another Way?

First attempts at queries aren't necessarily the most elegant. After all, we are following this route because we were stumped in the first place. Following the technique of solving the query by hand and describing the conditions helps you understand what you are trying to do. That often makes the query seem much easier than you first thought.

Having done the query as described in the previous section, I then realized that I could have thought of it this way: the manager just has to be in the set of coaches. I can easily find the list of coaches with a simple query, and then use that in a nested query, as shown in Listing 10-16.

Listing 10-16. *Finding Teams with Coaches As Managers (Another Way)*

```
SELECT t.TeamName FROM Team t
WHERE t.Manager IN
   (SELECT m.Coach FROM Member m)
```

For me, the query in Listing 10-16 is simpler and easier to understand than the one in Listing 10-15, so I would probably prefer to use that one.

As always, there are often many ways to achieve the same result. We could have done an inner join on the Team and Member tables with the join condition being t.Coach = m.Manager. The managers who don't appear in the Coach column will not appear in the inner join (see the section on outer joins in Chapter 3). The SQL for this approach is shown in Listing 10-17.

Listing 10-17. *Finding Teams with Coaches As Managers Using an Inner Join*

```
SELECT DISTINCT t.TeamName FROM Team t INNER JOIN Member m
ON t.Manager = m.Coach
```

Personally, I don't find the query in Listing 10-17 particularly intuitive. I doubt if someone else looking at the query would easily understand its purpose. I still like Listing 10-16 best in terms of ease of understanding.

You might also like to check the efficiency of each of the queries (discussed in Chapter 9), if you think that might be important (unlikely in this case). For SQL Server 2005, each of the queries in Listings 10-15, 10-16, and 10-17 had the same execution plan, so they were all carried out in exactly the same way under the hood.

Checking Queries

You've written a query, run it, and got some results. Is all well and good? Not necessarily. Just as first attempts at a query may not be elegant, neither might they be correct. Mistakes might arise from simple errors in the query syntax. These are usually easy to spot and correct. However, errors that result from subtle misunderstandings of the question or of the data can be more difficult to find.

I can't offer a foolproof way of checking that your query is correct, but I can give you some ideas for catching potential errors. Basically, they boil down to checking that you do not have extra, incorrect rows in your result and checking that you aren't missing any rows. In this section, we will look at ways to notice that your query has a problem. In the next chapter, we will look at some of the common mistakes that might be behind errors.

Check a Row That Should Be Returned

Take a look at your data and determine one record or row that should be returned by your query. For example, in our example about teams with managers as coaches, check through the tables and find at least one team that satisfies the query. In Figure 10-12, we see that TeamB satisfies the conditions, so check that this team is in your output.

Remember that some queries may quite legitimately have no output. For example, it's perfectly reasonable that, with the data we have at any particular time, no teams are managed by a coach. However, your query must work in all situations. If it is at all possible, make a copy of the tables, alter the data so that a row meets the condition, and check that it is returned correctly.

Check a Row That Should Not Be Returned

Similar to checking for a row that should be returned, look through the data and find a team that *doesn't* have a coach as a manager. TeamA's manager (member 239) does not appear as a coach in the Member table, so make sure that team is *not* included in your output. Once again, it is a good idea to use some dummy data to check this if the real data does not cover all eventualities.

Check Boundary Conditions

If your query has any sort of numeric comparison, you should check it carefully. Consider a query where we want to find people who have been members of our club for more than 10 years. To be certain of the correctness, we need to check three possibilities:

- Make sure no record is returned for someone with less than 10 years of membership (for example, 8 years of membership).

- Make sure that someone who has belonged to the club for 12 years does get his record retrieved.

- Check for someone who has been a member for exactly 10 years.

The last boundary condition is always tricky. It depends whether we use > or >= in the select condition. It might also mean reconsidering the original question. In this case, the request is probably for members with 10 or more years of membership. You should check with your users if there is any doubt.

Finding data in your tables that falls exactly on the boundaries is not always easy. However, you can always change the numeric value in your query. Find a particular member and change the value you are checking against in the query to match their years of membership.

If Harry has been a member for 16 years, change the query to check for 16 or more years of membership, and see if Harry is included (or not) as you expect.

Another important boundary condition, especially for aggregates and counts (covered in Chapter 8), is the value 0. Consider a query such as "Find members who have entered fewer than six tournaments." Doing a grouped-by count on the Entry table will return some rows for sure, and we can check for those who have less than, more than, or exactly six entries. However, what about members who have never entered a tournament? They won't appear in the Entry table at all and will be missing from the results. So whenever aggregates are involved, always check what happens for a count of 0. For example, does your query return members who have entered *no* tournaments?

Check Null Values

Be aware that some of the values you are checking against may be Nulls (discussed in Chapter 2). How does your query about team managers cope with the situation where the Manager field is Null? Try it out on some dummy data and see. What do we expect (or want) to happen if there is a Null in the JoinDate field when we run the query about length of membership?

Summary

The first rule about starting a query is don't panic. The next rule is to take small steps and look at the intermediate output to see if what you have done so far is helping you. Retain as many columns as possible in your initial queries, so you can check that you understand what is happening.

Figure 10-13 gives a summary of some of the steps you can take when first starting out on a query. The diagram doesn't cover the whole process, but you should be able to make a reasonable start with these steps. Refer to the relevant chapters for more help.

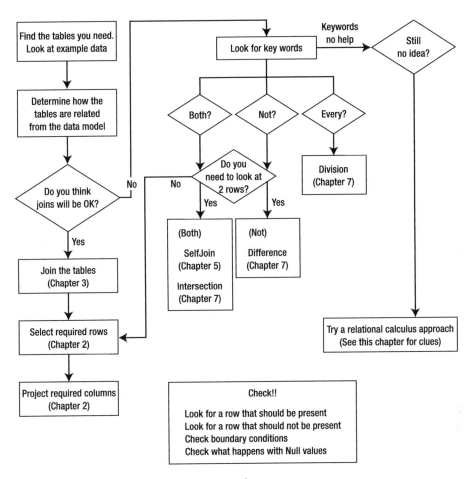

Figure 10-13. *Some steps to help you get started on a query*

■ ■ ■

Common Problems

In this book, you've seen many different ways to tackle a variety of categories of queries. However, even if a query retrieves some valid-looking rows, all may not be well. In the previous chapter, we looked at the importance of checking the output to confirm that (at least some of) the rows retrieved are correct, as well as checking to make sure that (at least some) incorrect (or irrelevant) rows are not being retrieved.

The problems that can befall queries are not just a matter of having the wrong syntax in your SQL statements, although that can certainly happen. Problems with the design of the tables or with data values can also affect the accuracy of queries. In this chapter, we will look at some common design and data problems, and also some of the most common syntactic mistakes.

Poor Database Design

Good database design is absolutely essential to being able to extract accurate information. Unfortunately, you will sometimes be faced with databases that are poorly designed and maintained. Often there is not a great deal you can do. Sometimes you can extract something that looks like the required information, but it should come with a caution that the underlying data was probably inconsistent.

Data That Is Not Normalized

One of the most common data design mistakes is to have tables that are not normalized. We looked at an example of this in Chapter 1. Rather than having two tables—one for members and one for membership information like fees—all this data was stored in one table, as in Figure 11-1.

MemberID	LastName	FirstName	Phone	Handicap	JoinDate	Gender	MemberType	Fee
118	McKenzie	Melissa	963270	30	10/05/1999	F	Junior	150
138	Stone	Michael	983223	30	13/05/2003	M	Senior	300
153	Nolan	Brenda	442649	11	25/07/2000	F	Senior	300
176	Branch	Helen	589419		18/11/2005	F	Social	50
178	Beck	Sarah	226596		6/01/2004	F	Social	50
228	Burton	Sandra	244493	26	21/06/2007	F	Junior	150
235	Cooper	William	722954	14	15/02/2002	M	Senior	300
239	Spence	Thomas	697720	10	4/06/2000	M	Senior	280
258	Olson	Barbara	370186	16	11/07/2007	F	Senior	300

Figure 11-1. *A nonnormalized Member table containing fee information*

What happens now if we are asked to find the fee for senior members? The query in Listing 11-1 will result in two values: 300 and 280.

Listing 11-1. *Finding the Fee for Senior Members*

```
SELECT DISTINCT Fee
FROM Member
WHERE MemberType = 'Senior'
```

Although the two values retrieved by Listing 11-1 may be surprising, nothing is wrong with the query or the result. The different value for senior member Thomas Spence gives us the additional fee result. That value may be a typographical error, or it may indicate some sort of discount for Thomas. In either case, there is a problem with the design. The design should allow for regular fees to be recorded consistently and, if necessary, allow for storage of additional discounting regimes. At this point, other than redesigning the tables, there is nothing we can do but return the list of fees that have been recorded against the senior members. It is just worth understanding the underlying issues.

Another problem you may encounter is a single table that stores multivalued data. Say our club has many different teams—interclub teams, social teams, pairs, foursomes, and so on—that members may belong to simultaneously. It is very common for tables to be redesigned to store additional values, as shown in Figure 11-2.

MemberID	LastName	FirstName	Team1	Team2	Team3
118	McKenzie	Melissa	TeamA		
138	Stone	Michael			
153	Nolan	Brenda	TeamB	TeamC	TeamA
176	Branch	Helen	TeamC	TeamB	
178	Beck	Sarah			
228	Burton	Sandra			

Figure 11-2. *Poor table design to store more than one team for a member*

Now suppose we are asked to find those members in TeamA. You can immediately see the problem. Melissa has "TeamA" in the Team1 column, and Brenda has "TeamA" in the Team3 column. We need to check every team column for the existence of TeamA. This isn't that difficult; the query in Listing 11-2 will do the trick.

Listing 11-2. *Finding Members of TeamA*

```
SELECT * FROM Member
WHERE Team1 = 'TeamA' OR Team2= 'TeamA' OR Team3 = 'TeamA'
```

While we can extract the information we require, the design in Figure 11-2 is clearly not the best way to store it. We will certainly start encountering problems if we need queries like "Find members who are in both TeamA and TeamB" or "Find members who are in more than two teams." You could probably devise queries that would answer these questions, but at this point, I would ask for the database to be redesigned properly before trying to fulfill such requests.

What is required is an intermediate Membership table to record relationships between members and teams. This is very like the Entry table, which records relationships between members and tournaments. The Membership table would look something like Figure 11-3.

MemberID	Team
118	TeamA
153	TeamC
153	TeamB
153	TeamA
176	TeamC
176	TeamB

Figure 11-3. *A Membership table that records the relationship between members and teams*

With the additional Membership table, we can now use all the relational operations, as described in previous chapters, to easily answer questions like "Who is in TeamA and TeamB?" and "Who is in three or more teams?"

We can create a Membership table with the SQL in Listing 11-3. The code includes foreign key constraints to the existing Member and Team tables and a concatenated primary key.

Listing 11-3. *Creating a New Membership Table*

```
CREATE TABLE Membership (
MemberID INT FOREIGN KEY REFERENCES Member,
Team Char(20) FOREIGN KEY REFERENCES Team,
PRIMARY KEY (MemberID, Team) )
```

If you don't mind a bit of manual fiddling about, you can populate the table with repeated update queries like the one in Listing 11-4. The query finds each member who is in TeamA and creates an appropriate row in the Membership table. If there are not too many teams, you can manually alter the second and last lines of the query for each team (TeamA, TeamB, and so on) and create a Membership table quite quickly. You then need to delete the Team columns from the Member table in Figure 11-2, and the database will look a whole lot better.

Listing 11-4. *Creating Rows in the Membership Table for TeamA*

```
INSERT INTO Membership (MemberID, Team)
SELECT MemberID, 'TeamA'
FROM Member
WHERE Team1 = 'TeamA' OR Team2= 'TeamA' OR Team3 = 'TeamA'
```

No Keys

The previous section gave an example of the problems you can run into if the underlying database has the inappropriate tables for your query. You sometimes find that the database has the appropriate tables, but without any primary or foreign key constraints. In these cases, you can run your queries, but the underlying data is likely to be inconsistent. In this section, you will see how you can find some of the inconsistencies by running a few queries.

Suppose that the Membership table in Figure 11-3 had been created without a primary key. Then we run the risk of having duplicate rows. For example, we might have two identical rows for member 118 in TeamA, which would cause a query that counts the number of members in TeamA to give the wrong result.

If you try to add a primary key when duplicates already exist, you will get an error, which is one way to find where the problems are! Another way is to do a GROUP BY query on the fields that should be in the primary key and use a HAVING clause to find those with two or more entries, as in Listing 11-5.

Listing 11-5. *Finding Rows with Duplicate Values in the Potential Primary Key*

```
SELECT MemberID, Team, Count(*)
FROM Membership
GROUP BY MemberID, Team
HAVING Count(*) > 1
```

Listing 11-5 will find the problem rows. When the table has fields other than the primary key fields, you need to manually inspect the values in those columns to decide which row should be deleted. The Membership table, which has only primary key fields, causes a different problem. How do we delete just one copy of the row for member 118 in TeamA? Because the entire rows are the same, we can't differentiate them, and so any query that deletes one will delete both. We can, in this situation, create a new table, and then insert just the distinct values with the query in Listing 11-6.

Listing 11-6. *Creating a New Table with Distinct Rows*

```
INSERT INTO NewMembership
SELECT DISTINCT MemberID,Team
FROM Membership
```

Another problem is having a `Membership` table (as in Figure 11-3) with no foreign key constraints. The first row could then have that member 1118 is in TeamA when no member 1118 is listed in the `Member` table. There are several ways to find such unmatched values in the `Membership` table. One way is to use a nested query (discussed in Chapter 4), as shown in Listing 11-7.

Listing 11-7. *Finding Unmatched MemberIDs in the Membership Table (Using Difference)*

```
SELECT ms.MemberID FROM Membership ms
WHERE ms.MemberID NOT IN
     (SELECT m.MemberID FROM Member m)
```

Similar Data in Two Tables

Sometimes a database has extra tables. An example for our club database would be to have a separate table for coaches or managers, as shown in Figure 11-4.

MemberID	LastName	FirstName	Phone
153	Nolan	Brenda	442649
235	Cooper	William	732954

MemberID	LastName	FirstName	Phone	Handicap	Gender
118	McKenzie	Melissa	963270	30	F
138	Stone	Michael	983223	30	M
153	Nolan	Brenda	442649	11	F
176	Branch	Helen	589419		F
178	Beck	Sarah	226596		F
228	Burton	Sandra	244493	26	F
235	Cooper	William	722954	14	M
239	Spence	Thomas	697720	10	M
258	Olson	Barbara	370186	16	F
286	Pollard	Robert	617681	19	M
290	Sexton	Thomas	268936	26	M

        Coach table   Some rows and columns from the Member table

Figure 11-4. *An additional table for coaches (poor design)*

For beginners, the extra table in Figure 11-4 makes it easy to create lists of coaches and their phone numbers (which would otherwise require a self join or nested query). However, the additional table soon causes problems. In Figure 11-4, we already see inconsistent data for William Cooper's phone number. The only real cure is to get rid of the extra table.

Using set operations (discussed in Chapter 7) can help us understand what the data contains. We can use the intersection operator to find rows for people who are in both tables, and the difference operator to find those who are in one and not the other. Once the design is correct, creating a view that shows the coach information would be helpful to your novice users. Listing 11-8 does the trick.

Listing 11-8. *A View to Retrieve Information About Coaches*

```
CREATE VIEW CoachInfo AS
SELECT * FROM Member
WHERE MemberID IN
    (SELECT Coach FROM Member )
```

Wrong Types

Having the fields in a table created with inappropriate types is another problem that can make queries look as though they are not behaving. I've seen whole databases where every field is a default text field.

Having the wrong field type means the data misses out on a whole lot of validity checking. For example, if our Member table had all text fields, we could end up with value like "16a" or "1o" in the Handicap column or text like "Brenda" in the Coach column.

Incorrectly entered values aside, inappropriate types give rise to other problems. Each type has its own rules for ordering values. Text types order alphabetically, numbers order numerically, and dates order chronologically. Different orderings clearly will be an issue if we add an ORDER BY clause to a query. A text field containing numbers will order alphabetically, giving an order like "1", "15", "109", "20" "245", "33", as described in Chapter 2.

Incorrect types also cause a problem with making comparisons. If we ask for values to be compared, the comparison used will depend on how the particular field type involved is sorted. For numbers entered in a text field, we will get comparisons such as "109" < "15" or "33" > "245". This will cause some odd output if we ask for people with handicaps less than 5, for example. It can be difficult to sort out what is going wrong, because the query syntax is fine and the data appears to be OK. Going behind the scenes to check out the data type is certainly not the first thing that may occur to you.

It is possible to change the type of a column in an existing table, but I find it a bit scary. For example, if you change from text to numeric values, "10" will probably be fine, but "1o" will cause an error. I prefer a more conservative approach: I make a new table with the appropriate types, and then insert the old values with the aid of a conversion function. Listing 11-9 shows how we could create a new table with a numeric value for the Handicap column.

Listing 11-9. *Adding (Some) Converted Values to a New Table*

```
INSERT INTO NewMember (MemberID, LastName, FirstName, Handicap)
SELECT MemberID, LastName, FirstName, CONVERT(INT Handicap)
FROM Member
```

This way, I still have the original data if the conversions do something I wasn't expecting.

Problems with Data Values

Even with a well-designed database, we still have the issue of the accuracy of the data that has been entered. As the query designer, you can't be held responsible for some accuracy problems. If a person's address has been entered incorrectly, there is not much anyone can do to find or fix the problem (apart from waiting for the mail to be returned to sender). However, you can be aware of a number of things, and even if you can't fix the problems, you can at least raise some alarms. In addition, it is sometimes possible to fix some problem data with careful use of update queries.

Unexpected Nulls

Nulls can cause all sorts of grief in databases. The real problem (as discussed in Chapter 2) is that a Null can mean either that the value is unknown or that the value doesn't apply for a particular record. If a member in our club has a Null value for his Team field, it could mean he isn't in a team or it could mean that he is in a team but we haven't recorded which one. As with other data problems, there is not much we can do about this. However, with something like the Gender field, we know that everyone does have a gender. The Nulls mean that for some members the gender has not been recorded. The same applies to fields like date of birth.

If, for example, you are asked for a list of the men in the club, it is often a good idea to also run another query for those rows where Gender IS Null. You can then say to your client, "Here are the men, and here are the members I'm not sure about." Such an approach can help avoid letters from aggrieved gentlemen who don't appear on the list.

Be aware of the differences between queries with COUNT(*) and say COUNT(Gender). The first will count all the rows in your database; the second will count all the rows with a non-Null value for gender. In the ideal world, these would be the same. In practice, they may not be.

Wrong or Inconsistent Spelling

Any database will have spelling mistakes in the data at some point. Mr. Philips may appear as Phillips, Philipps, or Philps for various reasons, ranging from illegible handwriting on the application form to a simple data-entry mistake. If you are trying to find information about Mr. Philips and you suspect there might be a problem, you can use functions or wildcards to find similar data. Different products have different ways of doing this.

We can use the keyword LIKE to find similar spellings. The wildcard symbol % (* in Access) stands for any group of characters. Our several versions of spelling for Philips would all be retrieved by the query in Listing 11-10.

Listing 11-10. *Using the Wildcard % to Retrieve Different Names Beginning with "Phil"*

```
SELECT * FROM Member
WHERE LastName LIKE 'Phil%'
```

Another problem involving incorrect or inconsistent spelling arises when you might be expecting a particular set of values or categories in a field. For example, in our Member table, we might be expecting values "M" and "F" in the Gender column, but there may be the odd "male" or "m" value. In the MemberType column, we expect a "Junior" value, "Senior" value, or "Associate" value, but in practice, it may have other values, such as "jnior" or "senor". If the tables have been designed with appropriate check constraints or foreign keys, this won't be a problem. However, often these constraints are not present, so it is useful to check for problematic entries with a query such as the one in Listing 11-11.

Listing 11-11. *Finding Inconsistent Data in a Categorical Column Such As MemberType*

```
SELECT * FROM Member
WHERE Gender NOT IN ('Senior','Junior','Associate')
```

Extraneous Characters in Text Fields

A common problem when trying to retrieve data that matches a text value is leading or trailing spaces and other nonprintable characters that have found their way into the data.

If we have a field like FirstName in our database, for example, we would usually declare it as a character field of some sort having a particular length. Because many values won't be exactly that stated length, there is room for additional characters to be included. Some implementations of SQL will deal with spaces before or after the text without intervention from the querier. For example, Access will retrieve " Dan" and "Dan " if asked to find rows where FirstName = 'Dan'. Some implementations might require you to specifically state that you don't want to consider the leading or trailing spaces, which you can do with various forms of a trim function. Check out your documentation to see what your implementation has. The RTRIM (right trim) function in Listing 11-12 will strip the spaces from the end (right) of the FirstName value before making the comparison.

Listing 11-12. *Trimming Trailing Spaces Before Making a Text Comparison*

```
SELECT * FROM Member
WHERE RTRIM(FirstName) = 'Dan'
```

You can use update queries to remedy some of these data inconsistencies. Listing 11-13 shows how to ensure no values in the FirstName column of the Member table have any leading (LTRIM) and trailing (RTRIM) spaces. It essentially replaces all the values with trimmed values.

Listing 11-13. *Removing All Leading and Trailing Spaces from the FirstName Values*

```
UPDATE Member
SET FirstName = RTRIM ( LTRIM (FirstName))
```

A more disturbing problem is characters that look like spaces but aren't. This sometimes occurs when data is moved around between various products and different implementations. I actually experienced this when generating and maintaining both an Access and SQL Server version of the tables for this book. All of a sudden, some of my queries to find rows with certain names weren't working. The name fields looked like they had gained some extra trailing spaces, but using trim functions wasn't helping. Eventually, I realized that the extra characters weren't spaces but some other unprintable character. By using a wildcard expression as in Listing 11-10, I managed to retrieve the right rows.

Two other data-entry "gotchas" are the numbers 0 (zero) and 1 (one) entered instead of the letters *o* and *l*. You can spend hours trying to debug a query that is looking for "John" or "Bill", but if the underlying data has been mistakenly entered as "J0hn" or "Bi11", you will search in vain.

The moral is that weird things can happen with data values, so when the troubleshooting of your query syntax fails, check the underlying data.

Inconsistent Case in Text Fields

If your SQL implementation is case-sensitive, you need to be aware that some data values may not have the expected case. Someone may have entered "dan" rather than "Dan" as a member's first name in the Member table. In case-sensitive implementations, a query with the clause WHERE FirstName = 'Dan' will not retrieve his information. As mentioned in Chapter 2, using a function that converts strings of characters to uppercase will help find the right rows. In Listing 11-14, we convert FirstName (temporarily) to uppercase, and then compare that with the uppercase rendition of what we are seeking.

Listing 11-14. *Finding Dan's Information Regardless of the Case in the Database Table*

```
SELECT * FROM Member
WHERE UPPER(FirstName) = 'DAN'
```

It is quite difficult to find problems with case in names because not all names conform to being lowercase with an uppercase first letter; for example, de Vere and McLennan. But for fields like Gender (M or F) or MemberType (Junior, Senior, or Associate), we know what we expect the values to be like. The best way to ensure that they are consistent is to put a check constraint on the field when the table is created to restrict the allowed values. This is shown in Listing 11-15.

Listing 11-15. *Including a Constraint on the Values of MemberType*

```
CREATE TABLE Member (
...
MemberType CHAR(20) CHECK MemberType in ('Junior', 'Senior', 'Associate')
...
)
```

If you are confronted with a table that has the values "JUNIOR", "Junior", and "junior", you can effect some repairs with the query in Listing 11-16. (But it's best to avoid getting into this situation if you can.)

Listing 11-16. *Getting Case Consistency for the Junior Member Types*

```
UPDATE Member
SET MemberType = 'Junior'
WHERE UPPER(MemberType)='JUNIOR'
```

Diagnosing Problems

In the previous sections, we looked at some problems you could possibly find with database design and inconsistent data. Most of the time, however, if the result of your query is not looking quite right, it is probably because you have the wrong SQL statement. Your statement may be retrieving rows that are different from what you were expecting. We looked at checking the query output in Chapter 10. I cannot overemphasize the importance of checking your query results, as sometimes two queries may be subtly different, and it can be tricky to spot if you have mistakenly asked the wrong question.

In the previous chapter, I suggested a way to approach queries that lets you build the query up slowly so you can check that each step is returning appropriate rows. However, if you are presented with a full-blown, complex query that is not delivering as expected, you need to pare it down until you find where the problem lies. If you have noticed a problem, then you have a good place to start. You have either noticed an expected row is missing or that an inappropriate row has been retrieved. Concentrate on finding where in the query that problem is. The following sections offer some suggestions.

Check Parts of Nested Queries Independently

Where you have one query nested inside another, the first thing to check is that the nested part is behaving itself. Take a look at Listing 11-17.

Listing 11-17. *SQL Statement to Retrieve Juniors with Handicaps Lower Than the Average*

```
SELECT *
FROM Member m
WHERE m.MemberType = 'Junior' AND Handicap <
      (SELECT AVG(Handicap)
       FROM Member)
```

If you are having trouble with a query like this, cut and paste the inner query and run it independently. Check to see if it is returning the correct result. If this is OK, you can try doing the outer query on its own. To do this, just put some value in place of the inner query—such as Handicap < 10—and see if that returns the correct results. If you can narrow down the problem to one part of the query, then use some of the ideas in the following sections.

This approach doesn't work if the inner and outer parts of the query are related (see Chapter 4), but some of the following techniques might help with that situation.

Understand How the Tables Are Being Combined

Many queries involve combining tables with some relational operation (join, union, and so on). Make sure you understand how the tables are being combined and if that is appropriate. Consider a query such as the one in Listing 11-18.

Listing 11-18. *How Are the Tables Being Combined?*

```
SELECT m.LastName, m.FirstName
FROM Member m, Entry e, Tournament t
WHERE m.MemberID = e.MemberID
AND e.TourID = t.TourID AND t.TourType = 'Open' AND e.Year = 2006
```

Three tables are involved in this query. It can take a moment to figure out that they are being joined. Make sure that is appropriate for the question being asked. Chapter 10 has examples of key words in questions and the appropriate ways to combine tables.

Remove Extra WHERE Clauses

After combining tables, usually only some of the resulting rows are required. In Listing 11-18, part of the WHERE clause is needed for the join operations. However, after the join, only the rows satisfying t.TourType = 'Open' AND e.Year = 2006 are retained. If you have rows missing from your result, it is often useful to remove the part of the WHERE clause that is selecting a final subset of the rows. If the rows are still missing, then you know that (for this example) the problem is occurring in the join.

Retain All the Columns

I'm a big fan of always saying `SELECT *` in the early stages of developing queries that involve joins. Consider the query in Listing 11-18. If we suspect a problem with the joins, then by leaving all the columns visible, we can see if the join conditions are behaving as expected. Once we are happy with the rows being retrieved, we can retain just the columns required.

However, if you are combining tables with set operations, this approach will be counter-productive, as projecting the right columns is critical (see the "Do You Have Correct Columns in Set Operations?" section later in this chapter).

Check Underlying Queries in Aggregates

If you have a problem with a query involving an aggregate—for example, `SELECT AVG(Handicap) FROM ... WHERE ...`—check that you have retrieved the correct rows first. Change the query to `SELECT * FROM ... WHERE ...`, and confirm that this returns the rows for which you want to find the average. In fact, I recommend always doing this with an aggregate, because it is difficult to otherwise check if the numbers being returned are correct.

Common Symptoms

Having tried some of the steps in the previous chapter, you will have simplified your query to isolate where the problem is. In this section, we will look at some specific symptoms and some likely causes.

No Rows Are Returned

It is usually easy to spot a problem with your query when no rows are returned and you know that some should be. Questions that involve "and" or "both" can often have this problem. Check that you have not mistakenly used a select operation instead of an intersection. For example, consider a question such as "Which members have entered tournaments 24 and 36?" A common first attempt (and I still catch myself doing this sometimes) is a query statement such as the one in Listing 11-19.

Listing 11-19. *Incorrectly Using a Select Condition for Questions Involving "And" or "Both"*

```
SELECT * FROM Entry
WHERE TourID = 24 AND TourID = 36
```

Listing 11-19 asks for a row from the Entry table where TourID simultaneously has two different values. This never happens, and so no rows are retrieved. The cure is to use a self join (covered in Chapter 5) or an intersection operation (covered in Chapter 7).

Getting no rows returned from a query may also be an extreme example of one of the problems in the next section.

Rows Are Missing

It can be difficult to spot if some rows are being missed by your query, especially when the set of retrieved rows is large. If you get a thousand rows returned, you might not notice that one is missing. Careful testing is required, and some ideas for how to do this were discussed in Chapter 10. It is often worthwhile to run through the following list of common errors to see if any might apply.

Should You Have an Outer Join?

Using an inner join when an outer join is required is a very common problem. Suppose that we are trying to get a list of member information, that includes names and fees. For this, we need the Member table (for the names) and the Type table (for the fees). A first attempt at a query is in Listing 11-20.

Listing 11-20. *First Attempt at Finding Name and Fee Information for Members*

```
SELECT m.LastName, m.FirstName, t.Fee
FROM Member m , Type t
WHERE m.MemberType = t.Type
```

We know there are (say) 135 members, but we are getting only 133 rows from the query in Listing 11-20. The issue here is that Listing 11-20 is performing an inner join (see Chapter 3), so any members with a Null value for member type will not appear in the result. Of course, this may be the result you want (those members who have a type and fee), but it is not the correct output if you want a list of all members and the fees for those who have them.

An outer join (also discussed in Chapter 3) that includes all the rows of the Member table will solve this problem. Whenever you have a join, it is worth thinking about the join fields and considering what you want to happen where a row has a Null value in that field.

Have Selection Conditions Dealt with Nulls Appropriately?

Nulls can cause quite a few headaches if you forget to consider their effect on your queries. The previous section looked at Nulls in a joining field. You also need to remember to check for comparisons involving fields that may contain Nulls. We looked at this in Chapter 2 and also earlier in this chapter.

Consider two queries on the Member table with selection conditions Gender = 'M' and Gender <> 'M'. It is reasonable to think that all rows in the Member table should be returned by one of these queries. However, rows with a Null in the Gender field will return false for both these conditions (any comparison with a Null returns false), and the row will not appear in either result.

Say we want to get a list of members of our club who are not particularly good players (to offer them coaching, perhaps). Someone may suggest a query like Listing 11-21 to find members who do not have a low handicap.

Listing 11-21. *Finding Members Without a Low Handicap*

```
SELECT *
FROM Member m
WHERE NOT (m.Handicap < 10)
```

The problem is that the query in Listing 11-21 will miss all the members with no handicap. Altering the WHERE condition to NOT (m.Handicap < 10) OR m.Handicap IS Null will help in this situation.

Are You Looking for a Match with a Text Value?

It is very disturbing to be trying to find rows for Jim, to be able to see Jim in the table, and to have your query return nothing. This may be caused by one of the problems we looked at in the "Problems with Data Values" section earlier in this chapter.

One quick way to eliminate the possibility of dodgy text values is to use LIKE for comparisons. For example, where you have = 'Jim', replace it with LIKE '%Jim%'. If the query then finds the row you were expecting (possibly along with some others), you know the problem is with the data. As noted earlier, putting the wildcard % (or * in Access) at the beginning and end of the string will find leading or trailing spaces and other nonprintable characters.

Have You Used AND Instead of OR?

We discussed the problem of queries involving "and" or "or" in the previous chapter (in the "Spotting Key Words in Questions" section). I'll recap briefly. The word "and" can be used in English to describe a union and an intersection. When we say "women *and* children," we really mean the *union* of the set of females and the set of young people. When we say "cars that are small *and* red," we mean the *intersection* of the set of small cars and the set of red cars.

If we are looking for "women and children" and use the selection condition Gender = 'F' AND age < 12, we are actually retrieving the intersection of women and children (or girls); the rows for older women and boys will be missing. We need the condition to be Gender = 'F' OR age < 12.

It is very easy to unwittingly translate the "and" in the English question to an AND in the query inappropriately, which can result in missing rows.

Do You Have Correct Columns in Set Operations?

If your query involves intersection or difference operations, the result may have fewer rows than expected because you have projected the wrong columns initially. We looked at this in Chapter 7. Here is a brief example for intersection; the same issue applies to difference operations as well.

We want to find out who has entered both tournaments 25 and 36. We realize that we need an intersection and try the query in Listing 11-22.

Listing 11-22. *First Attempt at Finding Members Who Have Entered Tournaments 25 and 36*

```
SELECT * FROM Entry
WHERE TourID = 25
INTERSECT
SELECT * FROM Entry
WHERE TourID = 36
```

No rows will be returned from the query in Listing 11-22, regardless of the underlying data. The intersection finds rows that are exactly the same in each set. However, all the rows in the first set will have TourID = 25, and all the rows in the second set will have TourID = 36. There can never be a row that is in both sets. We are looking for the member IDs that are in both sets, so the SELECT clauses in each part of the query should be SELECT MemberID FROM Entry.

Listing 11-22 is an extreme example of retaining the wrong columns, resulting in no rows being returned. The discussion around Figure 7-14 in Chapter 7 shows how retaining different columns can result in fewer rows than expected from a query.

More Rows Than There Should Be

It is often easier to spot extra rows than it is to notice that rows are missing from your query result. You only need to see one record that you weren't expecting, and you can concentrate on the different parts of your query to see where it failed to be excluded. Here are a couple of causes of extra rows.

Did You Use NOT Instead of Difference?

With questions containing the words "not" or "never," a sure way to get extra rows is to use a selection condition instead of a difference operator in the query. We looked at this issue in Chapter 4. To recap, consider a question like "Which members have never entered tournament 25?" A common first attempt using a select condition is shown in Listing 11-23.

Listing 11-23. *First Attempt at Finding Members Who Have Not Entered Tournament 25*

```
SELECT * FROM Entry
WHERE TourID <> 25
```

The condition in the WHERE clause checks rows one at a time to see if they should be included in the result. If there is a row for member 415 entering tournament 36, then that row will be retrieved, regardless of the possibility that another row shows member 415 entered tournament 25. For example, if member 415 has entered tournament 25 and four other tournaments, we will retrieve four rows when we were expecting none.

The correct query for this type of question is to use a nested query (see Chapter 4) or the EXCEPT difference operator (see Chapter 7). We need to find the set of all members (from the Member table) and remove the set of members who have entered tournament 25 (from the Entry table). Listings 11-24 and 11-25 show two possibilities.

Listing 11-24. *Finding Members Who Have Not Entered Tournament 25 with a Nested Query*

```
SELECT MemberID FROM Member
WHERE MemberID NOT IN
     (SELECT MemberID FROM Entry
      WHERE TourID = 25)
```

Listing 11-25. *Finding Members Who Have Not Entered Tournament 25 with a Difference Operator*

```
SELECT MemberID FROM Member
EXCEPT
SELECT MemberID FROM Entry
WHERE TourID = 25
```

Have You Dealt with Duplicates Appropriately?

It sometimes takes a little thought to decide what needs to be done with duplicate records retrieved from a query. By default, SQL will retain all duplicates. The following two requests sound similar:

- Give me a list of the names of my customers.

- Give me a list of the cities my customers live in.

In the first, we probably expect as many rows as we have customers; if we have several Johns, we expect them all to be retained. In the second, if we have 500 customers living in Christchurch, we don't expect 500 rows to be returned.

In the query to find the cities, we want only the distinct values. Listing 11-26 shows how to use the DISTINCT keyword.

Listing 11-26. *Finding the Cities Where Customers Reside*

```
SELECT DISTINCT (City) FROM Customer
```

Statistics or Aggregates Incorrect

All of the preceding problems can cause incorrect statistics. If you are counting, grouping, or averaging, and your underlying query misses rows or returns extra rows, then clearly the statistics will be affected. A couple of other things to consider are how Nulls and duplicates are being handled.

SQL will not include any Null fields in its statistics. For example, COUNT(Handicap) or AVG(Handicap) will ignore any rows with Nulls in the Handicap field. It is also important to consider what you want done with duplicates, especially for counting functions. COUNT(Handicap) will return the number of members who have a value in the Handicap column. COUNT(DISTINCT Handicap) will return the number of different values in the Handicap column—if all the members have a handicap of 20, it will return a count of 1.

The Order Is Wrong

If you have used an ORDER BY clause in your query and you are having problems with the order in which the rows are being presented, there is often a problem with the underlying data. Review the "Problems with Data Values" section earlier in this chapter. Check that the field types are appropriate (for example, numeric values aren't being stored in text fields) and that text values have consistent case and no extraneous characters.

Common Typos and Syntax Problems

Sometimes a query doesn't run because of some simple problem with the syntax—that is, the way the query is worded. Syntax problems involve things like missing brackets or incorrect spellings of fields or keywords. Your database will probably give you some error message that may or may not be helpful in finding and correcting the problem. Often the error message is not helpful, so here are a few things to check:

Quotation marks: Most versions of SQL require single quotation marks around text values, such as 'Smith' or 'Junior', although some use double quotation marks in some circumstances. If you are cutting and pasting queries, be sure the correct quotation marks have been transferred. When I cut and paste the queries in this book from Word to Access, the quotation marks look OK, but I need to reenter them. Also check that all the quotation marks are paired correctly. Don't use quotes around numeric values. Something like Handicap < '12' will cause problems if Handicap is a numeric field.

Parentheses: Parentheses are required in nested queries and also can be used to help readability in many queries (such as those with several joins). Check that all the brackets are paired correctly.

Names of tables and fields: It seems obvious that you need to get the names of tables and fields correct. However, sometimes a simple misspelling of a table name or field can cause an unintelligible error message. Check carefully.

Use of aliases: If you use an alias for table names (for example, Member m), check that you have associated the correct alias with each field name.

Spelling of keywords: Some software for constructing SQL queries will highlight keywords, so it is very apparent if you have spelled them incorrectly. If your version doesn't show this, then check keyword spelling, too. I often type FORM instead of FROM or AVERAGE() instead of AVG().

IS Null versus = Null: Some versions of SQL treat these quite differently. IS Null always works if you are trying to find fields with a Null value.

Summary

Before you can correct a query, you need to notice that it is wrong in the first place. Always check the rows returned from a query, as described in the previous chapter. When you do discover errors, the following are some ideas for tracking down the cause of the problem:

- Check that the underlying tables are combined appropriately (join, intersection, and so on).

- Simplify the query by removing selection conditions and aggregates to ensure the underlying rows are correct.

- Check each part of nested queries or queries involving set operations independently.

- Check queries for questions with the words "and" or "not" to ensure you have not used selection conditions when you need a set operation or nested query.

- Check that the columns retained in queries with set operations are appropriate.

- Check that Nulls and duplicates have been dealt with properly.

- Check that underlying data types are correct and that data values are consistent.

APPENDIX

■■■■

Sample Database

Most of the examples in this book use the golf club database. Figure A-1 shows how the tables in the database are related, and Figure A-2 shows the data in the tables.

An Access version of this database is available through the Apress web page for this book (http://www.apress.com/book/view/1590599438). You will also find SQL scripts for creating and populating the tables in common database management systems, such as Oracle Database; DB2 for Linux, Unix, and Windows; and MySQL.

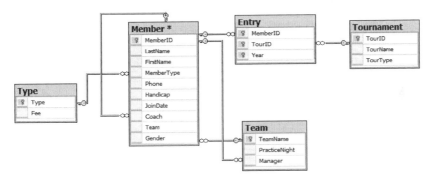

Figure A-1. *The data model for the golf club database*

MemberID	LastName	FirstName	Handicap	Gender	Team	MemberType	Coach	Phone	JoinDate
118	McKenzie	Melissa	30	F		Junior	153	963270	10-May-99
138	Stone	Michael	30	M		Senior		983223	13-May-03
153	Nolan	Brenda	11	F	TeamB	Senior		442649	25-Jul-00
176	Branch	Helen		F		Social		589419	18-Nov-05
178	Beck	Sarah		F		Social		226596	06-Jan-04
228	Burton	Sandra	26	F		Junior	153	244493	21-Jun-07
235	Cooper	William	14	M	TeamB	Senior	153	722954	15-Feb-02
239	Spence	Thomas	10	M		Senior		697720	04-Jun-00
258	Olson	Barbara	16	F		Senior		370186	11-Jul-07
286	Pollard	Robert	19	M	TeamB	Junior	235	617681	26-Jul-07
290	Sexton	Thomas	26	M		Senior	235	268936	10-Jul-02
323	Wilcox	Daniel	3	M	TeamA	Senior		665393	30-Apr-03
331	Schmidt	Thomas	25	M		Senior	153	867492	20-Mar-03
332	Bridges	Deborah	12	F		Senior	235	279087	05-Mar-01
339	Young	Betty	21	F	TeamB	Senior		507813	30-Mar-03
414	Gilmore	Jane	5	F	TeamA	Junior	153	459558	12-May-01
415	Taylor	William	7	M	TeamA	Senior	235	137353	09-Nov-01
461	Reed	Robert	3	M	TeamA	Senior	235	994664	18-Jul-99
469	Willis	Carolyn	29	F		Junior		688378	27-Dec-04
487	Kent	Susan		F		Social		707217	19-Sep-04

Member table

MemberID	TourID	Year
118	24	2005
228	24	2006
228	25	2006
228	36	2006
235	38	2004
235	38	2006
235	40	2005
235	40	2006
239	25	2006
239	40	2004
258	24	2005
258	38	2005
286	24	2004
286	24	2005
286	24	2006
415	24	2006
415	25	2004
415	36	2005
415	36	2006
415	38	2004
415	38	2006
415	40	2004
415	40	2005
415	40	2006

Entry table

TeamName	PracticeNight	Manager
TeamA	Tuesday	239
TeamB	Monday	153

Team table

TourID	TourName	TourType
24	Leeston	Social
25	Kaiapoi	Social
36	WestCoast	Open
38	Canterbury	Open
40	Otago	Open

Tournament table

Type	Fee
Associate	60
Junior	150
Senior	300
Social	50

Type table

Figure A-2. *The tables and data for the golf club database*

Index

Made in the USA
San Bernardino, CA
07 September 2014